Big Bang, Baby
Rock Trivia

Big Bang, Rock Trivia

HOUNSLOW PRESS
A MEMBER OF THE DUNDURN GROUP
TORONTO • OXFORD

Richard Crouse

Big Bang Baby

ELVIS

"Writing about music is like dancing about architecture."

— *Elvis Costello*

Design: V. John Lee
Printer: Transcontinental Printing Inc.

Canadian Cataloguing in Publication Data

Crouse, Richard, 1963-
Big bang, baby: rock trivia

ISBN 0-88882-219-7
1. Rock music — Miscellanea. I. Title.
ML3534.C953 2000   781.66   C00-930052-X

1   2   3   4   5   04   03   02   01   00

THE CANADA COUNCIL | LE CONSEIL DES ARTS
FOR THE ARTS | DU CANADA
SINCE 1957 | DEPUIS 1957

Canada

We acknowledge the support of the **Canada Council for the Arts**, the **Ontario Arts Council**, and the **Book Publishing Industry Development Program (BPIDP)** for our publishing activities.

Care has been taken to trace the ownership of copyright material used in this book. The author and the publisher welcome any information enabling them to rectify any references or credit in subsequent editions.

J. Kirk Howard, President

Printed and bound in Canada.

Dundurn Press
8 Market Street,
Suite 200
Toronto, Ontario, Canada
M5E 1M6

Dundurn Press
73 Lime Walk
Headington, Oxford,
England
OX3 7AD

Dundurn Press
2250 Military Road
Tonawanda, New York,
U.S.A. 14150

CONTENTS

How many music critics does it take to change
a light bulb?
One thousand — one to change it and 999 to
figure out its influences.

INTRODUCTION

ROCK AND ROLL IS NOW ALMOST FIFTY YEARS OLD. Like any other major sociological force, a great deal of history and trivia has sprouted amid the clatter of banging drums and howling guitars. In the fifties teeny-boppers were content to read about Elvis's favourite foods, or Fabian's eye colour, but as rock and roll grew up people's interests increased and deepened. The advent of the serious singer/songwriter types in the sixties saw rock music become the subject of earnest conversations in groups of sombre, beret-wearing, goateed bohemians. Suddenly Bob Dylan was being compared to Yeats, and Jim Morrison was publishing books of poetry. The music diversified and changed. Bands expanded their line-ups adding keyboards and horns; expanded their subject matter — no longer content to write about "chicks and cars" they drew from literature, mythology, and current events for their inspiration; and "expanded" their minds with drugs. Following them every step of the way were the journalists. In the beginning they were little more than groupies and fans, eager to report anything about their heroes, no matter how trivial. In the late sixties a new brand of rock writers emerged — intelligent, critical, and literate. They wrote the history of rock and roll as it was happening. Rock journalism flourished in the seventies and eighties. It was now possible to hear The Clash referred to as "Noble Savages," or to read pages and pages and pages of Sting's opinions on everything from E.M. Forster to the woes of the rainforest. By the 1990s several American universities, including Harvard, had added courses about Bob Dylan and Madonna to their curriculum. Rock music had grown up, and we had grown up with it. For many of us under 40 it is difficult to imagine a world without rock and roll, so pervasive is its impact on our lives. There are many who are more interested in Liam Gallagher's erratic behaviour than, say, recent events in the former USSR. This book is meant for people who grew up listening to the Stones, reading Lester Bangs and for those who think of Detroit as the home of Motown first, and General Motors second.

For her encouragement and support (electronic and otherwise) I would like to thank Ophira Eisenberg. I also wish to thank Dara Rowland and Rob Firing, whose early enthusiasm for this book encouraged me to proceed. A special nod goes to K-ROQ's Rodney Bingenheimer for supplying photographs from his personal collection. Thanks to Hilly Kristal at CBGB in New York, and Davy Jones. A further thanks to Greg Jones and Ann Yurek for their time and help, and for many of the photographs that appear in the following pages; and to PJ Wilson, Kelly McLaughlin, Greg MacDonald, and Matt Watts for their help.

DO YOU WANT TO DANCE?
The 1950s

1. What was the first rock and roll record to earn "gold" status?

A.) **"Hard Headed Woman"** (#1 6/30/58 *Billboard*), by Elvis Presley was the first rock and roll gold record. It was actually the fourth single of any genre to achieve gold status (i.e. $1,000,000 in sales) after Pat Boone, Gordon MacRae, and Laurie London, but still the first rock and roll record to sell in that quantity. There's a record for the record books.

2. What was the first rock and roll song on the *Billboard* charts?

A.) There is some debate, but most rock and roll historians agree that Bill Haley's **"Crazy, Man, Crazy"** in 1953 was the first rock and roll tune to crack the *Billboard* charts. For his next release, Bill cleaned up the raunchy lyrics to Big Joe Turner's "Shake, Rattle and Roll," which emphasized what Haley called the "rock and roll beat." Legend has it that disc jockey Alan Freed coined the phrase "rock and roll" while listening to Bill Haley's "Rock-A-Beatin' Boogie."

3. What was Elvis Presley's first single?

A.) On July 5, 1954, Elvis recorded **"That's Alright"** at Sun Studios (706 Union Avenue, Memphis, Tennessee). The session was intended as a rehearsal to work in the band, and to decide on the "Elvis Presley sound." Bassist Bill Black, guitarist Scotty Moore, and Elvis ran through uninspired cover versions of popular ballads before hitting on "That's Alright," an old blues song by Arthur "Big Boy" Crudup. After several takes they hit on a version that excited Sun Studios' owner, Sam Phillips. They produced a rhythm record described by Albert Goldman as "a remarkable feat of breathing in one cultural atmosphere and breathing out another." Scotty Moore was less academic in his reaction to the song. He thought they might get run out of town for playing this new rockabilly. Quite the opposite happened: they became local heroes. After the record had been on the market for one week, five thousand orders were placed, and by the end of July it had reached the number 3 spot on the local charts.

4. What was Roy Orbison's first single?

A.) Roy Orbison first recorded his unique voice on a self-penned record called **"Ooby Dooby,"** which was released by Sun Records in 1956. Roy then switched to the RCA Victor label, and while he had a flourishing songwriting career, he was unable to produce another hit single featuring his vocals. In 1958 he switched labels once again, this time going with the Monument Record Corporation. It was with Monument that Roy produced his classic string of hits, including "Only the Lonely," "Crying," "Blue Bayou," and "Oh Pretty Woman."

5. During his lifetime, what was Elvis Presley's only record to picture somebody other than Elvis on the cover?

A.) Elvis only shared an album cover once. ***Elvis Presley Sings Leiber and Stoller,*** a compilation album, featured Elvis and the songwriters on the cover. Leiber and Stoller were arguably the most influential songwriters of the early days of rock and roll. They started off in the early 1950s as two white kids who had a knack for writing hit R&B tunes. They penned hits for Wilbert Harrison, Willie Mae "Big Mama" Thornton, The Robins, and The Coasters before finding huge success with Elvis Presley. Elvis recorded the Leiber and Stoller tune "Hound Dog," then hired them to write the score for *Jailhouse Rock*. They continued to work with Elvis, while at the same time writing hits for The Drifters

("There Goes My Baby") and Ben E. King ("Stand By Me"). In the years that followed they did not rest on their laurels. In 1973 Stealer's Wheel scored a Top 10 hit with Leiber and Stoller's "Stuck in the Middle With You" (#6 3/31/73 *Billboard*). Later years saw them move into the realm of adult-oriented music. They composed an album's worth of songs for Peggy Lee, scored several musicals, and worked with Leonard Bernstein.

6. Who did Daisy almost drive crazy in 1956?

A.) Daisy almost drove **Little Richard** crazy in his 1956 hit "Tutti Frutti" (#17 1/28/56 *Billboard*). Little Richard had been performing this song in clubs for several years under the title "Wop-Bop-A-Loo-Bop," and with racy, obscene lyrics. The song brought down the house every night, but could never be committed to vinyl without drastically altering the words. Producer Bumps Blackwell brought in Dorothy LaBostrie to clean up the song and make it acceptable for conservative 1956 radio programmers. In about an hour she changed the words, and the title (which she claims to have borrowed from Tutti Frutti ice cream, a new flavour in 1956). Little Richard recorded the new clean version of this song in fifteen minutes, nailing it for posterity on the second take.

7. What was the first Elvis Presley record to feature The Jordanaires on background vocals?

A.) The Jordanaires debuted with Elvis on **"Hound Dog"** (#1 8/04/56 *Billboard*). Also recorded at this session were "Any Way You Want Me (That's How I Will Be)" (#20 11/10/56) and "Don't Be Cruel" (#1 8/04/56), which was number 1 for eleven weeks. The Jordanaires went on to work with Elvis until 1970, singing on virtually all of his records and appearing in twenty-eight movies with him.

8. What inspired the name for Rock-Ola jukeboxes?

11

Big Bang! Baby

A.) Rock-Ola jukeboxes were named for the founder of the Rock-Ola Company, **David C. Rockola**. While the old-style jukeboxes have become obsolete, and in great demand by collectors, there was a time when every bowling alley, gas station, and soda fountain had one. One statistic reports that between 1935 and 1950 there were 700,000 jukeboxes in the US alone. The first modern jukebox appeared in 1906 under the name "John Gabriel's Automatic Entertainer." The name "jukebox" was introduced in the thirties. The term "juke" was borrowed from the slang for a brothel, "juke house." As people's tastes changed, jukeboxes began to lose their popularity. In the sixties people's interest began to shift from singles to long-playing albums. Many bar jukeboxes were replaced by live d.j.'s, who had a greater selection of tunes, and could program the music for the mood of the crowd in the bar. In recent years jukeboxes, especially the ornate Wurlitzer's with their wooden casings and bubble lights, have become much in demand by collectors. Prices for reconditioned jukeboxes range from three thousand to fifteen thousand

Elvis Presley's backup singers The Jordanaires.

Photo courtesy of Gordon Stoker

dollars, depending on the aesthetic quality of the machine. Madonna, Elton John, Paul McCartney, and Huey Lewis are noted rock and rollers who collect antique "automatic entertainers."

9. Who are the only two acts ever to have nine or more songs in the American Top 100 at the same time?

A.) The only two acts to accomplish this feat were **Elvis Presley and The Beatles**. Near the middle of December 1956, Elvis had nine singles in the Top 100. They were: "Don't Be Cruel," "Hound Dog," "Love Me Tender," "Anyway You Want Me (That's How I Will Be)," "Love Me," "When My Blue Moon Turns to Gold Again," "Paralysed," "Old Shep," and "Poor Boy." On April 4, 1964, The Beatles had twelve singles on the chart, including all of the Top 5. The following week two more Lennon/McCartney compositions were entered to give them an unprecedented fourteen singles on the chart simultaneously. They were: "She Loves You," "I Want to Hold Your Hand," "Twist and Shout," "Please Please Me," "I Saw Her Standing There," "Can't Buy Me Love," "From Me to You," "All My Loving," "Roll Over Beethoven," "Do You Want to Know a Secret," "You Can't Do That," "Thank You Girl," "There's a Place," and "Love Me Do."

10. Who said: "In heaven, my name is still Richard Penniman. I call myself Marie down here, but in Glory, I'm still a man"?

A.) In Charles White's book *The Life and Times of **Little Richard,*** the outrageous singer is quoted as uttering this phrase. Little Richard, openly homosexual, also preaches from time to time, in the same exuberant manner he uses when singing rock and roll.

11. What popular dance show's manifesto was: "To reflect what's going on early enough to make a profit on it"?

A.) **Dick Clark's "American Bandstand"** always tried to accomplish this goal. The show lasted on air for over thirty years,

13

BiBang! Baby

taping over 6,000 hours of shows, playing more than 65,000 records, showcasing well over 10,000 singers and groups, and displaying the dancing prowess of over 600,000 teens.

12. Who said: "I can't picture Jesus Christ doin' a whole lotta shakin'"?

A.) **Jerry Lee Lewis** said this in rebuttal to Sun Records owner Sam Phillips' argument that you wouldn't go to hell for playing rock and roll music. Jerry Lee and his band were at Sun Records recording the follow-up single to "Whole Lotta Shakin' Goin' On." Jerry and his bandmates had been drinking, and Jerry announced that he was going to go to hell for singing "the devil's music." A lively conversation ensued between Sam Phillips, bass player Billy Lee Riley, and a drunken Jerry Lee. Someone in the control booth had the foresight to turn on a tape machine, thereby preserving the discussion for posterity. After a long argument Jerry Lee was finally convinced to record the song. By this point he was fired up from arguing and cut the song, "Great Balls of Fire," in one take. After the session someone joked that they should split the royalties with the Holy Ghost. Jerry Lee was not amused.

Jerry Lee Lewis, aka The Killer. Jerry Lee has long been torn between doing God's work and singing the devil's music. This dichotomy has plagued him throughout his checkered career. "I'm draggin' the audience to hell with me," he once said.

Photo courtesy of Kerrie Lewis

14

13. Who, according to James Brown, "taught white America to get down"?

A.) James Brown has been quoted as saying that **"Elvis Presley** taught white America to get down," thereby paving the way for black acts to find acceptance on the charts.

14. From the Sun Records stable of musicians, who did Sam Phillips think was going to be a bigger star than Elvis?

A.) Sun Records owner Sam Phillips felt that **Carl Perkins** had a better shot at stardom than Elvis Presley. In 1956, while Perkins was enjoying success with his recording of "Blue Suede Shoes," he drove to New York City to appear on "The Perry Como Show" and "The Ed Sullivan Show" to promote the record on network television. Along the way he had a car accident, which killed his brother, Jay Perkins, and his manager. Elvis covered "Blue Suede Shoes" and turned it into a huge hit, while Carl recuperated from four broken ribs and three breaks in the right shoulder. The accident slowed Carl's momentum, while Elvis quickly grabbed the spotlight and became a superstar.

15. What was Elvis's army serial number?

A.) Elvis Presley's army serial number was **US-53310761.** He was inducted into the US Army on March 24, 1958, and sent to Freiburg, West Germany. At the induction ceremony Elvis took this oath: "I, Elvis Presley, do solemnly swear that I will support and defend the Constitution of the United States against all enemies, foreign and domestic; that I will bear true faith and allegiance to the same; and that I will obey the orders of the President of the United States and the orders of the officers appointed over me, according to the regulations and uniform code of military justice. So help me God." At his post at Company D, 1st Battalion, 32nd Armor, 3rd Armored Division of the 7th Army, he was assigned to Lt. Col. Henry Grimm as a jeep driver. Elvis Presley was discharged on March 5, 1960.

16. What was Wolfman Jack's real name?

A.) Wolfman Jack was born **Bob Smith**. He adopted his colourful professional name because of his raspy voice and wild on-air antics. The Wolfman was the operator and main on-air personality of XERF, broadcasting from Mexico with a very powerful transmitter — far more powerful than would have been allowed in the US. He broadcast all over the continent, and it was said his show could be heard in Russia. The Wolfman and his unique brand of personality radio were brought to the silver screen in the hit film *American Graffiti*. The Guess Who immortalized the border-radio king in their song "Clap for the Wolfman" (#6 8/10/74 *Billboard*).

17. What famous rock and roll huckster and manager once painted sparrows yellow and sold them as canaries?

A.) Elvis's manager, **Colonel Tom Parker**, once painted sparrows yellow and tried to pass them off as canaries. He worked the carnival sideshow circuit for a time, once promoting an act of dancing chickens. In reality the chickens weren't dancing, but trying not to burn their feet on the electric hot plate they were standing on.

18. Who created The Chipmunks?

A.) The Chipmunks were created by songwriter **Ross Bagdasarian** in 1958. Using the stage name David Seville, he scored a hit with the song "Witch Doctor" (#1 4/14/58 *Billboard*), which stayed at number 1 for three weeks. The song featured a sped-up voice as the hook of the song. Trying to repeat the success of "Witch Doctor" he created The Chipmunks, who have sold over 25 million records to date.

19. What was Elvis Presley's mother's name? Is she still alive?

A.) Elvis Presley's mother's name was **Gladys Presley**, and she died on August 14, 1958. The former Gladys Smith eloped with Vernon

Presley on June 17, 1933, when she was 21 and he was 17. Elvis and his stillborn twin brother Jesse were born on January 8, 1935, with Dr. William Robert Hunt attending. As Elvis was growing up, he worshipped his mother, so much so that writer Albert Goldman called him the "classic mama's boy." One of the stranger aspects of their relationship was the secret language they used to converse. Elvis always called her "Satnin," and she would reply using a "language" made up of words that Elvis had used as a baby. This close relationship continued until her death in August of 1958. In 1974 Elvis said, "The bottom dropped out of my life the day my mother died. I thought I had nothing left. In a way, I was right."

20. How old was Myra Brown when she married Jerry Lee Lewis on December 12, 1957?

A.) Myra Brown was **thirteen years old** when she married Jerry Lee Lewis on December 12, 1957. When the press found out that Myra was only 13, and Jerry Lee's cousin to boot, they had a field day. It was also uncovered that he hadn't properly divorced his second wife. He started a tour of England shortly after the wedding, and was greeted by a hostile press, and jeers at his live performances. Lewis left England without completing the tour. The scandal put a damper on his meteoric career, which took many years to regain momentum. The marriage lasted until May 1971. Years later Ronnie Hawkins was quoted as saying, "None of us rock and rollers could understand all the fuss about Jerry Lee marrying a thirteen-year-old. All us Southern cats knew she was only 12."

21. Don McLean called February 3, 1959, "the day the music died" in his famous song "American Pie." What happened that day?

A.) Don McLean's line "the day the music died" refers to February 3, 1959, when **Ritchie Valens, Buddy Holly, and J.P. Richardson (The Big Bopper) were killed** when the single-engine plane they were travelling in crashed. The rockers were almost finished a short tour, and decided to fly ahead instead of taking the bus so they would have a chance to do some laundry.

22. Has Stevie Wonder been blind since birth?

A.) **Stevie Wonder has been blind since the first month of birth.** He was born on May 13, 1950, four weeks premature. Stevie was kept in an incubator for a month at a constant temperature of 80 degrees F, with a continuous supply of oxygen. His eyesight was destroyed by too much oxygen, a symptom known as retrolental fibroplasia, which occurs when an opaque fibrous membrane forms behind the lens of the eye.

23. Including documentaries, how many films did Elvis Presley star in?

A.) During his lifetime Elvis Presley starred in **thirty-three feature films and documentaries** from 1956 to 1972.

They were:
1.) *Love Me Tender*, 1956; 2.) *Loving You*, 1957; 3.) *Jailhouse Rock*, 1957; 4.) *King Creole*, 1958; 5.) *G.I. Blues*, 1960; 6.) *Flaming Star*, 1960; 7.) *Wild in the Country*, 1961; 8.) *Blue Hawaii*, 1961; 9.) *Follow That Dream*, 1962; 10.) *Kid Galahad*, 1962; 11.) *Girls! Girls! Girls!*, 1962; 12.) *It Happened at the World's Fair*, 1963; 13.) *Fun in Acapulco*, 1963; 14.) *Kissing Cousins*, 1964; 15.) *Viva Las Vegas*, 1964; 16.) *Roustabout*, 1964; 17.) *Girl Happy*, 1965; 18.) *Tickle Me*, 1965; 19.) *Harem Scarum*, 1965; 20.) *Frankie and Johnny*, 1966; 21.) *Paradise, Hawaii Style*, 1966; 22.) *Spinout*, 1966; 23.) *Easy Come, Easy Go*, 1967; 24.) *Double Trouble*, 1967; 25.) *Clambake*, 1967; 26.) *Stay Away, Joe*, 1968; 27.) *Speedway*, 1968; 28.) *Live a Little, Love a Little*, 1968; 29.) *Charro!*, 1969; 30.) *The Trouble With Girls (And How to Get Into It)*, 1969; 31.) *Change of Habit*, 1970; 32.) *Elvis: That's the Way It Is**, 1970; 33.) *Elvis on Tour**, 1972.
* numbers 32 and 33 were documentaries released by MGM.

24. Which Elvis movie was based on the Harold Robbins novel *A Stone for Danny Fisher?*

A.) Elvis Presley's fourth movie, *King Creole,* was based on the Harold Robbins best-seller *A Stone for Danny Fisher.* Set in New Orleans, Elvis plays nightclub singer Danny Fisher, who falls in love with a girl from the wrong side of town. Starring with Elvis is Carolyn ("The Addams Family") Jones and Walter Matthau. Elvis gives the best showing of his film career, and later said that this was the best film he was involved with.

25. Who was awarded back royalties for the 1956 hit "Why Do Fools Fall in Love"?

A.) In 1992 **Herman Santiago and Jimmy Merchant** were awarded millions of dollars in back royalties for the 1956 hit "Why Do Fools Fall in Love" (#6 2/18/56 *Billboard*). They wrote the tune while singing on street corners in their native New York. Later, when lead singer Frankie Lymon joined the group, which came to be known as Frankie Lymon and the Teenagers, they recorded the tune, and enjoyed a Top 10 hit in 1956. Unfortunately for them, the record business was still in its infancy, and songwriters were often cheated out of their royalties. The copyright for hit songs was quite often registered by record companies or producers, who would get rich, while the artists rarely saw any money from their work. The next thirty-six years saw Santiago and Merchant semi-retire from the music business and take odd jobs, like driving cabs. In 1987 they launched a suit against Morris Levy, the record company executive who owned the song. Levy died in 1989, and his estate settled the case (for an undisclosed sum, rumoured to be in the millions of dollars) in late 1992.

26. What 1956 movie features performances by Little Richard, Fats Domino, Gene Vincent, The Platters, Eddie Cochran, and Ray Anthony?

A.) 1956's **The Girl Can't Help It** features performances by these acts. The music serves as a background for the action; in one scene Eddie Cochran is seen on a television set. All the performances are excellent — worth a rental.

19

27. What was the first film to use rock and roll in its soundtrack?

A.) The first film to feature a rock and roll soundtrack was the 1955 MGM classic **Blackboard Jungle**. The film stars Glenn Ford as a young teacher in a tough school, struggling to win the respect of his juvenile delinquent students. The theme song is Bill Haley's "Rock Around the Clock." As a study of the juvenile delinquent problem of the 1950s *The New York Times* called it a "full throated, all out testimonial to the lurid headlines that appear from time to time, reporting acts of terrorism and violence by uncontrolled urban youths."

28. Who appears, singing the title track of 1958's *High School Confidential*, riding on the back of a truck playing piano?

A.) **Jerry Lee Lewis** sings the title track in this teen-exploitation classic. The film features all the aspects of true teenage trash: fast-talking hipsters, rock and roll, marijuana smoking, hotrods, and Mamie Van Doren. Of particular interest to all cool cats and chicks will be the movie's Beatnik free-form jazz/poem presentation of "Tomorrow is a Drag, Man." This movie was re-released in 1961 as *The Young Hellions*.

29. Which Elvis film featured the hit "Hard Headed Woman"?

A.) The hit "Hard Headed Woman" (#1 6/30/58 *Billboard*) was pulled from the soundtrack of **King Creole**. Although Elvis considered the film to be his best acting role, the soundtrack album didn't warrant great reviews. Rock writers Roy Carr and Mick Farren commented, "It was pretty much of a shame that one of Presley's better dramatic movies should have been saddled with music that was, with few exceptions, substandard."

30. What show marked Elvis Presley's first appearance on national television?

A.) Elvis Presley's first appearance on national television was **"Stage Show"** on CBS on January 28, 1956. He was paid $1,250 for the appearance. He sang two songs: "Blue Suede Shoes" (#20 4/28/56 *Billboard*) and "Heartbreak Hotel" (#1 3/10/56 *Billboard*), the latter with a dreadful orchestral arrangement by Tommy and Jimmy Dorsey. The show was beaten in the ratings by "The Perry Como Show," but still created quite a stir among those who saw it. Comedian Jackie Gleason said, "The kid has no right behaving like a sex maniac on a national show."

31. What year saw "Whole Lotta Shakin' Goin' On" by Jerry Lee Lewis, "You Send Me" by Sam Cooke, and "Bye Bye Love" by The Everly Brothers hit the charts?

A.) "Whole Lotta Shakin' Goin' On" (#3 7/15/57 *Billboard*) by Jerry Lee Lewis, "You Send Me" (#1 10/28/57 *Billboard*) by Sam Cooke, and "Bye Bye Love" (#2 5/27/57 *Billboard*) by The Everly Brothers all hit the charts in **1957**. That year also saw "Jailhouse Rock" b/w "Treat Me Nice" by Elvis Presley hit the top of the charts, while Buddy Knox had the number 1 US pop 45 with "Party Doll," and The Coasters hit the top of the R&B charts with "Searchin'" b/w "Young Blood."

32. What year saw "Johnny B. Goode" by Chuck Berry, "Lonely Teardrops" by Jackie Wilson, and "Summertime Blues" by Eddie Cochran hit the charts?

A.) "Johnny B. Goode" (#8 5/05/58 *Billboard*) by Chuck Berry, "Lonely Teardrops" (#7 12/08/58 *Billboard*) by Jackie Wilson, and "Summertime Blues" (#8 8/25/58 *Billboard*) by Eddie Cochran all hit the charts in **1958**. This year also saw The Champs' instrumental "Tequila" top the US pop 45 chart, while "Poor Little Fool" went all the way for Ricky Nelson, and The Coasters topped the R&B charts with "Yakety Yak." There was much rock and roll scandal in 1958: Jerry Lee Lewis's career skidded to a standstill when the British press discovered

21

BiBang! Baby

that his wife was a scant thirteen years old *and* his third cousin; Iran banned rock and roll, saying that it was against the concepts of Islam and a health hazard; and Alan Freed was arrested for allegedly inciting a riot at his rock and roll stage show at the Boston Arena.

33. Who did Arthur Rubenstein nominate as the finest high school pianist in the New York school system?

A.) **Neil Sedaka** started learning to play the piano at age 9, and by age 12 he had been accepted as a student at the Julliard Preparatory Division for Children. While studying at Julliard he wrote pop songs with his high school girlfriend Carole Klein (who later changed her name to Carole King) and Howard Greenfield. Neil enjoyed his first number 1 single in 1962 with "Breaking Up is Hard to Do" (#1 8/11/62 *Billboard*).

34. Who had a big hit in 1955 with "Moments to Remember"?

A.) **The Four Lads** scored a Top 5 hit with "Moments to Remember" (#2 9/03/55 *Billboard*) in 1955. They had a string of hits, including "No, Not Much" (#2 1/28/56 *Billboard*), "Standing on the Corner" (#3 4/28/56 *Billboard*), and "Who Needs You" (#9 2/02/57 *Billboard*). The Four Lads met in Toronto when they were choirboys at St. Michael's Cathedral.

35. Who topped the *Billboard* charts for nine weeks in 1959 with Brecht/Weill's "Mack the Knife"?

A.) Singer/actor **Bobby Darin** held the number 1 spot on the *Billboard* charts in 1959 with his take on Brecht/Weill's "Mack the Knife" (#1 9/07/59 *Billboard*) from *The Three Penny Opera*. Early in his professional life he announced to the press that he wanted to be "a legend by the time I'm 25." To that end he tried to become an all-round entertainer by recording various styles of music and branching off into motion pictures. His early hits were in the pop/rock vein. He broke into the Top 10 with "Splish Splash" (#3 6/30/58 *Billboard*) and "Queen of the Hop" (#9 10/27/58 *Billboard*) before moving on to Sinatra-style swing. During his marriage to starlet Sandra Dee he launched his film career. In 1963 he was nominated for an Academy Award for his portrayal of a drugged hospital patient in *Captain Newman MD*. 1961/62 saw another musical direction with the release of several R&B flavoured recordings from Darin, including "Multiplication" (#30 1/20/62 *Billboard*) from the film *Come September*. His last Top 10 hit came in 1966 with a folk reading of "If I Were a Carpenter" (#8 10/08/66 *Billboard*). Darin died in 1973 during a heart operation.

36. What was Chuck Berry's 1955 hit "Maybelline" originally called?

A.) Chuck Berry's 1955 hit "Maybelline" (#5 8/20/55 *Billboard*) was originally written as **"Ida May."** Berry recorded "Maybelline" on May 21, 1955, during his first session for Chess Records. A producer at Chess Records felt that "Ida May" sounded like a country song, and suggested that Berry change the title and give the song more of a rock and roll feel. Disc jockey Alan Freed was invited to the session to advise Berry on how to make the song more appealing to white audiences. Freed re-wrote the lyrics, and was rewarded with a writer's credit on the tune. By August the song had reached the number 5 spot on the *Billboard* charts, giving Berry his first rock and roll hit.

37. What was the first number 1 single to have the words "rock and roll" in its title?

A.) Kay Starr's **"Rock and Roll Waltz"** topped the *Billboard* charts on February 18, 1956. This song broke a lot of new ground: it was the first number 1 single for a female artist since the birth of rock and roll, and it was RCA's first number 1 record.

38. Who were the first black artists to have a number 1 single on the pop charts?

A.) **The Platters** were the first black singing group to top the pop charts when they released "My Prayer" (#1 8/04/56 *Billboard*), which was an adaptation of a French song called "Avant de Mourir." "My Prayer" topped the charts for two weeks. Under the guidance of producer Buck Ram, The Platters found success with remakes of standards and show tunes. Aside from "My Prayer" (a remake of a 1939 hit), they also reinterpreted "Harbor Lights," which was made famous by Rudy Vallee in 1937, and the Jerome Kern standard "Smoke Gets in Your Eyes." They were the most popular vocal group of the fifties, but their sound was soon eclipsed in the sixties by funkier vocal groups like The Temptations and The Supremes. The Platters, in one form or another, continued to perform (mostly in Europe and Asia) until the early eighties.

39. What was Arthur Andrew Kelm better known as?

A.) Arthur Andrew Kelm was well-known to record buyers and movie-goers as **Tab Hunter.** Tab scored his only number 1 hit in 1957 with "Young Love" (#1 3/02/1957 *Billboard*) on the Dot label. During the fifties he had a thriving Hollywood film career (*Island of Desire, Damn Yankees*) before moving to Europe to work in more artistically satisfying roles.

40. Who is the only native of Happy, Texas, to score a number 1 single?

A.) **Buddy Knox**, a native of Happy, Texas, topped the *Billboard* charts for the week of March 30, 1957, with his song "Party Doll." Knox co-wrote the song with bandmate Jimmy Bowen, and became the first artist to top the charts with a self-penned rock and roll song. Knox and his Rhythm Orchids placed several more songs in the Top 40, including "Hula Love" and "Somebody Touched Me," but the hits stopped coming in 1961.

41. Who was the inspiration for Paul Anka's 1957 number 1 hit "Diana"?

24

A.) A fifteen-year-old Paul Anka was infatuated with his younger sister and brother's babysitter, **Diana Ayoub**. She was 20 and wanted nothing to do with the skinny fifteen-year-old. To try and win her affection he composed a poem for her. This poem, when set to music, would give Anka his first number 1 hit on both sides of the Atlantic.

42. Who was the inspiration for Ritchie Valens's 1958 hit "Donna"?

A.) Ritchie Valens's first Top 5 hit, "Donna" (#2 12/15/58 *Billboard*), was a love song written for his high school sweetheart **Donna Ludwig**. Ritchie and Donna's romance was chronicled in the bio-pic *La Bamba*, starring Lou Diamond Phillips as the ill-fated singer. Valens's life was tragically cut short a few months after his success with this song when he was killed in the plane crash that also claimed Buddy Holly and The Big Bopper.

43. Who was the inspiration for Buddy Holly's 1957 Top 5 hit "Peggy Sue"?

A.) Buddy Holly almost immortalized the fictional "Cindy Lou" in his first Top 5 single. The title was changed to "Peggy Sue" (#3 11/11/57 *Billboard*) while they were recording. **Holly's drummer, Jerry Allison, was about to marry a girl named Peggy Sue**, and asked Buddy if he would change the title of the song as a tribute to her. Buddy agreed, and several months later penned "Peggy Sue Got Married" as a follow-up. This piece of rock and roll trivia was dramatized on the big screen in the Academy Award-nominated bio-pic *The Buddy Holly Story* starring Gary Busey.

44. Where was Buddy Holly born?

A.) Charles Hardin "Buddy" Holly was born on September 7, 1936, in **Lubbock, Texas.** Fans visiting Lubbock can visit many Buddy Holly landmarks — The Buddy Holly Recreation Area (on North University); Buddy Holly's Grave in Lubbock Cemetery (2011 East 31st), and the 1957 home of Buddy Holly (1305 37th Street). For more information on Lubbock call the Chamber of Commerce at (806) 763-4666 or the Buddy Holly Memorial Society (806) 799-4299.

45. Which gospel singer recorded the 1956 single "Lovable" under the pseudonym Dale Cooke?

A.) **Sam Cooke** released the 1956 pop single "Lovable" under the pseudonym Dale Cooke. At the time Sam was the lead singer for the gospel group The Soul Stirrers. In the fifties there was no crossover between gospel and secular music. Sam wanted to cut some pop records, but because he was part of a famous gospel group he was forced to use an alias. Once The Soul Stirrers found out that he was releasing pop records they let him go. His first secular single under his own name was 1957's "You Send Me" (#1 10/28/57 *Billboard*), which topped the charts for three weeks. He consistently placed singles in the Top 40 until his tragic shooting death in 1964.

46. What was the original title of Danny and the Juniors' 1958 hit "At the Hop"?

A.) Danny and the Juniors' 1958 hit "At the Hop" (#1 1/06/58 *Billboard*) was originally a dance song called **"Do the Bop."** The Bop was a very popular dance on Dick Clark's "American Bandstand" during the summer of 1957. Hoping to cash in on the dance craze, Danny and the Juniors took the song to Dick Clark to see if he could use it on his show. Clark, ever-mindful of teenage trends, advised them that The Bop was on the way out, and suggested they call the song "At the Hop." They took his advice, and "At the Hop" sat on the top of the charts for five weeks.

47. Which instrumental record won the first ever Grammy for "Best R&B Performance"?

A.) **"Tequila"** (#1 3/03/58 *Billboard*) by The Champs received this honour. The Champs were a group of session players who were recording tracks for a Jerry Wallace record. At the end of the session there were a few minutes to spare so they improvised on a song that saxophonist Danny Flores had written during a visit to Mexico. It was considered a throwaway track that would be released as filler on an instrumental album, or used as a b-side for a single. Certainly no one expected it to shoot to the top of the charts and hold the number 1 position for five weeks. The deep voice that shouts "tequila" during the song belonged to Danny Flores, who changed his name to Chuck Rio after the success of "Tequila."

48. Which novelty rocker played cattle-drive scout Pete Nolan opposite Clint Eastwood on television's "Rawhide"?

A.) Singer **Sheb Wooley** played Nolan for four and a half years on "Rawhide." Between roping steers on the show he found the time to record a novelty tune called "The Purple People Eater" (#1 6/09/58 *Billboard*), which lassoed the top of the charts for six weeks. Wooley made his film debut in 1950 with Errol Flynn in *Rocky Mountain* and can be seen in *Giant* opposite Rock Hudson, Elizabeth Taylor, and James Dean.

49. What was the first song to top *Billboard's* Hot 100 when it debuted as a regular feature in 1958?

A.) Since its beginning in August 1958 *Billboard Magazine's* Hot 100 chart has been the most reliable guide to the most popular discs in North America. The first record to top the Hot 100 was Ricky Nelson's **"Poor Little Fool"** (#1 7/07/58 *Billboard*).

50. Who inspired The Champs' name?

A.) The Champs were a group of session players who borrowed their name from **Gene Autry's horse Champion.** Guitarist Dave

27

Big Bang! Baby

Burgess was the only consistent member of the band, with other members coming and going continuously. Over the years several famous musicians passed through The Champs. Glen Campbell played guitar with them for a time before moving on to a solo career. Jim Seals and Dash Crofts both were members, although neither of them played on The Champs' biggest hit, "Tequila" (#1 3/17/58 *Billboard*). The Champs hung up their spurs in 1965 after the disappointing showings of their follow-up singles "El Rancho Rock" (#30 6/02/58 *Billboard*), "Too Much Tequila" (#30 2/08/60 *Billboard*), and "Limbo Rock" (#40 7/14/62 *Billboard*).

51. What is the only number 1 song written by a vice president of the United States?

A.) The music for the 1958 Tommy Edwards number 1 hit **"It's All in the Game"** (#1 9/29/58 *Billboard*) was written in 1912 by Charles Gates Dawes, who would become vice president of the United States under Calvin Coolidge. Thirty-nine years later songwriter Carl Sigman embellished the tune with some lyrics, the result being recorded by Sammy Kaye, Carmen Cavallaro, Dinah Shore, and Tommy Edwards. Edwards' version reached the Top 20 in 1951, but it wasn't until 1958 when he re-cut the song as a rock and roll ballad that he hit the top of the charts. In 1964 Cliff Richard's take on the song reached number 25, while The Four Tops' version touched down at number 24 in 1970.

52. How did Harold Jenkins choose his stage name?

A.) Harold Jenkins chose his stage name by **studying a map of the United States.** He chose place names of two southern towns for his stage moniker — Conway, Arkansas, and Twitty, Texas. In the fifties Conway Twitty was known as a rock and roll singer, and scored a number 1 hit in 1958 with "It's Only Make Believe" (#1 9/29/58 *Billboard*). His rock and roll image was so strong that the role model for Conrad Birdie in the musical *Bye Bye Birdie* was a cross between Twitty and Elvis Presley. It was in country music, however, that Twitty would make his mark, placing thirty-six consecutive Top 5 singles on the country charts from 1968 to 1977.

53. Which 1933 stage musical did "Smoke Gets in Your Eyes" appear in?

A.) "Smoke Gets in Your Eyes" was first heard in 1933's stage musical ***Roberta*** by Jerome Kern. In 1959 The Platters topped the charts with their Buck Ram-produced version of the old standard. Mrs. Kern, however, was not pleased that a modern group was recording a rock and roll version of her husband's song and tried to stop the release of the record. She relented when the song came out and started to climb the charts, and the royalty checks started coming in. In January of '58 the song sat at the top of the charts for three weeks, giving The Platters their last number 1 hit.

54. Who was known as "Mr. Personality"?

A.) New Orleans singer **Lloyd Price** was nicknamed "Mr. Personality" after his 1959 hit "Personality" (#2 5/11/59 *Billboard*), which sat at number 2 for three weeks. Price started in the music business as a jingle writer, but soon branched out into rock and roll. His best-known composition, "Lawdy Miss Clawdy," began life as a station break jingle for WBOK in New Orleans. Price's biggest hit was an R&B re-working of the traditional folk song "Stack-O-Lee," which he modified and retitled "Stagger Lee" (#1 2/09/59 *Billboard*).

55. What American city was home to Frankie Avalon, Bobby Rydell, Chubby Checker, and "American Bandstand"?

A.) **Philadelphia** was a breeding ground for talent in the fifties and early sixties. It is the city that gave us Frankie Avalon ("Venus," #1 3/09/59 *Billboard*), Bobby Rydell ("Wild One," #1 2/08/60 *Billboard*), James Darren ("Goodbye Cruel World," #3 11/06/61 *Billboard*), Chubby Checker ("The Twist," #1 8/08/60 *Billboard*), Fabian ("Tiger," #3 6/22/59 *Billboard*), and "American Bandstand."

Bang! Baby

Chubby Checker, born Earnest Evans in Philadelphia, Pennsylvania. Checker began his music career in 1959 while working at a local chicken market. He achieved national fame in 1960 with "The Twist."

56. What was the first number 1 rock single to pay tribute to an American city?

A.) The first number 1 rock single to pay tribute to an American city was Wilbert Harrison's **"Kansas City"** (#1 5/18/59 *Billboard*). The song was written by Jerry Leiber and Mike Stoller in the early fifties, and was issued under the name "K.C. Lovin'" by blues singer Little Willie Littlefield in 1952. The most famous version of the song appears on The Beatles' *For Sale* album, although it has been recorded by Hank Ballard and the Midnighters, Rocky Olson, Rockin' Ronald and the Rebels, and Little Richard.

57. This 1959 instrumental was called "Nuit Bleu" in France, "Loa" in Belguim, and "Grido" in Italy. What was the song called in North America?

A.) The 1959 number 1 Santo and Johnny hit **"Sleepwalk"** (#1 9/21/59 *Billboard*) was re-recorded as "Nuit Blue" by Caterina Valente in France; as "Loa" by Wim Van De Velde in Belgium; and "Grido" by Niki Davis in Italy. "Sleepwalk" was the last fifties instrumental to climb to the top the charts, where it sat for two weeks. Instrumentals were big business in rock's early years, with many of them going to number 1: "Tequila" by The Champs, "Telstar" by The Tornadoes, and "The Stripper" by David Rose to name a few. This trend continued until 1963 when the public seemed to lose interest in instrumental music. It wouldn't be until 1968 that another instrumental tune would make any

impact on the charts ("Love is Blue" by Paul Mauriat). In recent years only Vangelis's "Chariots of Fire" (#1 5/08/82 *Billboard*) has topped the charts, becoming only the twenty-third instrumental to hit number 1 since 1955.

58. What was the last song to reach number 1 on the *Billboard* charts in the fifties?

A.) The last number 1 song of the fifties was Frankie Avalon's **"Why"** (#1 12/28/59 *Billboard*). It was also Frankie Avalon's last number 1 hit. "Why" was co-written by Bob Marcucci, who was a legendary Philadelphia manager and talent scout. It was Marcucci who discovered and cultivated the talents of Frankie Avalon, Fabian, and a host of other teen idols. In 1980 Ray Sharkey played a character loosely based on Marcucci in *The Idolmaker*.

59. On which Buddy Holly song can a real, live cricket be heard?

A.) Careful listening will reveal a cricket's chirp near the end of **"I'm Gonna Love You Too"** by Buddy Holly and the Crickets. The sound is a real cricket that had found its way into the studio.

60. What movie inspired Buddy Holly to write "That'll be the Day"?

A.) Buddy Holly was inspired to write "That'll be the Day" (#1 8/19/57 *Billboard*) after watching the John Wayne movie ***The Searchers***. Wayne played a defiant anti-hero, and often said that it was his favourite film role. His catch-phrase in the movie was "That'll be the day," which he belligerently repeated throughout the film. Holly liked the sound of the phrase, and fashioned his first number 1 hit around it.

61. Who inspired The Bobbettes' 1957 Top 10 hit "Mr. Lee"?

A.) The Bobbettes were an all-female doo-wop group from New York. They all attended New York's P.S. 109 and studied with a **teacher**

Big Bang! Baby

named **Mr. Lee**. He wasn't very popular, so the girls wrote a song about him, with a verse that teased, "He's the ugliest teacher I ever did see." When it came time to record the song, Atlantic Records producer James Dailey suggested they change the words to something more complimentary. They did ("He's the handsomest sweetie I ever did see"), and "Mr. Lee" (#6 8/12/57 *Billboard*) became their only Top 40 song. Three years later, desperate for a hit, they released "I Shot Mr. Lee," which failed to emulate the success of the original song.

62. Who was known as "the Sheik of the Blues" in 1957?

A.) Georgia-based R&B singer **Chuck Willis** earned the title "the Sheik of the Blues" by scoring a string of top-selling R&B records and wearing a turban onstage and off. He later became "the King of the Stroll" when kids began doing the stroll to his songs "C.C. Rider" (#12 5/13/57 *Billboard*) and "Betty and Dupree" (#33 3/10/58 *Billboard*). Just as he was poised on the verge of major stardom he died from complications following a stomach ulcer operation. Ironically his posthumous hits were titled "What am I Living For" (#9 5/12/58 *Billboard*) and "Hang Up My Rock and Roll Shoes" (#24 5/26/58 *Billboard*).

63. What was J.P. Richardson better known as?

A.) Jiles Perry (J.P.) Richardson was known to audiences as **The Big Bopper.** Before becoming a recording star Richardson was a disc jockey. Inspired by the dance craze "The Bop," he changed his name. In 1957 The Big Bopper broke the record for continuous on-air broadcasting by staying on air for five days, two hours, and eight minutes. During his marathon he played 1,821 records, lost thirty-five pounds, and was paid $746.50 by his sponsor, station KTRM. While still d.j.-ing he wrote several hits for other artists, including George Jones's "White Lightening" (which hit number 1 on the country charts) and "Running Bear" (#1 12/21/59 *Billboard*) by Johnny Preston. The Bopper can be heard on "Running Bear" doing background vocals and providing Indian sounds. He released a

HELLOOO BABY!
THE BEST OF
THE BIG BOPPER

1954-1959

series of country tunes under the name Jape Richardson and the Japettes before a novelty tune, "Chantilly Lace" (#6 8/04/58 *Billboard*), gave The Big Bopper his biggest hit. Richardson died tragically at age 28 in the same plane crash that claimed Buddy Holly and Ritchie Valens.

64. Where did Buddy Holly, Ritchie Valens, and The Big Bopper play their last show?

While working as a disc jockey at KTRM radio, Jiles Perry Richardson needed a gimmick — something to spice up the show. At a college dance he saw all the kids doing a dance called "The Bop," so he lifted the name and became The Big Bopper.

Photo courtesy of Rhino Records

A.) Buddy Holly, Ritchie Valens, and The Big Bopper were the headliners on the Winter Dance Party Tour, which touched down at **The Surf Ballroom in Clear Lake City, Iowa,** on February 2, 1959. Admission to the show was $1.25 and almost 1,500 people showed up. Buddy Holly had booked a plane to transport he and his band on to the next stop on the tour after the show. He was fed up travelling in the broken-down old buses with the other musicians. The night before their Surf Ballroom show the unheated tour bus had quit completely outside Green Bay. The musicians tried in vain to keep warm by burning newspapers in the aisles, but several people got frostbite anyway. After this experience Buddy decided to make the next trip by plane both for comfort, and to provide time to do laundry, as the stage costumes hadn't been washed in a long time. After the show The Big Bopper and Ritchie Valens managed to connive their way onto the fateful plane, which crashed near Mason City, Iowa, on February 3,

1959, claiming the lives of all those on board. The Surf Ballroom still plays host to live music, and features many things of interest to a Buddy Holly fan. The payphone that Buddy and Ritchie Valens made their last phone calls on is in working order in the lobby, and there is a plaque commemorating the three musicians (plus their pilot, Roger Peterson) outside the building.

65. Who headlined the first rock and roll concert at New York's Carnegie Hall?

A.) The first rock and roll concert at Carnegie Hall (881 Seventh Avenue) was headlined by **Bill Haley and the Comets** in May 1955. The bill also included The McGuire Sisters, Les Paul and Mary Ford, Clifford Brown, and Max Roach. Since then many rock and roll concerts have been staged in America's premier concert hall, with different degrees of success. In 1961 Bob Dylan played in Carnegie's small side room, Chapter Hall. The November show only drew a crowd of sixty, and the promoter lost money. The Rolling Stones almost caused a riot when they played their first New York shows there in June 1964. Unimpressed with the Stones' fans, and their wild behaviour, Carnegie officials banned rock and roll shows the next day. This ban stood for almost a decade. Ray Charles summed up the mystique of the New York venue: "After Carnegie Hall," he wrote in his autobiography, "I've been more or less nonchalant about all the others."

66. What rock and roll landmark is located at 706 Union Street, Memphis, Tennessee?

A.) **Sun Studios** is located at this address. The studio was founded in the early fifties by Sam Phillips. The Sun Records label launched the first crop of superstars of the rock era — Elvis Presley, Carl Perkins, Jerry Lee Lewis, Roy Orbison, Johnny Cash, and a parade of lesser-known acts. Sun specialized in rockabilly, which fused blues, country, and honky tonk, all of which were prevalent in the Memphis area. Phillips sold Sun Studios in 1969, but the studio is still fully operational. Recently U2, Ringo Starr, and actor Dennis Quaid have recorded tracks in the legendary studio. The facility is open for tours. For information call (901) 521-9820.

67. What is the origin of Chuck Berry's famous duck walk?

A.) Chuck Berry first did his famous duck walk onstage during one of Alan Freed's rock and roll shows at the Brooklyn Paramount Theatre. Originally **the move was designed to camouflage the wrinkles in the cheap suit** he was wearing. By bending over and holding his guitar up high he could make the wrinkles less noticeable. The crowd cheered the unusual move, so he kept it in his show. Since then it has become a Chuck Berry trademark.

68. How much did Elvis Presley pay for Graceland in 1957?

A.) Elvis Presley was twenty-two years old when he paid **$100,000** for Graceland and its surrounding 13.8 acres in 1957. The house stands on the site of a five-hundred-acre farm owned by the Toof family during the Civil War. The mansion was built in 1939 by Dr. Thomas D. Moore who named it after his ancestor, Grace Toof. Elvis lived in the house from 1957 until his death in 1977. Since June 1982 Graceland has been open to the public. In those years it has become one of the most popular tourist attractions in America, drawing over 650,000 visitors a year. Graceland is the first rock and roll landmark to be registered with the National Register of Historic Places.

69. Who is buried in the Meditation Garden at Graceland?

A.) The final stop of the Graceland tour is the Meditation Garden. Here lie the bodies of **Elvis Presley, his mother Gladys, his father Vernon, and his grandmother Minnie.** There is also a cenotaph for Elvis's twin brother Jesse Garon, who is buried in an unmarked grave in Tupelo, Mississippi. The bodies of Elvis and his mother (who died in 1958) were originally interred at Forest Hills Cemetery in Memphis, but were moved to Graceland for security reasons. The misspelling of Elvis's middle name on his plaque (it reads Aaron — he spelled it Aron) threw fuel on the "Elvis is alive" fire. Those who believe Elvis is still alive think that he was too superstitious to put his real name on the grave, hence the misspelling of his middle name. Graceland officials don't offer any explanation for the extra "a".

70. Who were "The Million Dollar Quartet"?

A.) The Million Dollar Quartet was a group of Sun Records recording stars who jammed together for an afternoon in 1956. **Elvis Presley, Jerry Lee Lewis, Carl Perkins, and Johnny Cash** (who left the session early), were doodling in the Sun Studios on Tuesday, December 4, 1956, and someone happened to turn on a tape machine. The result was an album, *The Million Dollar Quartet* (a name coined by writer Bob Johnson, who wrote about the event), which includes a loose collection of studio chatter and fragments of songs. Johnny Cash had his photos taken with the Quartet, but does not actually appear on the record, although he apparently recorded two songs with them that have been lost over the years. The recordings have been digitally remastered, and were released on compact disc in 1990.

71. What song introduced the Bo Diddley beat to the world of rock and roll?

A.) The Bo Diddley beat — or "Bo Beat" as it is called — was first heard on **Bo Diddley's eponymous debut single**. Diddley was born Otha Ellas Bates on December 30, 1928, but was later adopted by the McDaniel family, becoming Ellas McDaniel. As a child of 10 he heard John Lee Hooker's version of "Boogie Children" and decided to play the guitar. His career took off when he earned a residency at Chicago's famous R&B nightspot the 708 Club. In 1955 he began recording for Chess Records in Chicago, and was possibly the first rock artist to sing a song about himself. More important than the content of the song, though, is the song's unusual chunka-chunka rhythm. The "Bo-Beat" has influenced many rock artists since then, and has become a staple of modern rock and roll.

72. Why did Bill Haley turn down his first offer to play outside the United States?

A.) Bill Haley rejected his first opportunity to play outside the United States because he was **afraid to fly**. An Australian promoter wanted to book a tour "down under" to coincide with the Australian release of "Rock Around the Clock." Even the guarantee of two thousand dollars a day for a fifteen-day tour couldn't persuade Haley to fly the coop. Haley overcame his fear of flying in 1957, when he embarked on a two-week tour of England, sharing the bill with Big Joe Turner and LaVern Baker.

73. Which founding father of rock and roll helped to create the Holiday Inn chain of hotels?

A.) In 1952 Sun Records owner and rock and roll founding father **Sam Phillips** invested $25,000 towards the building of the Memphis, Tennessee, Holiday Inn, the first in the giant chain of hotels. Since then the Holiday Inn has become a staple to any rock and roller on the road. In 1968 legendary rock rowdy man Keith Moon was celebrating his birthday at the Holiday Inn in Flint, Michigan, when he drove a Lincoln Continental into the swimming pool of the hotel. As he crawled out of the sinking car he threw the keys to the valet and asked him to park it. In the late eighties The Beastie Boys were banned from the entire chain for allegedly drilling a hole between their stacked suites for easier conversation.

74. Which outrageous father of rock and roll retired from the stage in 1957 to preach the word of God?

A.) **Little Richard** was on tour in Australia when he announced that he would retire from the music business. "If you want to live for the Lord," he said, "you can't rock and roll too." To prove his devotion to the sceptics in his band he threw four diamond rings, valued at over eight thousand dollars, into Sydney's Hunter River. In early 1958 he enrolled at the Seventh Day Adventist-run Oakwood College to study the Bible.

75. Which fifties rocker is credited with having discovered the guitar fuzz tone?

A.) Guitarist **Link Wray** ("Rumble" and "Rawhide") is credited with having discovered the guitar fuzz tone. Wray's records featured fat dirty riffs played on a distorted guitar. He achieved this sound purely by accident. The legend has it that Wray, angered by some malfunctioning equipment, punched a hole in his amplifier's speaker. The result was a dirty, distorted sound that would go on to become his trademark. Wray's patented sound would be an influence to a whole generation of guitar players like Jeff Beck, Pete Townshend, and Bob Dylan.

76. Who accompanied Jerry Lee Lewis on his 1958 tour of Britain?

A.) On his first tour of Britain in 1958 Jerry Lee Lewis was accompanied by his band and, against the wishes of his managers, **his thirteen-year-old wife (and third cousin) Myra.** The marriage had been hushed up in the United States, but the news made headlines in the United Kingdom when Lewis truthfully answered reporters' questions about his personal life. The result of the scandal was that thirty-four of the thirty-seven dates on the tour were cancelled, and the *London Evening Star* ran an editorial calling Lewis an "undesirable alien." He returned to more outrage in the United States, and a career that was quickly falling apart. He publicly announced to *Billboard* that if he was washed up as an entertainer, he hoped it wasn't "because of this bad publicity, because I can cry and wish all I want to, but I can't control the press or the sensationalism that these people will go to, to get a scandal started to sell papers." His career was stopped short, and it would be three years before he would break into the Top 40 again. After a tumultuous marriage Jerry Lee and Myra divorced in the early seventies.

77. What was Buddy Holly's last single before his death in 1959?

38

A. Buddy Holly's last single released during his lifetime was **"It Doesn't Matter Anymore"** (#13 3/09/59 *Billboard*). The song is unusual because it is not a Buddy Holly composition, having been written by Paul Anka with Holly in mind. Buddy rarely covered songs by other artists.

78. What was the world's first circular office building?

A. The world's first circular office building was the **Capitol Records Tower** at 1750 North Vine in Hollywood. The building was erected in 1956, designed to resemble a pile of records. If you watch closely you will notice that the light on top of Capitol Records' "needle" blinks the word H-O-L-L-Y-W-O-O-D in Morse code. At the time of the construction Capitol was just beginning to move into the rock and roll market, and had just signed Gene Vincent to their roster. Since then they have been leaders in promoting rock music, having signed The Beatles, The Band, Bob Seger, Duran Duran, The Beach Boys, and Steve Miller. The Capitol Records Tower still houses the West Coast offices of Capitol, and the famous studio in the basement is still operational.

The Capitol Records building at 1750 North Vine in Hollywood. Designed by architect Welton Becket, construction on "the stack of records" building began in 1956.

Photo by Richard Crouse

79. What was Elvis Presley's favourite snack?

A. Elvis Presley's favourite snack was a **fried peanut butter and banana sandwich.** To make one of Elvis's "nanner" sandwiches you will need two slices of white bread, one ripe banana, 45 mL of peanut butter, and 30 mL of butter. First mash up the banana,

39

the riper the banana the better. Next toast the bread lightly, then spread the mashed banana on one piece, the peanut butter on the other. Finally melt the butter in a skillet, and fry the sandwich until golden brown. Cut in quarters and serve.

80. What is skiffle music?

A.) The skiffle music craze swept through Britain in 1957, and made stars of Lonnie Donegan, The Vipers, and The Chas McDevitt Skiffle Group. Skiffle was a **do-it-yourself folk music,** often played on acoustic guitars, washboards, kazoos, washbasin string basses, and other homemade instruments. The arrangements of the songs were simple, and lent themselves to singing along. Skiffle remained a British phenomenon, although Lonnie Donegan and his Skiffle Group made a dent in the US charts with "Rock Island Line" (#8 3/31/56 *Billboard)* and the novelty "Does Your Chewing Gun Lose Its Flavour (on the Bedpost Over Night)" (#5 8/14/61 *Billboard*). Donegan reported that he found the chewing gum song "buried within the yellowed pages of a boy scout songbook."

81. Who released the lascivious "Work With Me Annie" in 1954?

A.) **Hank Ballard and the Midnighters** scored their first big R&B hit with the suggestive "Work With Me Annie" in 1954. The lyrics bragged about the sexual stamina of the singer, and as a result the song was banned by many radio stations. That would have been the end of the story, except that Etta James recorded an answer to Ballard's tune, "Roll With Me Henry," in which she questioned some of his boasts. To end the argument, and prove that his boasts were true, Henry shot back with "Annie Had a Baby." Etta James had the last word in this vinyl argument with "Henry's Got Flat Feet."

82. What was the lowest score a record could receive on "American Bandstand"'s Rate-a-Record? What was the highest?

A.) One of "American Bandstand"'s greatest traditions was the Rate-a-Record segment. A teenage jury of four would listen to two records and rate them for listenability and danceability. Host Dick Clark would select four kids from the audience to judge two records — three to judge, one to keep score. The most famous Bandstand phrase was born during this segment of the show: "It's got a good beat and you can dance to it. I'll give it a 90." Clark imposed rules for rating the records: No song could score less than **thirty-five** or more than **ninety-eight**, based on the theory that no record was completely terrible or completely perfect. Usually dead-on, the Rate-a-Record segment was a good way for record

Hank Ballard, the originator of The Twist. His cousin, Florence Ballard, also found fame as a member of The Supremes.

company insiders to test a song's popularity. It wasn't always infallible, however. One of the lowest-rated songs ever to appear on "American Bandstand" was "The Chipmunk Song" by Alvin and the Chipmunks. It was one of the few records to receive a 35 and then go on to become a major hit. It reached number 1 on the pop charts and sold millions of copies. In the fall of 1963 "She Loves You" by The Beatles scored a paltry 71, with one audience member commenting, "It doesn't seem to be anything special ... the best I can give it is a 70."

83. Who originally recorded "The Twist"?

A.) "The Twist" was originally recorded by **Hank Ballard and the Midnighters** in 1959. Hank, who wrote the song, wanted to release it as a single, but his record company chose instead to issue it as a b-side to "Teardrops on Your

41

BiBang! Baby

Letter." Meanwhile, The Twist was fast becoming a dance craze among big city kids and on television dance shows. Chubby Checker covered the song, appeared on "American Bandstand," and quickly became the ambassador of The Twist. During the Twist craze Ballard's version limped to number 28 on the charts, but it was Checker who made a name for himself with the song.

84. Which game show host had a Top 10 hit with 1959's "Deck of Cards"?

A.) Game show host **Wink Martindale** (real name: Winston Conrad) had a number 7 hit with "Deck of Cards" in 1959. The spoken-word song about a lonely soldier who finds solace with a pack of cards was a cover of T. Texas Tyler's 1948 country hit. Martindale's recording career didn't take off — "Deck of Cards" was his only hit — but he did find fame as master of ceremonies of such game shows as "Tic Tac Dough" and "Last Word."

85. Which comedy duo introduced "break-in" records like "The Flying Saucer Parts 1 and 2" and "Santa and the Satellite"?

A.) **Bill Buchanan and Dickie Goodman** have a dubious musical claim to fame. Songs such as "The Flying Saucer Parts 1 and 2" (#3 8/11/56 *Billboard*), "Flying Saucer the 2nd" b/w "Martian Melody" (#18 7/29/57 *Billboard*), and "Flying Saucer Goes West" b/w "Saucer Serenade" gave birth to two new genres of music. Firstly, with these releases Buchanan and Goodman created the "break-in" record. These singles featured a narrator asking questions, with answers supplied by clips (or "break-ins") from hit songs to tell the story. Secondly (and most obviously), the duo pioneered "space rock" — songs about outer space. They weren't alone, however: also cashing in on America's fascination with all things alien were Billy Lee Riley ("Flying Saucer Rock 'N' Roll") and Jesse Lee Turner ("Odes to the Little Girl" and "Her Father.") Space themes also abounded in late-fifties and early-sixties singles by Sheb Wooley, Jose Jimenez, and Gene Vincent and the Ran-Dels.

42

86. Who was known as "Mr. Excitement, Mr. Delightment"?

A.) Soul singer **Jackie Wilson** was known as "Mr. Excitement, Mr. Delightment" during his peak years in the early sixties. Wilson's most memorable vocal performances mixed the excitement of gospel singing and the sexuality of soul crooning to create his unique and irresistible sound. He first entered the Top 10 in 1958 with "Lonely Teardrops" (#7 12/08/58 *Billboard*), and despite some personal setbacks (including a bizarre and almost fatal shooting accident) he continued to place songs in the Top 40 for the next ten years. In 1975 tragedy struck when Wilson had a stroke onstage at the Latin Casino in Cherry Hill, New Jersey. He had just sung the words "my heart is crying" (from his signature song "Lonely Teardrops") when he collapsed. The audience, thinking it was part of his dramatic act, applauded wildly while the band continued to play. After thirty seconds or so the band realized something was wrong, and attempted to revive him. Wilson survived the stroke, but never recovered fully, and he died on January 21, 1984.

87. What fifties doo-wop band did Johnny Mastrangelo lead?

A.) Using the stage name Johnny Maestro, Johnny Mastrangelo was the leader of the doo-wop band **The Crests**. They are best known for their 1958 hit "16 Candles" (#2 12/22/58 *Billboard*), which became *the* make-out song of that year. The Crests chugged along for another three hitless years before Maestro split for a solo career. It would be eight years before he would hit the charts again, this time as the leader of the one-hit wonders The Brooklyn Bridge. Their only chart entry, "The Worst That Could Happen" (#3 1/04/69 *Billboard*), was a remake of an old Fifth Dimension number. The follow-up single "Welcome Me, Love" didn't chart. Maestro found himself without a recording contract by the early seventies, but made a living playing his old hits on the rock revival circuit.

88. What is Fabian's last name?

BiBang! Baby

A.) When "idolmaker" Bob Marcucci was gearing Fabiano **Forte** for teen stardom, the first thing he did was shorten his name to the less-ethnic-sounding Fabian. In 1959–60 Fabian's last name was one of the most closely guarded secrets in rock and roll. His lack of formal musical training is apparent on his early records, but he had a nice smile, and fit the teenage idol mould perfectly. After his initial chart success ("Turn Me Loose," "Tiger") he set his sights on movie stardom. His big screen debut, *Hound Dog Man,* was a critical flop, but did respectable business and the theme provided Fabian with his last Top 10 hit.

89. What name is on Bobby Rydell's birth certificate?

A.) Bobby Rydell's real name is **Robert Ridarelli.** After a successful singing career ("Wild One," "Swingin' School," and "Volare") Rydell moved into motion pictures. His biggest hit was the film adaptation of the Broadway musical *Bye Bye Birdie*, about a rock singer, Conrad Birdie, who gets drafted.

90. Whose debut single on the Brunswick label was "Reet Petite"?

A.) **Jackie Wilson** launched his solo career by releasing "Reet Petite" on the Brunswick label in 1957. Wilson had been a Golden Gloves boxing champion at age 16, but hung up his gloves to replace Clyde McPhatter in The Dominoes. He enjoyed the fame he earned as lead singer of The Dominoes, and wanted a solo career. He left The Dominoes in 1957, and signed a deal with Brunswick to make solo recordings. It was around this time he met a young Berry (Motown) Gordy Jr., who offered Jackie a song he had just written. The song, "Reet Petite," climbed into the Top 10 in Britain, but barely managed to dent the Top 75 in the United States. After a prolific recording career Wilson suffered a stroke on stage in 1975, and died in 1984 at age 49.

91. Who began their singing career as The Robins?

A.) **The Coasters** were originally called The Robins. They chose the name to cash in on the avian name craze among L.A. doo-wop groups like The Orioles, The Crows, The Penguins, The Wrens, The Flamingos, and The Ravens. The Robins scored a few minor hits with "Riot in Cell Block #9," "Framed," and "Smokey Joe's Cafe" before reorganizing and forming The Coasters in 1956. Their West Coast home inspired their new name. The Coasters, with writers/producers Leiber and Stoller, enjoyed a string of hits like "Young Blood" (#8 5/20/57 *Billboard*), "Yakety Yak" (#1 6/09/58 *Billboard*), "Poison Ivy" (#7 9/07/59 *Billboard*), and "Charlie Brown" (#2 2/09/59 *Billboard*). Their humorous songs earned them a reputation as the comedians of rock and roll. They disbanded in the early sixties.

92. Who was the deep voiced narrator on The Robins' hit "Riot in Cell Block #9"?

A.) **Richard Berry,** who wrote one of rock's most famous songs, "Louie Louie," is the deep voiced narrator on The Robins' hit "Riot in Cell Block #9." Berry can also be heard as the "voice" of Henry on Etta James's "Roll With Me Henry" (1955). The Robins changed their name to The Coasters in 1956. Their stock in trade were humorous singles, many of which were penned by Leiber and Stoller, who

The Coasters, early rock and roll's pre-eminent vocal group. They built their career on a series of cleverly comic R&B songs written by their producers, Leiber and Stoller.

Photo courtesy of Rhino Records

45

Big Bang! Baby

also wrote "Hound Dog," "Stand By Me," "There Goes My Baby," and "Jailhouse Rock," among others. The Coasters split in the early sixties.

93. In which Coasters hit did they enlist the help of Charlie Chan, Bulldog Drummond, and the Royal Canadian Mounted Police to help them find the girl of their dreams?

A.) The Coasters enlisted the help of Charlie Chan, Bulldog Drummond, and the Royal Canadian Mounted Police to help them find the girl of their dreams in the 1957 hit **"Searchin'"** (#3 5/20/57 *Billboard*). "Searchin'" was the a-side of a double-sided single (coupled with "Young Blood" — #8 5/20/57 *Billboard*) that hung near the top of the charts for most of the summer of 1957. Their humorous approach to the songs, and King Curtis's prominent saxophone, kept them on the charts for the rest of the decade.

94. What was Ross Bagdasarian's pseudonym?

A.) Ross Bagdasarian's stage name was **David Seville.** As David Seville he introduced the phrase "Ooo eee ooo ah ah, ting tang walla walla bing bang" to our vocabulary. The song was "Witch Doctor" (#1 4/14/58 *Billboard*), a novelty hit, which sat at number 1 for three weeks. With this tune Seville perfected his method of varying tape speeds to create unusual sounds and vocal tracks. The Witch Doctor's singing voice was actually Seville, with his voice sped up several times. Seville would find great success with this technique during the Christmas season of 1958 with the release of "The Chipmunk Song" (#1 12/08/58 *Billboard*). "The Chipmunk Song" was one of the fastest-selling records of 1958, selling 2,500,000 records in the month of December alone. It topped the charts for four weeks in December of '58, and entered the Top 40 again in January of 1962.

95. Who was William Saroyan's writing partner on the 1951 Rosemary Clooney hit "Come On-A My House"?

A.) William Saroyan co-wrote the 1951 Rosemary Clooney hit "Come On-A My House" with his cousin **Ross Bagdasarian**. Bagdasarian is better known as David Seville, creator of The Witch Doctor and The Chipmunks.

96. Who gave his seat to The Big Bopper on the fatal flight of February 3, 1959?

A.) On February 2, 1959, Buddy Holly was on tour as the headliner of the Winter Dance Party. The tour had been plagued by transportation problems, which Buddy found very irritating. One night the unheated tour bus broke down, and several musicians got frostbite while waiting for help to arrive. Fed up with the poor conditions, Buddy chartered a small plane to ferry his band from gig to gig. After a packed show at The Surf Ballroom in Clear Lake, Iowa, The Big Bopper (real name: J.P. Richardson) convinced Buddy's bassist, **Waylon Jennings,** to give up his seat on the plane. Meanwhile Ritchie Valens won Tommy Alsop's seat by tossing a coin. The four-seat Beechcraft Bonanza crashed at 1 a.m. on February 3, 1959, killing everyone on board. Waylon Jennings went on to become one of the most influential country artists of the 1970s. Jennings and Willie Nelson closed the gap between country and rock music as leaders in the "outlaw" country movement of the mid-seventies.

97. Which fifties rock legend was jailed by order of the Mann Act in 1959?

A.) **Chuck Berry** was charged on December 21, 1959, with violating the Mann Act. Earlier that year he had transported a fourteen-year-old Mexican girl to St. Louis. He alleged that he thought she was 21, and he was going to hire her at his club. The police didn't believe him, and advised Chuck to get a lawyer. In January 1960 he was charged with another Mann Act violation, this one stemming from an incident in 1958. He was convicted and served two years, from 1962 to 1964.

Bi Bang! Baby

98. Which story-telling singer hit the charts in 1957 with "Honeycomb" and "Kisses Sweeter Than Wine"?

A.) **Jimmie Rodgers** hit the charts in 1957 with "Honeycomb" (#1 8/19/57 *Billboard*) and "Kisses Sweeter Than Wine" (#3 11/18/57 *Billboard*). After a stint in the Air Force, James Frederick Rodgers decided to try his hand at singing professionally. He had won several Air Force talent competitions, and enjoyed performing for others. A winning performance on the "Arthur Godfrey's Talent Scouts" television program led to a record deal and a string of hits. Rodgers was known for his story-telling songs, which where quite often updated versions of traditional folk songs.

99. Who is the only artist to ever score a number 1 UK single in each decade from the 1950s through to the 1990s?

A.) **Cliff Richard** is the only artist to ever place songs in the number 1 spot on the UK charts in five successive decades. He hit the top spot in 1959 with "Living Doll" and "Travellin' Light," followed by two number 1 songs in 1960 — "Please Don't Tease" and "I Love You." He continued to ride high in the charts throughout the sixties with hits like "The Young Ones," "The Next Time," "Summer Holiday," "The Minute You're Gone," and "Congratulations." The seventies saw him hit the top of the charts once, with the disco-flavoured 1978 hit "We Don't Talk Any More." In the eighties he teamed with The Young Ones for a remake of "Living Doll" in 1986, and produced a Christmas chart topper with "Mistletoe and Wine." In 1990 Cliff Richard set a new record — one that is unlikely to be equalled — when "Savior's Day" took the top spot.

100. What is "Grammy" short for?

A.) Grammy is an abbreviation of **"gramophone."** The Grammys are awarded each year at a televised ceremony to honour excellence in the music business. The first Grammys were awarded in 1958. The first Grammy winners were: Henry Mancini's "The Music from Peter Gunn"

48

and "Nel Blu Dipinto Di Blu" — or "Volare" as it is better known. The biggest overall winner of Grammys is Chicago Symphony conductor George Solti, who has twenty-nine Grammys on his shelf at home. In the pop world Quincy Jones leads the pack with twenty-five Grammys to his credit.

101. According to Harvey and the Moonglows, what are "The Ten Commandments of Love"?

A.) According to the 1958 Harvey and the Moonglow's hit, "The Ten Commandments of Love" (#22 10/20/58 *Billboard*) are:
1. **"Thou shall never love another"**
2. **"Stand by me all the while"**
3. **"Take happiness with heartaches"**
4. **"Go through life wearing a smile"**
5. **"Thou shall always have faith in me in everything I say and do"**
6. **"Love me with all your heart and soul until our life on earth is through"**
7. **"Come to me when I am lonely"**
8. **"Kiss me when you hold me tight"**
9. **"Treat me sweet and gentle"**
10. **The song leaves the tenth commandment of love up to the listener's imagination.**

The Moonglows hailed from Louisville, Kentucky, and featured lead singers Bobby Lester and Harvey Fuqua, with background vocals supplied by Alexander "Pete" Graves, Prentiss Barnes, and Billy Johnson. As The Moonglows they placed two songs in the Top 30: "Sincerely" (#20 3/26/55 *Billboard*) and "See Saw" (#25 10/13/56 *Billboard*). By 1958 Fuqua's popularity outshone the rest of the band, so they changed their name to Harvey and the Moonglows, and entered the charts for the final time with "The Ten Commandments of Love."

Big Bang! Baby

102. What is the shortest song ever to make the Top 40?

A.)At 1:17, the shortest song to ever reach the Top 40 was **"Some Kind-a Earthquake,"** a 1959 Duane Eddy instrumental that hit number 39.

103. How did R&B singer Johnny Ace die?

A.)Johnny Ace (real name: John Marshall Alexander Jr.) was at the top of his game on Christmas Eve 1954, with two Top 10 R&B hits — "Please Forgive Me" (number 6) and "Never Let Me Go" (number 9) — under his belt. Ace gave his last performance on that night at the Civic Auditorium in Houston, Texas. Also on the bill were B.B. King and Willie Mae "Big Mama" Thornton. Backstage he participated in a game of Russian Roulette with his own gun. **He accidentally shot himself**, dying instantly. His first posthumous single, "Pledging My Love," released three weeks after his death, became his biggest hit, reaching number 1 on the R&B chart, number 17 on the pop chart.

104. What rock and roll landmark is located at 1619 Broadway in New York City?

A.)This is the address of **The Brill Building**. In the 1950s and 60s this building was a songwriting factory, housing dozens of music publishers. Jerry Leiber and Mike Stoller wrote many of Elvis Presley's hits here; Tony Orlando was a singer on demo records produced in the Brill; and before forming Steely Dan, Walter Becker and Donald Fagan worked here as songwriters. The most famous tenant of the rock and roll era was Aldon Music. While that name might not be familiar, Aldon's employees comprised a who's who of sixties and seventies music. Aldon's songwriting staff included Neil Sedaka, Barry Mann, Cynthia Weil, Carole King, and Gerry Goffin. Between them they pumped out some of the most enduring music of the sixties, including "The Loco-Motion," "One Fine Day," "Up on the Roof," "Kicks," and "Will You Still Love Me Tomorrow?".

50

105. What music landmark is located at 2648 West Grand Boulevard in Detroit?

A.) **Hitsville, USA**, the home of Motown Records, is located at this address. Label founder Berry Gordy Jr. used an eight-hundred-dollar loan from his family to purchase the unassuming bungalow in 1959. Installing offices and a recording studio, he turned the building into the vortex of his recording empire. Virtually all Motown hits released between 1960 and 1972 were recorded here before the entire Motown operation moved to Los Angeles. Today the building is open to the public as The Motown Museum.

106. What hotel was the site of Elvis's first performance in Las Vegas?

A.) Elvis Presley first played Las Vegas at the **Frontier Hotel** in 1956. The shows were disastrous. After just a few performances Elvis was moved down the bill to make way for a new headliner, Shecky Greene. It would be thirteen years before Elvis would triumphantly return to Las Vegas as the star of the Las Vegas Hilton. The Frontier was also the setting for another significant event in music history: it was during a series of 1970 performances at the hotel that Diana Ross announced that she was leaving The Supremes.

The Motown Museum, housed in the original bungalow at 2648 West Grand Boulevard that Berry Gordy Jr. purchased in 1959.

Photos by Greg Jones

107. What was the first record played on the first network airing of "American Bandstand"?

A.) The first record played on "American Bandstand"'s August 5, 1957, debut was "**Whole Lotta Shakin' Goin' On**" by

Jerry Lee Lewis. Musical guests on that first show were R&B singer Billy Williams and all-girl group The Chordettes.

108. Where was the first electric guitar manufactured?

A.) The first electric guitar was manufactured at the **Gibson Guitar Factory in Kalamazoo, Michigan**. Orville Gibson first opened his stringed-instruments shop in Kalamazoo in the late nineteenth century. The business grew and prospered, and in 1917 moved to a factory space at 225 Parsons Street. It was here in 1952 that the first electric guitar, the Les Paul model, was manufactured. In 1980, after sixty-three years at Parsons Street, the Gibson factory moved to Nashville.

WHAT'S NEW PUSSYCAT?
The 1960s

1. In 1963 Jan and Dean released "Linda" (#28 4/20/63 *Billboard*). Who was this song written for?

A.) "Linda" was written for entertainment lawyer **Lee Eastman's daughter Linda.** Little Linda eventually became a groupie, a photographer, and the wife of Paul McCartney. As a teenager she picked up a camera because, as she later said in an interview with Patrick Watson, "Taking pictures makes me less shy." Her professional photographic career was launched in New York while working as a receptionist at *Town and Country Magazine.* She talked her way into a party The Rolling Stones were hosting on the Hudson River. Her candid photos of the Stones were the only photos taken at the event, and they sold very quickly. She discovered there was a demand for her impromptu snaps of rock stars, and went on to shoot Jimi Hendrix, The Rolling Stones, and Janis Joplin. In 1967 Linda was on assignment in London, photographing Stevie Winwood and Traffic, when she met Paul McCartney. Living up to her nickname, "the Park Avenue groupie," she pursued Paul, and on March 12, 1969, they were married. In 1992 she released a well-received volume of her 1960s rock and roll

Paul and Linda McCartney in 1984. "Linda was, and still is the love of my life," said Paul in a statement released after Linda's death in April 1998. "She was unique and the world is a better place for having known her."

Photo courtesy of MPL Communications

53

Big Bang! Baby

photographs called *Linda McCartney's Sixties: Portrait of an Era*. Linda McCartney succumbed to breast cancer on Friday, April 17, 1998 at the age of 56.

2. Who inspired the Beatles song "When I'm Sixty-Four"?

A.) Paul's father, **James McCartney**, inspired the song "When I'm Sixty-Four" on the *Sgt. Pepper's Lonely Hearts Club Band* album. James sired both Paul and his singing brother Michael. A musician himself, James McCartney fronted both The Masked Melody Makers and the Jim Mac Band. One of the elder McCartney's compositions, "Walking in the Park With Eloise," was recorded by Paul in 1974 under the name The Country Hams.

3. Who did John Lennon write "Sexy Sadie" about?

A.) "Sexy Sadie" was John Lennon's bitter tribute to the **Maharishi Mahesh Yogi,** a guru The Beatles studied with for a time. The Maharishi had allegedly made advances on actress Mia Farrow, prompting John Lennon to write, "Sexy Sadie [Maharishi] what have you done/Made a fool of everyone." In an interview with *Playboy* Lennon said that this was the last song he wrote before leaving India disillusioned. He penned the song while they were packing their bags.

4. What was the first song David Bowie released on record?

A.) David Bowie's first vinyl release was a song called **"Liza Jane"** in June 1964. His name was still Davie Jones, and his backup group was called The King Bees. The song was released on the Vocalion label (a subsidiary of Decca) on June 5, 1964. On June 6 it was featured on Britain's popular television show "Juke Box Jury." The song was chosen as a hit by a panel that included Diana Dors and comedian Charlie Drake. The public didn't agree, however, and the song sunk without a trace. It has been reissued several times since.

5. What was Cassius Clay's (Muhammad Ali) first single?

A.) Columbia Records released Cassius Clay's album *I'm the Greatest* in 1964. The single release was a remake of the Ben E. King classic **"Stand By Me,"** and failed to make the charts. The pugilist had been recruited by the William Morris Agency to record an album of his boastful poetry and several upbeat rock and soul songs. The resulting album was released just before Cassius Clay's victory over Sonny Liston, his conversion to the Nation of Islam, and his name change to Muhammad Ali. Sensing controversy, Columbia pulled the disc from the stores and cancelled all of Ali's personal appearances. *I'm the Greatest* sank without a trace, and without making any impression on the charts. This was, however, not the end of Ali's singing career. In 1976 he teamed up with Frank Sinatra and Howard Cosell to cut *Ali and His Gang vs. Mr. Tooth Decay.* Both these discs are hard to find, but "Stand By Me" has been reissued by the people at Rhino Records as part of their *Golden Throats* series.

6. Who played guitar on The Who's first hit, "I Can't Explain" (#25 2/14/65 *New Musical Express*) ?

A.) **Jimmy Page,** later to become a guitar legend, cut his teeth playing sessions for many bands, and can be heard on records by The Who and The Kinks. "I Can't Explain" was recorded at the Pye Studios in London in January 1965. The producer of the record was a little unsure of Pete Townshend's ability as a lead guitarist, so he brought in Page, who plays lead guitar to Pete Townshend's rhythm. Page also added guitar parts to Them's "Baby Please Don't Go," "It's Not Unusual" (#9 5/01/65 *Billboard*) by Tom Jones, and "With a Little Help from My Friends" by Joe Cocker.

7. What was the first song to feature the sitar as a rock and roll instrument?

A.) The sitar was introduced to pop music by The Beatles in 1965's **"Norwegian Wood."** The song was written by John Lennon about a mistress. He was married to his first wife Cynthia, and rather than confessing in person, he decided to tell her about it in the song. When asked about the song in 1980 Lennon said that he could not remember the woman he was involved with, or the inspiration for the song's cryptic title.

8. Who was the first British group to have a number 1 hit single in America?

A.) The first group from over 'ome to score a number 1 in the US was **The Tornadoes** with the instrumental "Telstar" (#1 11/17/62 *Billboard*). In 1962 the United States introduced the Telstar satellite to relay television signals between the US and Europe. The Tornadoes ripped a page out of the newspapers of the day, releasing an instrumental homage to the communications satellite, complete with spacey sounds. The Tornadoes were a five-piece band who backed up Billy Fury when not releasing instrumental hits. The first British solo artist to score a number 1 hit in the US was clarinettist Mr. Acker Bilk, with "Stranger on the Shore" (#1 5/26/63 *Billboard*). Years later British pop rock band Squeeze paid tribute to Mr. Bilk with "Stranger Than the Stranger on the Shore."

9. Before they were called The Who, the band released a single under the name The Highnumbers. What was the name of this song?

A.) The Highnumbers took a stab at chart success with 1964's **"Zoot Suit,"** written by their manager Pete Meadon. Legend has it that the single only sold five hundred copies. It is said that Meadon bought 250 of them, John Entwistle's grandmother bought two, leaving 248 copies to be snapped up by a rather lethargic record-buying public.

10. What was the first single released by The Rolling Stones?

A.) The Rolling Stones first came to the attention of record buyers with **"Come On" b/w "I Want to be Loved"** released on June 7, 1963. Both songs were Chuck Berry covers, and only reached 50 on the charts. The press was not kind to the young Stones. Craig Douglas wrote in *Melody Maker*: "Very ordinary. I can't hear a word they are saying. If they had a Liverpool accent it might get somewhere." The band was not pleased with the result either. They refused to play the songs at their live shows, with Jagger adding, "I don't think 'Come On' was very good. In fact it was shit."

11. What was the name of Alice Cooper's first record?

A.) Alice Cooper was sprung on an unsuspecting public in 1969 with *Pretties for You.* The album was recorded for Frank Zappa in 1968, not released until 1969, and really should not have been released at all. *Pretties for You* was recorded in fourteen hours, with Frank Zappa as producer for eight of the songs. Zappa left the studio and Alice and the band were forced to complete the remaining two cuts without the aid of a producer. Many stories surround the recording of this album. Sources close to the Cooper camp believed that Zappa was not prepared to work with the group, and didn't know what to do with their complex, weird music. It has also been suggested that Zappa felt that they should release the album as a novelty item. Critics and consumers ignored the disc. Years later Lenny Kaye wrote, "To say the album was flawed is to be charitable." The album was only Cooper's second appearance on vinyl; in 1965 Alice (then known as Vince Furnier) released a song called "Don't Blow Your Mind" with a band called The Spiders. The song was a number 1 regional hit in Phoenix.

12. What was The Jackson 5's first single?

A.) The Jackson 5, featuring future superstar Michael on vocals, debuted with **"I Want You Back"** (#1 12/06/69 *Billboard*) in 1969. In his book *The Motown Story* writer Don Waller says, "'I Want You Back' is probably the best pop record ever made." The song bumped B.J. Thomas's "Raindrops Keep Falling on My Head" from the top spot.

13. Who was the first Beatle to release a solo single?

Big Bang! Baby

A.) **John Lennon** was the first Beatle to release a solo single with "Give Peace a Chance" (#14 8/09/69 *Billboard*) in 1969. The single was recorded at Montreal's Queen Elizabeth Hotel in room 1742 on June 1, 1969. It was the first Lennon/Yoko composition, although on the record it was credited to Lennon/McCartney. John decided to record the song immediately after writing it, so he ordered an eight track recorder and just a few hours later they had finished the song with John and Yoko on vocals, John and Tommy Smothers on guitars, and Yoko providing rhythm by banging on a wardrobe. The chorus features Allen Ginsberg, Rosemary and Timothy Leary, Murray the K, Dick Gregory, Petula Clark, Derek Taylor, some hotel staff, a few reporters, and a film crew from the Canadian Chapter of the Radna Krishna Temple.

George Harrison was the first Beatle to release a solo album. The long-player was the soundtrack to a film by Joe Massot and was called *Wonderwall Music*.

14. What was the first LP release on Apple Records?

A.) Apple's first long playing release was George Harrison's ***Wonderwall Music***, recorded in 1967, but not released until August 11, 1968. *Wonderwall Music* is a soundtrack album to Joe Massot's 1969 movie *Wonderwall*, starring Jack MacGowran, Jane Birkin, Irene Handl, Richard Wattis, Beatrix Lehmann, and Iain Quarrier. The soundtrack was partially recorded in Bombay, India, during the same sessions that produced The Beatles' "The Inner Light." George used a mix of Indian musicians and English superstars to make this eclectic album. Ashish Khan and Mahapurush Misra play side-by-side with Eric Clapton and Ringo Starr. The record did not chart, and was the first Beatle solo project to fall out of print in Britain.

15. Who was the first singer to make the top position simultaneously on the pop singles chart, the pop album chart, and the R&B chart?

A.) **Stevie Wonder** simultaneously topped both the pop singles and pop album charts, while also resting atop the R&B chart. The year was 1963, and Stevie had just released the album *The Twelve Year Old Genius* and the single "Fingertips Part Two" (#1 7/06/63 *Billboard*), which stayed at number 1 on the *Billboard* charts for three weeks.

16. Whose 1966 debut album was called *Freak Out*?

A.) **Frank Zappa** debuted with *Freak Out*, which was the first double rock album ever, and possibly the first concept album. The LP cost $21,000 to produce, which was considered an outrageous amount in 1966. *Freak Out*, with its wide range of musical influences, was a radical statement, even in 1966. The album jumped stylistically from R&B to avant garde to jazz, with satirical lyrics, and a pinch of social protest thrown in. At Zappa's suggestion producer Tom Wilson linked the songs with unusual sound effects.

17. Who is the woman on the cover of *The Freewheelin' Bob Dylan*?

A.) The mysterious girl on the cover of *The Freewheelin' Bob Dylan* is **Suze Rotolo**, an on-again-off-again girlfriend of Dylan's. He chronicled their break-up in "Ballad in Plain D" in which he called Suze "the could-be dream lover of my lifetime."

18. What were each of The Beatles wearing on the cover of *Abbey Road*?

A.) The famous cover of *Abbey Road* features from left to right: **George Harrison in denim, Paul barefoot and wearing a grey suit and a white shirt, Ringo donning a black formal suit, and John Lennon wearing a white suit and sneakers.** The cover fuelled the "Paul is Dead" fire, as proponents of this bizarre theory seem to think The Beatles are walking in a mock funeral procession. George, in jeans, is the gravedigger; Ringo, dressed in black, is the undertaker; John is the minister, dressed as he is in white. Beatle watchdogs also note that Paul's eyes are closed; that he is out of step with the others; that he is barefoot (which, Beatle-conspiracy theorists say would seem to represent the corpse in Eastern religion); and that he holds a cigarette in his right hand, even though he is left-handed. In 1992 Linda McCartney told People that there was no symbolism behind Paul's lack of footwear. He had been wearing sandals, but it was a hot day, and he kicked them off just before the photo was snapped.

19. What is John Lennon holding on the cover of *Sgt. Pepper's Lonely Hearts Club Band?*

A.) The cover of *Sgt. Pepper's Lonely Hearts Club Band* shows John Lennon holding **a French horn,** Ringo a trumpet, Paul McCartney a clarinet, and George Harrison a flute. Also pictured on the cover photo (by Michael Cooper) are a doll with "Welcome The Rolling Stones" embroidered on its sweater, and a photo montage of fifty-seven photographs of some of The Beatles' favourite people. They are (starting from the back row at the left): Unknown, Aleister Crowley, Mae West, Lenny Bruce, Karlheinz Stockhausen, W.C. Fields, Carl Gustav Jung, Edgar Allen Poe, Fred Satire, Merkin, Binnie Barnes, Huntz Hall, Simon Rodia, Bob Dylan; (second row from left) Aubrey Beardsley, Sir Robert Peel, Aldous Huxley, Terry Southern, Tony Curtis, Wallace Borman, Tommy Handley, Marilyn Monroe, William Burroughs, Unknown, Richard Lindner, Oliver Hardy, Karl Heinrich Marx, H.G. Wells, Unknown, Unknown; (third row from left) Stuart Sutcliffe, Unknown, Dylan Thomas, Dion, Dr. David Livingstone, Stan Laurel, George Bernard Shaw, Julie Adams, Max Miller, Unknown, Marlon Brando, Tom Mix, Oscar Wilde, Tyrone Power, Larry Bell, Johnny Weissmuller, Stephen Crane, Issy Bonn, Albert Stubbins, Unknown, Albert Einstein, Lewis Carroll, T.E. Lawrence; (fourth row from left) Sonny Liston, George, John, Ringo, Paul, Unknown, John, Ringo, Paul, George, Bobby Breen, Marlene Dietrich, Unknown, Diana Dors, Shirley Temple.

20. On the inside of *Sgt. Pepper's Lonely Hearts Club Band,* which police force's badge is Paul McCartney wearing?

A.) On the inside of *Sgt. Pepper's Lonely Hearts Club Band* Paul McCartney has an **OPP badge** on his arm. The badge is the logo for the Ontario Provincial Police, although the perpetrators of the "Paul is

60

Dead" myth claimed that it stood for "Officially Pronounced Dead" because the patch is folded in such a way that it looks like the second "P" is a "D." Those who believed that Paul was dead also took the back cover photo as proof that he had passed on. In the photo he is the only Beatle with his back turned to the camera. Actually, it isn't Paul at all. At the time of the photo sessions for the back cover, McCartney was in America celebrating Jane Asher's twenty-first birthday. The photographs for the album jacket had to go to the printers, so Mal Evans stepped in and posed as Paul. He turned his back to the camera so no one would realize the switch. The colourful costumes worn by The Beatles were custom made by Berman's, one of London's premier costumers. The band members selected the material for the suits themselves, instructing the designers to style the suits after those worn by the Salvation Army.

21. What was Maxwell Edison majoring in, according to The Beatles?

A.) Maxwell Edison was majoring in **medicine,** according to The Beatles' "Maxwell's Silver Hammer." Years later John Lennon said that he hated this song. He claimed that during the recording sessions they had to play it over and over until McCartney was satisfied. Lennon thinks that it was probably one of their most expensive songs to record. Released as a single, it failed to make the Top 40 in America.

22. What did John and Yoko eat "in a bag"?

A.) In "The Ballad of John and Yoko" (#8 6/21/69 *Billboard*) they eat **chocolate cake** in a bag. Lennon wrote this song while on honeymoon in Paris and considered it to be a journalistic account of his wedding to Yoko.

23. How do northern girls keep their boyfriends warm at night?

A.) Northern girls generate some heat with **the way they kiss,** according to Brian Wilson in The Beach Boys' "California Girls" (#3 8/07/65 *Billboard*).

Big Bang! Baby

24. Where did John Lennon and Paul McCartney meet?

A.) John Lennon and Paul McCartney met **at a church picnic** in the Liverpool suburb of Woolton in July 1957. The entertainment that day was provided by John's skiffle band The Quarrymen. McCartney, who was an aspiring musician, introduced himself to Lennon, and between sets taught him how to play Eddie Cochran's "Twenty Flight Rock" and Gene Vincent's "Be-Bop-a-Lula." They stayed in touch, and Paul eventually joined The Quarrymen, who later evolved into The Beatles.

25. Where did Petula Clark say things would be great?

A.) Petula Clark thought things would be great **"Downtown"** (#1 1/02/65 *Billboard*).

26. Where do The Beach Boys go to find romance in "Barbara Ann"?

A.) The Beach Boys go looking for romance **at a dance** in "Barbara Ann" (#2 1/15/66 *Billboard*).

27. Where were Bob Dylan's famous Basement Tapes recorded?

A.) The aptly named Basement Tapes were recorded in the **basement of Big Pink** in West Saugerties, New York. Dylan was recuperating from a broken neck, and re-thinking his sound by working with Robbie Robertson and The Band. The tapes were not officially released until 1975, but by that time they had already been turned into one of the most widely bootlegged records ever. Several artists had hits with songs from these sessions — Julie Driscoll and Brian Auger scored with "This Wheel's On Fire," while Manfred Mann covered "The Mighty Quinn."

28. Which Beatles song did Mick Jagger and Keith Richards sing background vocals on?

A.) Keith Richards and Mick Jagger sang on **"All You Need is Love,"** The Beatles' fifteenth single. Other background singers included Marianne Faithful, Jane Asher, Patti Harrison, Keith Moon, and Graham Nash. The record also features John Lennon on harpsichord, Paul on string bass, Ringo on drums, and George Harrison on violin. "All You Need is Love" was commissioned for the television show *Our World*, which was broadcast on June 25, 1967, to an estimated worldwide viewing audience of 400 million. It was the first time a satellite hook-up of this magnitude had been attempted — linking twenty-six nations and five continents. Careful listening will reveal four other songs heard within the fabric of "All You Need is Love." A sampling of "The Marseillaise" (the French national anthem) can be heard alongside several bars of Glenn Miller's "In the Mood"; Lennon and McCartney also borrowed a section of "Greensleeves" and placed it next to a chorus of "She Loves You," which Paul sings on the fade out. In a 1993 interview with Peter Howell of *The Toronto Star*, Mick Jagger confirmed that he also sang backup on "Baby, You're a Rich Man," but not on "Hey Jude" as some rock and roll historians claim.

29. Name the first Beatles album comprised of all Lennon and McCartney songs.

A.) The first Beatles album to be comprised of all Lennon and McCartney tunes was 1965's **Rubber Soul.** With this album The Beatles broke all of their previous sales records, selling 1,200,000 copies in the first nine days in the US alone. *Rubber Soul* topped the album charts for six weeks, and remained in the Top 200 for fifty-one weeks. "Michelle," taken from side one of *Rubber Soul,* went on to become one of the most recorded Lennon and McCartney songs of all time. One month after the release of the album there were already twenty-five cover versions of the song worldwide. In the years since, that number has risen to almost seven hundred, making "Michelle" second only to "Yesterday" in cover versions.

30. How old was Stevie Wonder when he recorded *The Twelve Year Old Genius?*

BiBang! Baby

A.) Stevie Wonder was **thirteen** years old when he recorded *The Twelve Year Old Genius*, his record-breaking debut for Motown Records.

31. Who sang lead vocal on The Beach Boys' hit "Barbara Ann"?

A.) **Dean Torrence** of Jan and Dean sang the lead vocal on the Beach Boys' hit "Barbara Ann" (#2 12/11/65 *Billboard*). Jan and Dean enjoyed chart success for a few years starting with 1963's "Surf City" (#1 6/22/63 *Billboard*). But in 1966 Jan Berry had a near fatal auto accident that snuffed out their recording career. Torrence went on to play with The Legendary Masked Surfers, and opened his own design studio in Hollywood.

32. In 1967 United Artists released the LP *How I Won the War* by Musketeer Gripweed and the Third Troop. Who was Musketeer Gripweed?

A.) **John Lennon,** who played Musketeer Gripweed in the film *How I Won the War*, was also featured on the album of the same name. The album is mostly instrumental, but Lennon can be heard on several cuts.

33. What was the working title of Cat Stevens' 1969 album *Mona Boe Jakon*?

A.) Cat Stevens' *Mona Boe Jakon* was to have been called **The Dustbin Cried the Day the Dustman Died,** but that title was thought to be too long. The album was eventually named after one of the tunes on the record.

34. What game-show host wrote Freddy Cannon's hit "Palisades Park"?

A.) Freddy Cannon (real name: Freddy Picariello) scored a hit with "Palisades Park" (#3 5/26/62 *Billboard*), written by "The Gong Show"'s **Chuck Barris**. After a string of hits in the early sixties, "the Explosive Freddy Cannon" was one of the early victims of the British

Invasion, finding his releases buried by singles from English bands like The Beatles and The Dave Clark Five. By the 1970s Cannon was a staple on the rock revival circuit, playing his old hits for crowds old enough to remember his glory days. In the early 1980s he teamed with The Belmonts (ex of Dion and the) to release "Let's Put the Fun Back in Rock and Roll," which was a minor hit in Britain.

35. What famous Beatles song was released in Germany as "Sie Liebt Dich"?

A.) "Sie Liebt Dich" was The Beatles' Germanized version of **"She Loves You."** They re-recorded several of their biggest hits for German airplay, including "Komm, Gib Mir Deine Hand" ("I Want to Hold Your Hand"). The band recorded these songs at the urging of their record company's German executives, who argued that The Beatles wouldn't be successful in Germany unless they sang in the native tongue. The Beatles were against the suggestion, but the record company, and producer George Martin, insisted it was a good idea. Finally on January 29, 1964, they went into the studio and recorded the German tracks. After hearing the result, George Martin admitted that the band may have been right. He commented that "Sie Liebt Dich" sounded like a Peter Sellers style send-up of the popular tune.

36. Ted Nugent first came to prominence with a Detroit band called The Amboy Dukes. What was the name of their 1968 hit record?

A.) The Amboy Dukes broke into *Billboard*'s Top 20 with **"Journey to the Center of Your Mind,"** a heavy metal psychedelic record. They were never again able to reach the Top 10. Amboy Dukes guitar player Ted Nugent released his first solo record in 1975 after recording eleven albums with the Dukes.

37. Did Creedence Clearwater Revival ever have a number 1 hit single?

A.) Creedence Clearwater Revival **never managed to top the charts.** They came close several times during their heyday from the spring of 1969 to late 1970. The highest spot they reached was number 2. Of their nine Top 10 singles, five of them climbed to number 2 only to be beaten out by "I Think I Love You" by the Partridge Family, "In the Year 2525" by Zager and Evans, and "The Love Theme from Romeo and Juliet" by master rock and roller Henry Mancini.

38. Name the company whose slogan was: The Sound of Young America.

A.) The Sound of Young America belonged to **Motown Records**. Berry Gordy Jr. started Motown Records in a house on West Grand Boulevard in Detroit, and turned it into one of the most successful record companies in the world. The Sound of Young America was Gordy's vision. He redefined black music, smoothing out the rough edges of blues and R&B and forming a sanitized R&B that came to be known as the Motown Sound.

39. What music tabloid billed itself as "America's Only Rock 'N' Roll Magazine" ?

A.) Founded in Detroit in 1969, *Creem Magazine* billed itself as "America's Only Rock 'N' Roll Magazine." *Creem*, under the editorship of Dave Marsh, attracted some of the best rock and roll writers around, including the king of rock journalism, Lester Bangs. *Creem* was also the only major magazine to support the Underground Press Syndicate by using the syndicate's distinctive spelling of "Amerika" on its cover.

40. Who did British Prime Minister Sir Alec Douglas-Home call "our best exports"?

A.) Douglas-Home paid this honour to **The Beatles,** referring to their uncanny ability to sell millions of records all over the world and generate millions of pounds in income tax payments.

41. What does Pete Townshend yell at the end of The Who's "Happy Jack"?

A.) You can hear Pete Townshend saying **"I saw you"** at the end of The Who's "Happy Jack" (#24 5/20/67 *Billboard*). Legend has it that Keith Moon (who was not allowed to sing on the record) was hiding in the sound booth, and trying to make the band laugh during the recording.

42. Why does Pete Townshend claim he learned to play guitar?

A.) Pete Townshend gives two reasons for learning to play guitar: **A: his nose, and B: to meet girls.** About his nose he once said, "It was huge. It was the reason I played guitar." He also noted that bands (even band-members with large noses) always got the best girls.

43. Where was Bob Dylan's first professional gig?

A.) On April 11, 1961, a twenty-year-old Dylan took the stage at **Gerde's Folk City** in New York's Greenwich Village for his first paying gig ever. He opened the show for John Lee Hooker. Gerde's was a popular folk-music hangout, featuring the likes of Judy Collins, John Phillips, Peter, Paul and Mary, and Richie Havens. It was a performance here that led to John Hammond signing Dylan for Columbia Records.

44. Who were the first rock and rollers to have their likenesses placed in Madame Tussaud's Wax Museum in London?

A.) The first wax figures of rock and rollers appeared at the world famous Madame Tussaud's in March 1964 when likenesses of **John, Paul, George, and Ringo** were unveiled. These statues appear as background filler on the cover of *Sgt. Pepper's Lonely Hearts Club Band*. The next rocker to be cast in wax at Tussaud's was Elton John in 1976. In 1999 Tussaud's added wax figures of The Spice Girls to their display at London's Rock Circus. The group is reportedly the first full band to have models made in their image since The Beatles. Each of The Spice Girls donated a pair of shoes for the wax statues to wear. "I've actually just had a grope of myself," said Posh Spice. "So that's what it must feel like for David [soccer player Beckham, Posh Spice's husband]."

45. What was the name of the first band Jimi Hendrix played with consistently?

A.) The first band Jimi Hendrix played with consistently was **The Rocking Kings** in Seattle, Washington. The band was formed by a high school friend of Jimi's called Fred Rollins, and played the popular hits of the year (1958–59), such as "Yakety Yak," "Along Came Jones," "The Twist," "The Peter Gunn Theme," and "Do You Want to Dance." Jimi's career in The Rocking Kings was cut short when he took a fancy to the drummer's girlfriend. He was kicked out of the band, and apparently beaten up by the drummer.

46. What was the name of Bruce Springsteen's first band?

A.) Bruce Springsteen's first band was called **The Castiles.** The band borrowed its name from the brand of soap that the rhythm guitar player, George Theiss, used. The Castiles played at high school dances and roller rinks; at one show they were the openers for the movie *The Russians are Coming, the Russians are Coming*; another time they played at the opening of a Shoprite Supermarket. Playing the hits of the day (1965–66), they occasionally had the chance to open a show for established stars like Dion or Little Anthony and the Imperials. Referring to this time Bruce told Robert Hilburn of the *Los Angeles Times*, "Music became my purpose in life." He went on to say that it was more than a hobby, "it was a reason to live."

47. What was the original name of The Who?

A.) The Who went through several name changes. They were originally called **The Detours,** then briefly called The Who, then The Highnumbers. They settled on The Who in October 1964 when maniac Keith Moon joined.

68

48. Why did David Bowie and the Mannish Boys almost lose a headlining spot on the English television show "Gadzooks! It's All Happening" in 1965?

A.) David Bowie refused to appear on "Gadzooks! It's All Happening" when the producers of the show insisted he **cut his fifteen-inch hair.** "I would rather die than get my hair cut," announced Bowie. Only after fans picketed the BBC studios with signs that read "Be Fair to Long Hair" did the producers consent to show David's locks.

49. Jimi Hendrix and Tommy Chong (of Cheech and Chong fame) worked together in an R&B band for a time. Name the band.

A.) Jimi Hendrix and Tommy Chong played together in **Bobby Taylor and the Vancouvers.** Jimi was wooed away from The Vancouvers by one of his heroes, Little Richard. Tommy Chong teamed with Cheech Marin for a string of successful drug-comedy records and movies. Bobby Taylor enjoyed some chart action in 1968 with "Does Your Mamma Know About Me?", which dealt with interracial dating.

50. How did Daryl Hall and John Oates meet?

A.) In 1967 Daryl Hall and John Oates were competing against one another in a **Battle of the Bands** being held at the Adelphi Ballroom in West Philadelphia. A fight broke out and there were gunshots. John and Daryl, sensing personal danger, ran to hide and met in a freight elevator. The two became friends that night, and have been working together ever since.

51. Name the Monkees.

A.) After auditioning 437 young hopefuls (including Stephen Stills, John Sebastian, and allegedly Charles Manson), "Monkees" producers settled on **Mickey Dolenz, Davy Jones, Peter Tork, and Mike Nesmith.** Dolenz was the son of character-actor George Dolenz, who is best known as television's "Count of Monte Cristo." Using the

Bang! Baby

The Monkees —
"four insane boys
aged 17 to 21."
Clockwise from
top: Mike
Nesmith, Peter
Tork, Davy Jones,
and Mickey
Dolenz.

Photo courtesy of Rhino
Records

stage name Mickey Braddock, the future Monkee was a child star, having played the lead role in the series "Circus Boy." Davy Jones had trained to become a jockey in his native England, before turning to show business at age 14. After several appearances on "Coronation Street," and other BBC television shows, he starred in the Broadway show *Oliver*. He was nominated for a Tony Award for his portrayal of the Artful Dodger, and became very popular with the teeny-boppers who read *16 Magazine*. In 1964 he and the cast of *Oliver* performed on "The Ed Sullivan Show," sharing the bill with The Beatles, who garnered all the attention that night. At the time of the auditions for "The Monkees," he was under contract to Screen-Gems Productions. Peter Tork (real name: Pater Halsten Torkelson) made a living in the early sixties as a busker in New York City's Greenwich Village. It was during this time, playing on the street and in tiny folk clubs, that he developed the easy-going likeable personality that won him a part on the television show. Michael Nesmith was the only "serious" musician to become a Monkee, having released several singles under the name Michael Blessing, and having signed a publishing deal with Colpix Records. He made a name for himself as a songwriter, penning "Different Drum" (#13 12/09/67 *Billboard*) for The Stone Poneys, featuring Linda Ronstadt. When asked why he was chosen for the role, he said, "They asked me to play a guitar player named Michael Nesmith, which was a part I did quite well." Nesmith was also the only Monkee to enjoy

any significant success after "The Monkees." He scored a Top 30 hit with "Joanne" (#21 9/05/70 *Billboard*) under the name Michael Nesmith and the First National Band.

52. Who lived at 251 Menlove Avenue in Liverpool, England?

A.) A young **John Lennon** lived at 251 Menlove Avenue in Liverpool, England. This site, along with 10 Admiral Grove (Ringo's house), 174 Mackets Lane (George's residence), and 20 Forthlin Road (Paul's place), are all on The Beatle Trail, a special bus tour recommended by the Liverpool City Council.

53. Near the end of January 1964 The Rolling Stones recorded Buddy Holly's "Not Fade Away" and "Little By Little" at Regent Sound Studios. In addition to the Stones, who played on these cuts?

A.) During the recording sessions for "Not Fade Away" at Regent Sound Studios, The Rolling Stones expanded to include **Alan Clark and Graham Nash** of The Hollies on background vocals, and producer **Phil Spector** on maracas. **Gene** "A Town Without Pity" **Pitney** played piano on "Little By Little."

54. Jeremy Spencer, guitar player for Fleetwood Mac, went missing during an American tour. Where did he turn up?

A.) Jeremy Spencer, one of the founding members of Fleetwood Mac, was obsessed with American blues guitarist Elmore James, whose style suited the early Fleetwood Mac's R&B and blues sound. His fluid slide-guitar work can be heard on "Albatross," a 1968 UK hit for the band. He disappeared during an American tour just hours before a 1970 gig in Los Angeles, only to turn up **as a member of The Children of God**, an American-based cult. Spencer was replaced by Peter Green for the remainder of the tour. Bob Welch joined in 1971, staying with the band for four years.

71

55. Who replaced Syd Barrett in Pink Floyd in April 1968?

A.) Syd Barrett was replaced by guitarist **David Gilmour** after his mental condition deteriorated to such a degree that he became a detriment to the workings of the band. Barrett was responsible for Floyd's first two hit singles, "Arnold Lane" and "See Emily Play" in 1967, and their first album, *Piper at the Gates of Dawn*. As a solo artist he recorded two albums, *The Madcap Laughs* and *Barrett*, both in 1970.

56. Peter Frampton was the guitar player for what late-1960s teeny-bopper band?

A.) Peter Frampton played with teen heart-throbs **The Herd**, who scored chart hits with "From the Underworld" in 1967, and "Paradise Lost" and "I Don't Want Our Loving to Die" in 1968. Later in '68 he quit The Herd and formed Humble Pie. Frampton left Humble Pie in 1971 to go solo. It wasn't until 1975 that he hit the big time with a double live collection, *Frampton Comes Alive*, which became one of the biggest-selling discs of all time.

57. Who were The Mugwumps?

A.) The Mugwumps were formed in the early 1960s in New York City, and featured **John Sebastian** and **Zalman Yanovsky**, who later became The Lovin' Spoonful, and **Cass Elliot** and **Denny Doherty**, who formed the nucleus of The Mamas and the Papas. After The Mugwumps split and the members went on to fame, Warner Brothers released an album of early recordings called *An Historic Recording of The Mugwumps*.

58. What songs did Paul McCartney teach John Lennon the first time they met?

A.) John Lennon and Paul McCartney met at a church picnic in Woolton, a suburb of Liverpool. Lennon's band, The Quarrymen, was playing in the church basement. McCartney taught Lennon to play

"Twenty Flight Rock" and "Be-Bop-A-Lula," and they became friends.

59. What do Cilla Black, Gerry and the Pacemakers, Billy J. Kramer, and The Beatles have in common?

A.) Cilla Black, Gerry and the Pacemakers, Billy J. Kramer, and The Beatles all shared **Brian Epstein as a manager, and they all hailed from Liverpool, England**. In 1962 Epstein formed NEMS (Northern England Music Stores) Enterprises to administer to the business needs of The Beatles, and manage his stable of Liverpudlian stars. While steering John, Paul, George, and Ringo along the road to superstardom, he became disillusioned when none of his other acts enjoyed the same success as The Beatles. Fearing he was a one-hit wonder, he sunk into depression and drug taking. Brian Epstein died of an overdose of barbituates in the summer of 1967.

60. By what names are Mark Volman and Howard Kaylan better known?

A.) Mark Volman and Howard Kaylan are better known as **Flo and Eddie.** They had a string of hits from 1965 to 1969 with The Turtles. They hailed from Los Angeles and had a hit in 1965 with Bob Dylan's "It Ain't Me Babe." The Turtles had their biggest hit in 1967 with "Happy Together." They

The Turtles broke up in the mid-seventies, leaving Howard Kaylan (first on left) and Mark Volman (fourth from left) to strike out on their own as The Phlorescent Leech and Eddie. In due course the name was shortened to Flo and Eddie.

Photo courtesy of Rhino Records

73

enjoyed several more hits (including "She'd Rather Be With Me" and "Elenore") before breaking up the band in 1970. Legal reasons forbad them to use the name The Turtles, so they worked under the name The Phlorescent Leech and Eddie, which in time was shortened to Flo and Eddie.

61. What was the name of Brian Epstein's record shop in Liverpool in the early 1960s?

A.) Brian Epstein ran the **NEMS Music Store** in Liverpool, England. His policy was that no customer would go unsatisfied. This led him to tracking down a record called "My Bonnie" by The Beatles to meet requests from fans. He became interested in the band, and soon became a very satisfied customer himself when he steered The Beatles to mega-stardom.

62. In 1966 Peter and Gordon released a song called "Woman," written by Bernard Webb, who was described as a college student in Paris. What was Webb's real name?

A.) Bernard Webb was a pseudonym for **Paul McCartney.** He insisted that his writing credit on "Woman" (#14 3/12/66 *Billboard*) be listed under the name Webb, to see if the song could be a hit if nobody knew who wrote it. Peter and Gordon were actually Peter Asher and Gordon Waller. McCartney was dating Peter's sister Jane at the time of the release of this record.

63. Who is the "A" in A and M records? Who is the "M"?

A.) The "A" and "M" of A and M records are **Herb Alpert and Jerry Moss**. The partners started the company in 1962 in Alpert's garage, where they shared one desk. Since then the company has released records by Joe Cocker, Supertramp, Janet Jackson, and The Carpenters to name just a few.

64. Who is L'Angelo Misterioso?

A.) L'Angelo Misterioso is one of **George Harrison**'s recording pseudonyms. He used this name when he played rhythm guitar on Cream's "Badge" (he also co-wrote that song with Eric Clapton). L'Angelo pops up again on Jack Bruce's "Never Tell Your Mother She's Out of Tune."

65. In Beatles circles, what was "Arthur"?

A.) "Arthur" was George Harrison's nickname for the **Beatle haircut.** A reporter was questioning George on what he called The Beatles' hairstyle, and he flippantly replied "Arthur."

66. What were Motown writers Holland/Dozier/Holland's first names?

A.) Holland/Dozier/Holland were known to their parents as **Brian and Eddie Holland and Lamont Dozier.** As a songwriting team, the two brothers and Lamont Dozier provided Motown with some of their biggest hits. The Four Tops recorded "Baby, I Need Your Loving" (1964), "I Can't Help Myself" (1965), and "It's the Same Old Song" (1965). The Supremes benefited the most from the team's songwriting magic, scoring thirteen number 1 hits, most written by Holland/Dozier/Holland. In 1970 the trio of writers split from Motown and formed their own label, Invictus.

67. What did The Beatles do just before receiving their M.B.E.'s (Members of the Order of the British Empire) on June 12, 1965?

A.) Just before receiving their M.B.E.'s The Beatles ducked into a Buckingham Palace washroom to **smoke a joint** to calm their nerves. Giving The Beatles M.B.E.'s sparked a storm of protest from past recipients. Paul Pearson, a war hero, returned his M.B.E. because "it has become debased," and former Canadian Member of Parliament Hector Dupuis sent his M.B.E. back, causing George to quip that if Mr. Dupuis didn't want his award, "he had better give it to us. Then we can give it to our manager, Brian Epstein. M.B.E. really stands for Mr. Brian Epstein."

BiGBang! Baby

68. What was the claim to fame of The Plaster Casters?

A.) The Plaster Casters of Chicago — Cynthia, Dianne, and Marilyn — were **1960s super-groupies** who made and collected plaster models of the erect penises of rock stars. Over the years they collected dozens (if not hundreds) of casts of everyone and anyone who was someone in the music business. Apparently Jimi Hendrix was a willing participant who produced a very impressive cast. All the details of the castings were recorded in diaries. In recent years there has been an on-going court battle to determine ownership of the casts.

69. Who is credited with creating the Beatle haircut?

A.) Former Beatle Stuart Sutcliffe's girlfriend **Astrid Kirschner** is credited with creating the Beatle haircut. She called the cut "the French style," because it featured (for the time) unusually long bangs, which she thought were most continental.

70. What was the title of John Lennon's first book?

A.) John Lennon's first book was titled **In His Own Write**, and was released in 1964. In a review for the book *Newsweek* said that the book, "suggests that when John Lennon sings 'I Want to Hold Your Hand,' he is wishing he could bite it." The book contains very inventive nonsense verse, and much word play. Stories such as "The Fingletoad Resort of Teddyviscious" and "On This Churly Morn" showcase Lennon's love of puns and childish language. Buoyed by The Beatles' popularity, the book did extremely well on both sides of the Atlantic, and was translated into French.

71. What book did John Lennon borrow the line "goo goo boo joob" from for his song "I am the Walrus"?

A.) John Lennon quoted Humpty Dumpty's last lines — "goo goo boo joob" — in **Finnegan's Wake** for his *Magical Mystery Tour* tune

"I am the Walrus." The background vocals on this tune were supplied by the Mike Sammes Singers — six boys sing "Oompah, oompah, stick it up your jumper," while six girls chant, "Everybody's got one."

72. In 1964 Charlie Watts released a book as a tribute to Charlie Parker. What was the book called?

A.) Rolling Stones drummer (and former graphic artist) Charlie Watts' 1964 tribute to Charlie Parker was called ***Ode to a High Flying Bird.*** At the time of the book's release Watts said, "It doesn't matter if you know anything about Parker because it's about this little bird. In fact, it's the kind of book you can buy for a kid." The book, with an accompanying CD, was re-released in 1991.

73. How many times was Elvis Presley married? Did he have any children?

A.) Elvis Presley was only married **once** to Priscilla Beaulieu. He met her while he was stationed in Germany with the army. The underage Priscilla came to live with Elvis at Graceland until she finished school, and was old enough to marry. They were wed in Las Vegas at the Aladdin Hotel on May 1, 1967. Lisa Marie, the couple's one and only child, was born at the Baptist Memorial Hospital (where Elvis was pronounced dead in 1977) in Memphis in February 1968. Elvis has two grandchildren by Lisa Marie and her then-husband Danny Keough — a girl Danielle (born 1989) and a son Benjamin Storm Keough (born 1992).

74. What was Elton John's real name? What is his mother's name?

A.) Elton John's real name is **Reginald Kenneth Dwight.** He changed his name in 1969, shortly before the release of the *Empty Sky* album. The name Reg Dwight, he reasoned, sounded like a cement mixer, not a singer. He "borrowed" the name from two people he had previously played with in Bluesology, a London-based blues combo. He nicked sax player Elton Dean's first name, and combined it with Long

John Baldry's handle to create his unusual moniker. He contemplated changing it later, however he was at a loss to come up with anything better, so it stuck. His mother's name is Sheila.

75. Where did Iggy Pop get married?

A.) Iggy Pop married Wendy Weisberg on the front lawn of the **Stooges Farmhouse** in Michigan. Neither set of parents showed up for the wedding. Iggy's best man was Stooge Ronnie Asheton, who wore an authentic SS colonel's uniform. The minister was Iggy's manager, who had sent twelve dollars away to the Universal Life Church so he could legally perform the ceremony.

76. The Rolling Stones were arrested and fined on March 18, 1965. Why were they picked up?

A.) The Rolling Stones were arrested on March 18, 1965, for **publicly urinating** on the Stratford Garage in Essex. The garage owner refused them entry to the washrooms because of their long hair. They literally took matters into their own hands, and were arrested and fined five pounds each.

77. Where were John Lennon and Yoko Ono married?

A.) While on vacation in Paris, John Lennon and Yoko Ono made a stopover in **Gibraltar** where they said their vows on March 20, 1969, with Peter Brown and David Nottal (both of Apple) as witnesses. Their wedding escapades are described in The Beatles' tune "The Ballad of John and Yoko" (#8 6/21/69 *Billboard*). George Harrison and Ringo Starr were not present at the April 22, 1969, recording session for "The Ballad of John and Yoko," so John plays guitar and sings while Paul McCartney plays drums and piano, and adds some vocals at the end.

78. Who is Jane Asher's famous brother?

A.) Jane Asher's famous brother is producer, songwriter, manager, and performer **Peter Asher**. He began his career in the singing duo Peter and Gordon. Because of his friendship with Paul McCartney (Jane had dated Paul for four years) he was made head of artists and repertoire (A&R) at Apple Records. He then moved to L.A. to produce James Taylor and Linda Ronstadt, who he still works with.

79. Where was Meredith Hunter killed? Who is alleged to have killed him?

A.) Meredith Hunter was killed while attending the **Rolling Stones concert at the Altamont Speedway** near San Francisco on December 6, 1969. He allegedly pulled a gun and pointed it at the stage, whereupon the Hell's Angels, who were acting as security at the event, beat him to death with pool cues, fists, and chains and stabbed him five times. The gun Hunter was allegedly pointing at Jagger was never recovered, and a verdict of justifiable homicide was handed down by the courts. Marvin Belli, lawyer for the Stones, commented, "They (the Angels) might have been a little too enthusiastic." Jagger chimed in, saying, "If Jesus had been there, he would have been crucified." Hell's Angel Alan David Passaro, who was tried and acquitted in the case, later sued The Rolling Stones, claiming that because *Gimme Shelter*, the film of the concert, showed the stabbing, he suffered an invasion of privacy.

80. Who scored a posthumous hit with "Three Steps to Heaven" in 1960?

A.) **Eddie Cochran**'s last single release was the ironically titled "Three Steps to Heaven" in 1960. His career and his life were cut short by a car accident in England on April 17, 1960. Cochran had just wrapped up a hugely successful tour of England and was riding to London Airport at the time of the crash. In the car with him were his fiancée Sharon Sheeley and rocker Gene Vincent. Sheeley and Cochran were on their way to the United States to get married, while Vincent was to fly to Paris for a series of concerts. Their car blew a tire and skidded backwards into a lamppost. The impact killed Eddie and injured Sheeley, who went into

Big Bang! Baby

shock, and wandered around the crash site mumbling, "Where's Eddie? Where's Eddie?" Vincent suffered a leg injury, which eventually became ulcerated and painful, leading to his alcoholism and death in 1971. Cochran was inducted into the Rock and Roll Hall of Fame in 1987.

81. What do Elvis Presley, David Bowie, and Jimmy Page all have in common?

A.) Elvis Presley, David Bowie, and Jimmy Page all share a **common birthday** — January 8. Elvis was born in 1935, Bowie in 1947, and Page in 1944.

82. Where did Brian Jones die?

A.) Rolling Stones guitarist Brian Jones was found dead **in the swimming pool of his home, The House at Pooh Corner, Cotchford Farm,** on July 3, 1969. The house once belonged to A.A. Milne, author of the Winnie the Pooh books. Jones's funeral was on July 10, 1969, at the Hatherly Road Parish Church, Cheltenham, Gloucestershire, and he was buried in the town's Priory Road Cemetery.

83. On July 5, 1969, The Rolling Stones held a memorial concert in London's Hyde Park for Brian Jones. Two hundred and fifty thousand people sat silently while Mick Jagger read a eulogy for his late guitar player. What did Jagger read?

A.) At the Hyde Park Memorial Concert Mick Jagger read part of **Shelley's *Adonais*** as a eulogy for Brian Jones. "The One remains, the many change and pass," read Jagger. "Heaven's light forever shines, Earth's shadows fly; Life, like a dome of white radiance of Eternity, Until death tramples it to fragments. — Die! If thou wouldst be with that which thou dost seek!"

84. Did The Band appear in the movie of the Woodstock Festival?

A.) **No,** The Band did not appear in the film of the Woodstock Festival. They played at the concert, but did not make it into the final print. Other artists who performed at the festival but did not make the final print were: Blood, Sweat and Tears, Paul Butterfield, Creedence Clearwater Revival, The Grateful Dead, Keef Hartley, The Incredible String Band, The Jefferson Airplane, Janis Joplin, Melanie, Mountain, Ravi Shankar, Bert Sommer, and Johnny Winter.

85. What was the name of the film that marked David Bowie's first appearance on celluloid?

A.) David Bowie's first foray into film was **The Image** for Border Films in September 1967. It tells the story of a painter who is working on a portrait from a photograph. We get the impression that the painter is in some sort of danger from the rather pained look on his face as he hears noises in the studio. He investigates by poking around in the studio and looking out the window, but he finds nothing, and continues his work. As he is working a face appears in the window — David Bowie's mug. We then realize that the artist is painting the portrait of a dead man who has come to life. The film runs for about fourteen minutes, and Bowie was paid thirty pounds for his contribution.

86. Which Beatles film was included in a Californian time capsule to be opened in the year 2960?

A.) The Beatles film **A Hard Day's Night** was included in a Californian time capsule, which will be opened in the year 2960. The Richard Lester-directed film was released by United Artists in 1964 as a musical rockumentary guiding us through a day with The Beatles. It was well-received critically, with *The New York Post* calling it "the surprise of the century." *A Hard Day's Night* garnered two Academy Award nominations — for adaptation of a musical score and for screenplay written directly for the screen — but walked away empty-handed.

87. Who invades Pepperland in the 1968 animated Beatles film *Yellow*

Big Bang! Baby

Submarine?

A.) **The Blue Meanies** invade Pepperland in the 1968 animated Beatles film *Yellow Submarine*. Pepperland is a paradise, led by Sgt. Pepper's Lonely Hearts Club Band. The land is invaded, so the Yellow Submarine is dispatched to find The Beatles to restore harmony. Although the real Beatles do make an appearance in a live-action segment at the end of the film, they were not closely involved with the production.

88. Which Beatles film was "respectfully dedicated to the memory of Mr. Elias Howe, who in 1846 invented the sewing machine"?

A.) The 1965 Beatle film ***Help!*** was "respectfully dedicated to the memory of Mr. Elias Howe, who in 1846 invented the sewing machine." The humour in this movie (directed by Richard Lester) was largely influenced by the British comedy troupe The Goons. Led by Peter Sellers and Spike Milligan, The Goons parodied everything, and were often completely irreverent.

89. In late 1968 John and Yoko produced a film for Australian television. What was the name of this film?

A.) John and Yoko produced ***Rape*** for Australian television in 1968. In the film a woman is harassed by the camera until she is in tears. "We are showing how all of us are exposed and under pressure in the contemporary world," said Lennon. "What is happening to the girl on screen is happening in Biafra, Vietnam, everywhere."

90. Who choreographed The Monkees' movie *Head*?

A.) **Toni Basil** choreographed The Monkees' movie *Head*. In an interview with *Sight and Sound* the director, Bob Rafelson, summed up the movie: "*Head* was supposed to be an exploitation film but it was not that at all. It opened metaphorically with The Monkees committing suicide; it was a complete exposure of my relationship to the group. *Head* is an

82

utterly and totally fragmented film. Among other reasons for making it was that I thought I would never get to make another movie, so I might as well make fifty to start out with and put them all in the same feature. I was, in a sense, emulating or satirising the styles of various American pictures — there was a kind of history of American movies in there." Whatever Rafelson's intentions might have been, the movie was savaged by critics, with Pauline Kael of *The New Yorker* saying, "The doubling up of greed and pretentious-to-depth is enough to make even a pinhead walk out." Fortunately Basil bounced back, enjoying chart success in 1982 with her hit single (and video) "Mickey" (#1 10/09/82 *Billboard*). Her choreography credits include the dance sequences for George Lucas's *American Graffiti*, and tours for David Bowie (*Diamond Dogs*), Devo, and Bette Midler.

91. What was Frank Zappa's Studio Z?

A.) Frank Zappa's Studio Z was a **film house** run by Frank Zappa and Lorraine Belcher, formerly located at 8040 N. Archibald Avenue, Cucamonga, California. The house specialized in making blue movies to order for three hundred dollars a piece. Zappa and Belcher were arrested and booked on the "Suspicion of conspiracy to manufacture pornographic materials and the suspicion of sex perversion." Shortly after the arrest Zappa moved to Hollywood and founded the Mothers of Invention.

92. In the 1969 United Artists film *Alice's Restaurant*, what is Alice's last name?

A.) Alice **Brock** is the owner of Alice's Restaurant. In the movie she is played by Pat Quinn. Based on the famous Arlo Guthrie tune, the movie tells the story of Guthrie's evasion of the draft, his quest to be with his dying father, and the birth of Alice's Restaurant from a hippie commune. Folkie Pete Seeger makes a guest appearance, singing two songs: "Car Car Song" and "Pastures of Plenty."

93. Who is the popular sixties band featured in Michelangelo Antonioni's

Big Bang! Baby

1966 film *Blow Up?*

A. Michelangelo Antonioni's first film in English, *Blow Up,* features a performance by **The Yardbirds.** Set in the Swinging London of the mid-sixties, it is the story of a fashion photographer played by David Hemmings. The plot develops into a murder mystery, with the bulk of the film spent on a tour through London in search of the solution to the crime. The Yardbirds (featuring Jimmy Page and Jeff Beck) appear in a club scene playing "Stroll On." In homage to Pete Townshend, Beck smashes his guitar onstage.

94. Name the film that starred Marlon Brando, Richard Burton, James Coburn, John Huston, Walter Matthau, and Ringo Starr.

A. The six entertainers all co-starred in 1968's *Candy.* This star-"studded" movie tells the story of Candy (Ewa Aulin), and her search for happiness through sex. For his portrayal of the Mexican gardener, Ringo (in his first feature without John, Paul, or George) had to have his hair dyed jet black.

95. Which 1968 American International release tells the story of Max Frost, a rock singer who becomes President of the United States?

A. American International Pictures released *Wild in the Streets* in 1968. The ad copy on the movie poster tells the whole story: "This is the story of Max Frost, 24 years old, President of the United States, who created the world in his own image. To him, 30 is over the hill. 52% of the nation is under 25... and they've got the power. That's how he became President...." He runs an anarchistic government, and orders everyone over the age of 30 to be arrested and fed LSD. The film was inspired by an article in *Esquire* called "The Day it All Happened Baby," and features good performances from Shelley Winters, Hal Holbrook, and Richard Pryor.

96. Who sang the title song of 1967's drama *To Sir With Love?*

A.) The title song of *To Sir With Love* was a hit for **Lulu** in 1967, topping the *Billboard* charts for five weeks. Lulu began her career in 1964 in a band called Lulu and the Lovers, but it wasn't until her marriage to Bee Gee Maurice Gibb and her role as Barbara Pegg in *To Sir With Love* that she found any success.

97. In 1968 who earned a commendation from the White House for appearing on national television with a plea for peace after the assassination of Dr. Martin Luther King?

A.) **James Brown.**

98. In what year did The Rolling Stones make their debut on "The Ed Sullivan Show"?

A.) The Rolling Stones debuted on "The Ed Sullivan Show" on October 25, **1964.** They performed "Around and Around" and "Time is on My Side" to a crazed reaction from the young fans in the audience. Television critics attacked their "grubby" appearance, and remarked that Mick lacked "fire and depth, and was otherwise very unconvincing." Even Sullivan got in on the Stones-bashing, pledging, "So help me, the untidy Rolling Stones will never again darken our portals." The Rolling Stones were in fact invited back, several times.

99. Why was Stephen Stills rejected by the producers of "The Monkees"?

A.) In 1966, 437 people auditioned to be part of a new television show, "The Monkees." John "Lovin' Spoonful" Sebastian, Charles Manson, and Stephen Stills all auditioned, but were turned away. Stephen Stills was rejected because **his teeth were too crooked**.

100. Why did Bob Dylan refuse to appear on "The Ed Sullivan Show" in May 1963?

BiBang! Baby

A.) Bob Dylan walked off "The Ed Sullivan Show" when **censors told him he would not be able to sing "Talking John Birch Society Blues."** The song is a parody of a man who believes that there are communists everywhere. In the course of the song everyone comes under suspicion — even Betsy Ross is guilty because she sewed red stripes on the American flag. By the end of the song, the man is so paranoid he isn't sure if even his own record is clean. Sullivan liked the song, but the CBS censors were afraid of a lawsuit from The John Birch Society. Sullivan released a statement that read, "We told CBS, 'It's your network, but we want to state that the decision is wrong and the policy behind it is wrong.'"

101. Who wrote the 1967 novel *Mott the Hoople*?

The first edition dust jacket of Willard Manus's *Mott the Hoople*, published in 1967.

A.) The 1967 novel *Mott the Hoople* was written by **Willard Manus**. When bassist Overend Watts (real name: Peter Watts), guitarist Mick Ralphs, organist Verden Allen, and drummer Dale Griffin first met singer Ian Hunter they were using the band name Silence. After Hunter joined the band, their producer, Guy Stevens, felt they needed a snappier sounding name. He christened the band Mott the Hoople after the Manus book. It's a wonder that Stevens had ever seen the book. As Manus himself admits, "The book was published in England, where it got rave reviews from all four major Sunday papers (on the same day) — and didn't sell a single copy."

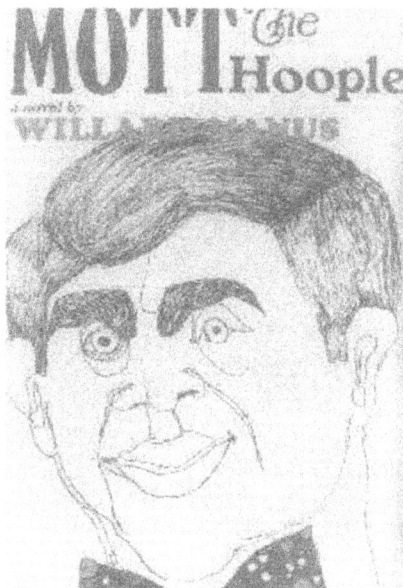

MOTT the Hoople
a novel by WILLARD MANUS

102. Which one-hit wonders appeared on "The Munsters" in 1965?

A.) **The Standells** appeared in the twenty-sixth episode of "The Munsters," titled "Far Out Munster," which aired March 18, 1965. In the show The Standells rent the Munster house for a weekend hideaway from their fans. The Munsters, who have been staying in a hotel, return home to find a wild party in progress. After the initial conflict, the Munsters grow to like The Standells, who perform "I Wanna Hold Your Hand" in the Munsters' livingroom. The Standells hit the *Billboard* Top 40 once in 1966 with the garage rock classic "Dirty Water" (#11 6/11/66 *Billboard*).

103. Which 1965 musical album featured *The Munsters*?

A.) *At Home With the Munsters* was released in 1965 on A.A. Records/Golden Records. Issued to cash in on the Munster craze, it features Herman crooning "It Takes All Kinds of People," and "I Wish Everyone was Born This Way" as sung by Eddie. A children's chorus adds vocals to the Munsters theme, with lyrics written specially for the album by Bob Mosher. In 1983 Butch "Eddie" Patrick tried his hand at rock music with the release of "What Ever Happened to Eddie?"

104. What year saw Otis Redding score a number 1 posthumous hit with "(Sittin' On) The Dock of the Bay"?

A.) Otis Redding was killed in a plane crash on December 10, 1967. He scored his first number 1 hit single with the posthumous release of "(Sittin' On) The Dock of the Bay" (#1 2/10/68 *Billboard*) in **1968.** The single stayed at number 1 for four weeks. Other chart toppers that year included "Mrs. Robinson" by Simon and Garfunkel, The Doors' "Hello I Love You," and "People Got to be Free" by The Rascals.

105. What year saw Zager and Evans hit the top of the charts with "In the Year 2525"?

A.) Denny Zager and Rick Evans hit the top of the US pop charts in **1969** for six weeks with "In the Year 2525" (#1 6/28/69 *Billboard*). Other songs

Otis Redding started his career as a teenaged Little Richard imitator, but later came to redefine the development of southern soul music in the 1960s.

Photo courtesy of Rhino Records

BiBang! BaBy

to top the charts that year include, "Crimson and Clover" by Tommy James and the Shondells (two weeks), "Everyday People" by Sly and the Family Stone (four weeks), "Dizzy" by Tommy Roe (four weeks), "Aquarius/Let the Sunshine In" by The Fifth Dimension (six weeks), "Get Back" by The Beatles with Billy Preston (five weeks), "Love Theme from Romeo and Juliet" by Henry Mancini (two weeks), "Honk Tonk Women" by The Rolling Stones (four weeks), "Sugar Sugar" by The Archies (four weeks), "I Can't Get Next to You" by The Temptations (two weeks), "Suspicious Minds" by Elvis Presley (one week), "Wedding Bell Blues" by The Fifth Dimension (three weeks), "Come Together"/ "Something" by The Beatles (one week), "Na Na Hey Hey Kiss Him Goodbye" by Steam (two weeks), "Leaving on a Jet Plane" by Peter, Paul and Mary (one week), and "Someday We'll Be Together" by Diana Ross and the Supremes (one week).

106. What popular mid-sixties band was originally called The Alan Price Combo?

A.) **The Animals** began life as The Alan Price Combo in 1961. By 1963 they decided they needed a snazzier name, and borrowed the moniker of Newcastle-upon-Tyne tough guy "Animal" Hog. Under the guidance of producer Mickie Most they became a regular fixture on the British charts with songs like "Don't Let Me Be Misunderstood," "We Gotta Get Out of This Place," "House of the Rising Sun," and "It's My Life." The original Animals had great success until 1965 when keyboardist Price left the band. Several minor hits followed, but the band broke up in late 1966. Singer Eric Burdon reformed the band in 1967, and relocated to Los Angeles. Instead of the R&B flavourings that had made the band chart toppers, he swung towards a psychedelic sound that would grant him several more hits ("When I was Young," "Sky Pilot," and "San Franciscan Nights"). This band (which at one point included future Police guitarist Andy Summers) was retired in 1969. After a failed attempt at a film career, Eric Burdon went on to work with the funk band War, and made several attempts to reform The Animals.

107. Who replaced Eric Clapton in The Yardbirds?

A.) Eric Clapton left The Yardbirds in 1965 when he felt they were starting to stray from their blues roots into more commercial territory. His replacement was **Jeff Beck,** who had already made a name for himself in English blues bands like The Deltones and The Tridents. Beck played on several of The Yardbirds' hits ("Heart Full of Soul," "Evil Hearted You," and "Shapes of Things"), and shared guitar duties with Jimmy Page, who had also joined the group. The only recording featuring both Beck and Page is 1966's psychedelic "Happenings Ten Years Time Ago." Both guitarists can be seen in the Antonioni movie *Blow Up.* The Yardbirds play in a club scene, and smash their instruments a la The Who. Beck left The Yardbirds for a solo career in 1966.

108. Who penned the 1969 best-selling collection of poetry *Warlock of Love*?

A.) **Marc Bolan** of T-Rex fame wrote *Warlock of Love,* a best-selling collection of his poems, in 1969. A fantasy theme runs throughout the sixty-three-page work, influenced by books like *The Lord of the Rings* and Oriental legends. In the book's preface he writes:

  We hide behind the masks of the Orient,
  because the sullen, lumbering shapes of
  the western world strike fear and terror
  into our limbs, and all is ungrown.
  Legends we long for and legends there are
  in the east of our heads.

After the book became a best-seller (it sold over forty thousand copies in Britain) Bolan admitted that it "took me about two weeks to write" *Warlock of Love.* He credited his speedy work to a previous life as a Celtic troubadour. The book was re-issued in 1992. For more information write: T-Rex Appreciation Society, P.O. Box 297, Newhaven, E Sussex, BN9 9NX.

109. What did Neil Young's father do for a living?

89

Big Bang! Baby

A.) Neil Young's father, Scott Young, was a well-known **Canadian sports writer.** He was the recipient of the Canadian National Newspaper Award for sports writing, and a CBC Wilderness Award for excellence in a television script. His short stories have been printed in magazines and anthologies all over the world, and have been translated into many different languages. In 1985 he wrote a book titled *Neil and Me* about his life with his superstar son. *The Vancouver Sun* called the work "a universal book about fathers and sons and the pains and joys they bring to each other."

110. Who was the only Canadian member of The Lovin' Spoonful?

A.) Guitarist and vocalist **Zal Yanovsky** was the only Canadian member of The Lovin' Spoonful. He was born in Toronto on December 19, 1944. Before quitting the band he played on all their big hits, including "Do You Believe in Magic" (#9 9/18/65 *Billboard*), "Daydream" (#2 3/12/66 *Billboard*), "Did You Ever Have to Make Up Your Mind?" (#2 5/14/66 *Billboard*), and "Summer in the City" (#1 7/23/66 *Billboard*). He now runs a restaurant and bakery in Kingston, Ontario.

111. What was the original name of The Spencer Davis Group?

A.) The Spencer Davis Group was originally called **The Rhythm and Blues Quartet.** They came together in Birmingham in 1963, and built up a local following, signing to Island Records in 1964. Their early records are remarkable for sixteen-year-old Stevie Winwood's striking R&B vocals, which many reviewers likened to Ray Charles. Winwood and his brother Muff (bass) left after 1967's Top 10 hit "I'm a Man" (#10 4/08/67 *Billboard*). Stevie formed Traffic, while Muff moved into record production. The Spencer Davis Group struggled along for several years without them with little success. Davis recruited several top players to replace the departed brothers including Eddie Hardin, Dee Murray, and Nigel Olsson before dissolving the band in 1968.

112. Who was the song "Jennifer Juniper" written for?

A.) Donovan wrote "Jennifer Juniper" (#26 3/30/68 *Billboard*) for **Jennifer Boyd**, who was sister-in-law to George Harrison and later married Mick Fleetwood. Jennifer's sister Patti was the subject of Eric Clapton's song "Layla" (#10 6/17/72 *Billboard*). Clapton pinched the name Layla from "Layla and Mashoun," a Persian love story. While Patti was married to George Harrison, his best friend, Eric Clapton, fell in love with her. Patti eventually left the Beatle for Clapton, which put an understandable strain on the friendship of the two guitar heroes. They must have mended their fences, because both Patti and Eric Clapton appear on George's version of "Bye Bye Love." George re-wrote the lyrics, making reference to Patti ("our lady") and "old Clapper." Clapton and Patti have since divorced, while George and Eric have remained friends, and have even toured the Far East together.

113. Who had a hit with 1968's "Baby Come Back"?

A.) **The Equals**, featuring singer and lead guitarist Eddie Grant, scored a hit with "Baby Come Back" (#32 9/28/68 *Billboard*) in 1968. The Equals broke up in 1970, but Grant continued on the charts with 1983's "Electric Avenue" (#2 5/21/83 *Billboard*), which sat at number two for five weeks, and 1984's "Romancing the Stone" (#26 6/30/84 *Billboard*). Grant, a native of British Guiana, also owns a studio complex in Barbados that counts some of the world's most popular bands among its clients.

114. What was the name of Napoleon XIV's only hit single?

A.) One-hit wonder Napoleon XIV (real name: Jerry Samuels) climbed up the charts in 1966 with **"They're Coming to Take Me Away, Ha-Haaa!"** (#3 7/30/66 *Billboard*), a song about a man who goes insane after his dog runs away. "They're Coming to Take Me Away, Ha-Haaa!" was banned by several radio stations, who felt that it offended the mentally ill, but in spite of the controversy, or perhaps because of it, the song became the fastest-selling single in history to that date. "I knew it was touchy, but I was never afraid of it," says Jerry "Napoleon XIV" Samuels. "I figured we'd probably get away with it for about a month, then somebody would say, 'Hey this guy is making fun of the sickies.' I never felt there was a problem with the thing. The reason I put (the dog) in is that I thought it might throw off the naysayers long enough to give us a little more time. Somebody would say, 'Oh wait, it's about a dog. That's alright.' If you're talking about something that pokes fun at insanity, it doesn't make any difference who or what the object is — whether it is a human being or a dog or anything else. You either object to the premise or you don't. I felt it would cause some people to say, 'Well, it's alright.' And it did. It worked." Follow-up singles like "Marching Off to Bedlam," and "I'm in Love with My Little Red Tricycle" failed to garner any public support.

115. Who was "the God of Hellfire"?

A.) One-hit wonders **(The Crazy World of) Arthur Brown** declared themselves to be "the God of Hellfire" on their 1968 Pete Townshend-produced single "Fire" (#2 9/21/68 *Billboard*). The band was unable to repeat their chart success, and Arthur Brown (real name: Arthur Wilton) quit performing to teach music in Burundi, Africa.

116. Who sang about the "Eve of Destruction" in 1965?

A.) Former New Christy Minstrel **Barry McGuire** placed "Eve of Destruction" (#1 8/28/65 *Billboard*) at the top of the charts in 1965. The song faced

A cartoon rendering of Jerry "Napoleon XIV" Samuels on the cover of Rhino Records' compilation disc *The Second Coming*. Samuels, who had a hit with the novelty record "They're Coming to Take Me Away, Ha-Haaa!", has never been photographed in costume, preferring the public to conjure up their own idea of what the character Napoleon XIV looks like.

Photo courtesy of Rhino Records

92

opposition at first, with radio stations refusing to program it because of its depressing subject matter. Despite radio's apathy the song caught on, and gave McGuire his only chart entry. Follow-up singles like "Child of Our Times" and "Cloudy Summer Afternoon (Raindrops)" failed to make an impression.

117. What was Herbert Khaury better known as?

A.) Herbert Khaury was known to the millions as **Tiny Tim.** In 1968 he enjoyed his only chart success with the novelty hit "Tip-Toe Through the Tulips with Me" (#17 6/08/68 *Billboard*). He became a media darling for a short time, going so far as to get married on "The Tonight Show with Johnny Carson" in front of 39 million people. The marriage lasted as long as his success, and by 1969 Tiny Tim was already a has-been. In the years prior to his death (of cardiac arrest) in 1996 he tried to stay in the public eye, releasing records sporadically and acting in slasher movies.

118. What is Dion's last name?

A.) Dion's last name is **DiMucci**. As the lead voice of Dion and the Belmonts (named after Belmont Avenue in the Bronx), DiMucci sold millions of doo-wop records (including "A Teenager in Love" and "Where or When") before the group split in 1960. His solo recordings in the early sixties shifted gears from the doo-wop sound of The Belmonts to a rockier dance-oriented sound. He topped the chart several times ("Runaround Sue" and "The Wanderer") before drug problems slowed his career momentum. In the late sixties he re-emerged with a folkie sound and another big hit, "Abraham, Martin and John" (#4 11/02/68 *Billboard*). Dion recorded light rock and folk albums until he embraced Christianity at the end of the seventies. His output since then has largely been inspirational albums for small Christian labels.

119. What is Michael Lubowitz better known as?

93

A.) Michael Lubowitz is known to British Invasion buffs as **Manfred Mann.** The South African-born Mann began his British musical career as a jazz pianist before forming a blues combo with drummer Mike Hugg. They scored a few hits in Britain, and reached the top of the charts in America with "Do Wah Diddy Diddy" (#1 9/12/64 *Billboard*), which sat at the top of the heap for two weeks. Mann was among the first rock artists to interpret Bob Dylan's songs, giving them the electric treatment. He reached the number 2 spot in Britain with his take on Dylan's "If You Gotta Go, Go Now." In 1968 Manfred Mann raided the Bob Dylan catalogue once again and issued "Mighty Quinn (Quinn the Eskimo)" (#10 3/09/68 *Billboard*), which Dylan had recorded on *The Basement Tapes*.

120. What did The Beatles do to cause fans to picket their gigs, shouting "Pete Forever, Ringo Never!"?

A.) Fans picketed Beatles gigs shouting "Pete Forever, Ringo Never" **when John, Paul, and George fired drummer Pete Best and hired Ringo Starr to replace him** in August 1962. Best was the band's original drummer, and was very popular with Liverpool fans, who demanded to know why he was let go. No reason was ever made public, but Beatles insiders have intimated that Best's unwillingness to change his hairstyle led to his sacking. Best stayed in the music business for a time, even touring the US with his own band before quitting show business and becoming a baker.

121. Who did George Harrison say was the "fifth Beatle"?

A.) George Harrison dubbed disc jockey **Murray the K** (for Kaufman) the fifth Beatle after their first American tour. Murray, who was a highly rated announcer with WINS in New York, followed them on tour and broadcast live from their press conferences and hotel rooms. He spent so much time with the band it was almost as if he was a member, hence George's nickname for him. The title stuck, and for the next twenty years (he died in 1982) Murray the K was the acknowledged fifth Beatle.

122. Where did the following late sixties psychedelic bands hail from:

Colossal Pomegranate, Shiva's Headband, and The Cleanliness and Godliness Skiffle Band?

A.) According to *The Jefferson Airplane and the San Francisco Sound* by Ralph Gleason, Colossal Pomegranate, Shiva's Headband, and The Cleanliness and Godliness Skiffle Band all hailed from **San Francisco**. While these groups may not have left much of a mark on popular music, the Bay Area did produce some of the sixties' biggest names — Big Brother and the Holding Company, Country Joe and the Fish, The Grateful Dead, and The Jefferson Airplane.

123. Who had a 1961 Top 10 hit with "Those Oldies but Goodies (Remind Me of You)"?

A.) The 1961 Top 10 hit "Those Oldies but Goodies (Remind Me of You)" (#9 5/29/61 *Billboard*) was performed by **Little Caesar and the Romans.** Singer Carl Burnett (Little Caesar) was unable to match the success of this hit, and the band never made the Top 40 again.

124. Who was Gary Lewis's famous father?

A.) Comedian **Jerry Lewis** was the father of Gary Lewis, who, with The Playboys, became one of the biggest-selling acts of 1965. Their debut single, "This Diamond Ring" (#1 1/23/65 *Billboard*) topped the charts, and in 1965–66 they managed to consistently plant singles in the Top 10 ("Count Me In," "Everybody Loves a Clown," and "Sure Gonna Miss Her"). Their career was dealt a mortal blow in 1967 when Gary Lewis was drafted into the US Army. He did his hitch as a military clerk in Korea, and upon release tried to resume his singing career. He was

Los Angeles R&B quintet Little Caesar and the Romans, led by David "Little Caesar" Johnson (middle).

95

Big Bang! Baby

unable to repeat his earlier success, and now performs on the nostalgia circuit, singing his old songs.

125. What does the name Procol Harum mean?

A.) The name Procol Harum, when roughly translated from Latin, means **"beyond these things."** Led by guitarist Robin Trower, and singer/keyboardist Gary Brooker, the band developed the Procol Harum sound, a mix of Gothic classic and modern pop sensibilities. Their biggest hit, "A Whiter Shade of Pale" (#5 7/01/67 *Billboard*), hit the Top 5 in 1967.

126. Who wrote The Bobby Fuller Four hit "I Fought the Law"?

A.) The Bobby Fuller Four hit "I Fought the Law" (#9 2/12/66 *Billboard*) was written by former Buddy Holly and the Crickets member **Sonny Curtis,** who had first recorded the tune after Holly's death. Curtis is also well-known for penning "Love is All Around" — the theme song for "The Mary Tyler Moore Show."

127. What was Bob Dylan's first all-electric album?

A.) Bob Dylan's first all-electric album was 1965's **Highway 61 Revisited.** The album introduced the now-classic "Like a Rolling Stone," which clocked in at six minutes — a 1965 record breaker. *Rolling Stone*'s Dave Marsh calls the album one of Dylan's best, and one of the greatest of the rock era. Included with "Like a Rolling Stone" are two other Dylan classics, "Ballad of a Thin Man" and "Just Like Tom Thumbs Blues."

128. Which West Coast band did Alan "Blind Owl" Wilson and Bob "The Bear" Hite form in the mid-sixties?

A.) Alan "Blind Owl" Wilson and Bob "The Bear" Hite formed **Canned Heat** in Los Angeles in 1965. Hite, an enthusiastic record collector,

96

was a fan of Tommy Johnson's "Canned Heat Blues," which inspired the
name for his new band. They scored their first boogie woogie blues hit with
"On the Road Again" (#16 9/07/68 *Billboard*), which featured Wilson's
"Kermit the Frog" falsetto. Their follow-up hit, "Going Up the Country"
(#11 12/21/68 *Billboard*) was featured on the Woodstock soundtrack.
Wilson, who lent the band his distinctive harmonica playing and unusual
falsetto voice, committed suicide in 1970 at age 27. The group continued
on without him until the death of Bob "The Bear" Hite in 1981.

129. Which 1965 film features James Brown and His Fabulous Flames
singing on a snow-covered mountain?

A.) In the 1965 film ***Ski Party*** James Brown and His Fabulous
Flames perform on a snow-covered mountain, dressed in ski gear.
Ski Party is basically a "beach party" movie moved to a different locale.
American International Pictures, the producers of the beach movies
(*Muscle Beach Party, How to Stuff a Wild Bikini*, and *Bikini Beach*)
had hoped to start a new trend as the beach party movies seemed to be
on the way out. It was advertised as "The COOLEST way to keep warm at
20 below," but audiences didn't agree. Also starring are Frankie Avalon,
Leslie Gore, and Dwayne Hickman.

130. Who scored a 1962 hit with a reworking of the Walt Disney chestnut
"Zip-A-Dee Doo-Dah"?

A.) **Bob B. Soxx and the Blue Jeans** (Bobby Sheen, Darlene Love,
and Fanita James) hit the Top 10 in 1962 with the Walt Disney
classic "Zip-A-Dee Doo-Dah" (#8 12/08/62 *Billboard*). The group had
been brought together by producer Phil Spector, who met Love and
James when they were members of an L.A. vocal group called The
Blossoms. Sheen was a soloist, in the Clyde McPhatter tradition, who had
cut several unsuccessful records at Liberty before hooking up with
Spector. Their album, *Zip-A-Dee Doo Dah*, was a collection of standards
("This Land is Your Land," "White Cliffs of Dover," and "Let the Good
Times Roll") done in their own soulful style. Further chart success eluded

Big Bang! Baby

Bob B. Soxx and the Blue Jeans, although they appear on the 1963 classic seasonal album *A Christmas Gift for You From Phil Spector*.

131. Where was Jim Morrison arrested and charged with open profanity, indecent exposure, public drunkenness, and lewd and lascivious behaviour in March 1969?

A.) Jim Morrison was arrested and charged for allegedly exposing his sexual organ onstage at the **Dinner Key Auditorium in Miami, Florida.** This event is the subject of much speculation. Many claim that he did not expose himself, although there are those who vehemently claim he did. As legend has it (and as Oliver Stone dramatised it in the 1991 movie *The Doors*) the band was playing "Touch Me," while an inebriated Morrison fumbled with his belt buckle, shouting, "I'm talking about having some fun! I'm talking about love your neighbour!" A roadie restrained him before he was able to drop his pants completely, but the damage was done. After the charges were laid the band had to cancel the rest of their tour until the case came to trial in September. At the trial Morrison was found guilty on the profanity and exposure charges, and was fined five hundred dollars and sentenced to six months in jail. The case was on appeal at the time of Morrison's death in 1971.

132. Where did the Woodstock Festival take place?

A.) The Woodstock Festival took place on **Max Yasgar's farm** in the upstate New York town of Bethel on August 15, 16, and 17, 1969. More than 400,000 people showed up to witness the incredible musical line-up that included Jimi Hendrix, The Who, Santana, Joan Baez, Sly and the Family Stone, Sha Na Na, The Grateful Dead, John Sebastian, Janis Joplin, The Jefferson Airplane, Ten Years After, Canned Heat, Country Joe and the Fish, Crosby, Stills, Nash and Young, Ravi Shankar, The Paul Butterfield Blues Band, Joe Cocker, and Richie Havens. During the three days there were three deaths, two births, and four miscarriages. A plaque now stands at the site of the festival.

133. What was the first African song to hit number 1 on the *Billboard* charts?

A.) The first African song to hit number 1 on the *Billboard* charts was **"The Lion Sleeps Tonight"** (#1 11/27/61 *Billboard*) by The Tokens. The song was translated from an African folk song called "Mbube" (or sometimes "Wimoweh"). Traditional versions of the tune had been released by The Weavers and Miriam Makeba to no great success. In 1972 ex-Token Robert John would resurrect the song, and score a Top 5 hit with the remake.

134. Who played the garbage can on the first Beach Boys release?

A.) The Beach Boys' first recording, "Surfin'" was written by Brian Wilson. It featured Carl Wilson on acoustic guitar, Al Jardine on double bass, Mike Love and Dennis Wilson on vocals, and **Brian Wilson** singing lead while banging out the beat on a garbage can. "Surfin'" was released by a small Los Angeles company called Candix Records, and rode a wave to the *Billboard* charts, touching down at number 118.

135. In 1963 who did Richard Buckle, a writer for London's *Sunday Times,* call "the greatest composers since Beethoven"?

A.) London *Sunday Times* writer Richard Buckle called **John Lennon and Paul McCartney** "the greatest composers since Beethoven" in 1963. Two days before Mr. Buckle's startling pronouncement, the Music Critics of the London *Times* dubbed Lennon and McCartney "The Outstanding Composers of 1963." The Beatles were also voted the Number One Group of the Year in the 1963 *New Musical Express*'s Twelfth Annual International Popularity Poll, which also named their song "She Loves You" Record of the Year.

136. Who made Princess Margaret laugh by saying, "Will you people in the cheaper seats clap your hands? All the rest of you, if you'll just rattle your jewellery"?

A.) **John Lennon** made Princess Margaret laugh at a 1963 Royal Command performance when he made this request from the stage. The British press reported the next day that "The Royal box was stomping."

137. Translate these British Invasion band names from Latin to English: Lapides Provolventes, and Cimictus.

A.) In Latin **The Rolling Stones** are known as Lapides Provolventes and **The Beatles** are called Cimictus. Here are some other Latin translations you can use to impress your friends: The Grateful Dead translates into Mortui Grati, while Pueri Litoris is the Latin name for The Beach Boys, and The Monkees would be called Simitatores in ancient Rome.

138. Which top-rated-sitcom star released the single "Granny's Mini-Skirt" in 1965?

A.) **Irene Ryan,** better known as Granny from the long-running sitcom "The Beverly Hillbillies," took a shot at singing stardom in 1965 with "Granny's Mini-Skirt." Done in a bluegrass style, this song tells the story of Grandpa's outrage at Grandma's new mini-skirt. "He can't stand to look at my bony knees," she sings, explaining Grandpa's disdain at her new outfit. Not surprisingly, the song did not make the charts.

139. Who were the only father and son team to ever host NBC's "Hullabaloo"?

A.) **Gary Lewis** and his comedian father **Jerry Lewis** were the only father and son team to ever host NBC's rock show "Hullabaloo." Gary Lewis and the Playboys were one of America's biggest-selling acts during the 1965–66 season, scoring nine Top 20 singles in two years. Their career came to an abrupt end when Gary was drafted and sent to Korea. After his discharge Lewis tried to kick-start his singing career, but the times had changed, and he failed to make any headway on the charts.

140. Why did "Along Comes Mary" by The Association shock some Americans in 1966?

A.) The Association's "Along Comes Mary" (#7 6/25/66 *Billboard*) shocked some Americans when it was revealed that **the "Mary" of the song wasn't a girl, but actually marijuana.** The controversy surrounding the song actually hiked sales of the song to the under-20 set, who enjoyed the drug reference. The band had a string of pop/rock million-sellers ("Cherish," "Windy," "Never My Love," and "Everything That Touches You") until 1968 when they were overshadowed by more progressive acts like The Doors and Jimi Hendrix. The band refused to give up, and stayed on the road despite the drug-related death of bassist Brian Cole. The Association (with a mostly new line-up) can still be seen at rock revival concerts.

141. Where did the name "The Shirelles" come from?

A.) The name "The Shirelles" is a combination of lead singer **Shirley Alston's first name and the French feminine word "elle."** The Shirelles hit the top of the charts for the first time with "Will You Still Love Me Tomorrow" (#1 10/17/60 *Billboard*), written by future soft-rock superstar Carole King. After the huge success of the single The Shirelles became regulars on the Dick Clark Caravan of Stars travelling shows, and appeared on "American Bandstand" frequently. They defined the early-sixties girl group sound with classic tunes like "Dedicated to the One I Love" (#3 2/06/61 *Billboard*), "Baby It's You" (#8 1/06/62 *Billboard*), and the time-honoured story of a broken heart, "Soldier Boy" (#1 3/31/62 *Billboard*). Shirley Alston left The Shirelles in 1975 and recorded under the name Lady Rose.

142. Which producer called his records "little symphonies for the kids"?

A.) Producer **Phil Spector** called his records "little symphonies for the kids." Spector's records are identifiable by his "Wall of Sound" — a blast of Wagnerian clatter that literally jumped out of the radio at you. He achieved this grandiose sound by layering a throbbing rhythm track against a prominent string section, adding lots of echo, and turning the volume way up. Spector was the mastermind behind many of rock's classic hits. He manned the board for (among others) The Crystals' "He's a Rebel" (#1 10/06/62 *Billboard*), The Ronettes' "Be My Baby" (#2 9/14/63 *Billboard*), and The Righteous Brothers' "You've Lost That Lovin' Feeling" (#1 12/26/64 *Billboard*).

143. Who is famous for recording in Los Angeles's Gold Star Studios?

A.) **Phil Spector** put Los Angeles's Gold Star Studios on the map. Spector originally came to Gold Star in 1958, and soon worked here almost exclusively. It was here that Spector perfected his "Wall of Sound" on recordings by The Crystals, The Ronettes, and The Righteous Brothers. Spector's last production at this studio was the 1980 Ramones' album *End of the Century*. Gold Star Studios was torn down to make way for a mini-mall in 1984.

144. Who wrote the 1961 Ricky Nelson hit "Hello Mary Lou"?

A.) **Gene Pitney** wrote Ricky Nelson's 1961 hit "Hello Mary Lou" (#9 5/08/61 *Billboard*). Pitney made his name as a songwriter, penning hits for Ricky Nelson, The Crystals ("He's a Rebel") and others before heading out on his own. During the sixties Pitney placed sixteen hits in the Top 40, including "A Town Without Pity" (#13 12/18/61 *Billboard*), "(The Man Who Shot) Liberty Valance" (#4 5/19/62 *Billboard*), and "It Hurts to be in Love" (#7 8/29/64 *Billboard*).

145. Who had a string of hits with "Devil or Angel," "Rubber Ball," and "Take Good Care of My Baby"?

A.) Teen idol **Bobby Vee** (real name: Bobby Velline) had a string of hits in the early sixties with "Devil or Angel" (#6 9/05/60 *Billboard*), "Rubber Ball" (#6 12/12/60 *Billboard*), and "Take Good

Care of My Baby" (#1 8/21/61 *Billboard*). Vee stayed in the lower end of the Top 40 for most of the sixties while also making movies (like *Swinging Along*) and guest shots on national television. Bobby Vee retired from recording, and now tours on the nostalgia circuit.

146. What 1963 hit did the courts rule that George Harrison had "subconsciously plagiarized"?

A.) In 1976 a judge ruled that George Harrison had "subconsciously plagiarized" the 1963 Chiffons' hit **"He's So Fine"** (#1 3/09/63 *Billboard*) for his 1970 single "My Sweet Lord" (#1 12/05/70 *Billboard*). Bright Tunes Publishing, who owns "He's So Fine," felt that George's ode to Eastern religion sounded a bit too close for comfort. Harrison was sued for infringement of copyright, and was found guilty — sort of. It was judged that he didn't intentionally rip off The Chiffons' hit, but copied the song unknowingly. He still had to pay, but his artistic integrity was left intact. The long and drawn-out court battle left Harrison with writer's block. He broke through his block with a sarcastic musical comment on his legal woes. In "This Song" (#25 12/11/76 *Billboard*) George summed up his position in one line: "This tune has nothing Bright about it." Monty Python's Eric Idle can be heard chatting in the middle of the song.

147. Where is Dead Man's Curve?

A.) The Dead Man's Curve made famous by Jan and Dean was on **Sunset Boulevard, west from Groverton**, and across from the UCLA football field in Los Angeles. The city regraded the curve in the early sixties after comedian Mel Blanc was almost killed in a car accident here. Jan Berry was partially paralysed in a car accident further down on Sunset in Beverly Hills two years after the release of "Dead Man's Curve" (#8 3/28/64 *Billboard*).

148. What tale of teen tragedy closes with, "I'll never kiss your lips again/

Big Bang! Baby

They buried you today"?

A.) Mark Dinning's tale of teen tragedy **"Teen Angel"** (#1 1/04/60 *Billboard*) closes with the line "I'll never kiss your lips again/They buried you today." Dinning was a pioneer in the morbid field of car crash songs. These tunes have morbid lyrics (see above), usually centring around an unrequited love, and in all of them someone dies a horrible death. Other 1960s car crash songs include Jan and Dean's "Dead Man's Curve" (#8 3/28/64 *Billboard*), The Shangri-La's "Leader of the Pack" (#1 10/24/64 *Billboard*), Ray Peterson's "Tell Laura I Love Her" (#7 6/27/60 *Billboard*), and J. Frank Wilson and the Cavaliers' "Last Kiss" (#2 9/26/64 *Billboard*). Death discs made a brief comeback in 1971 with Bloodrock's "D.O.A." (#36 2/27/71 *Billboard*), the most gut-wrenchingly graphic crash song ever.

149. What is the only song sung entirely in Japanese to reach number 1 on the *Billboard* charts?

A.) Kyu Sakamoto's **"Sukiyaki"** (number 1, 1963) is the only song sung entirely in Japanese to hit the number 1 spot on the *Billboard* charts. Sakamoto was among the 520 people who lost their lives in the 1985 crash of a Japan Airlines 747 near Tokyo.

150. Who wrote "Popsicles and Icicles" for the 1960s one-hit wonder band Murmaids?

A.) Future **Bread front man David Gates** wrote the 1965 hit "Popsicles and Icicles" (number 3, 1963) for Murmaids. Murmaids consisted of two sisters, Carol and Terry Fischer, and their neighbour Sally Gordon. When the song hit the charts the threesome were just starting college and unavailable to tour to promote the record. Several poorly produced singles were released to capitalize on the success of "Popsicles and Icicles," but to no avail, and the group broke up. In 1966 Chattahoochee Records resurrected the "Murmaids" name with different singers for the unsuccessful folk-rock offering "Go Away."

151. What was The Standells' only hit song?

A.)One of rock's great garage bands, The Standells were only able to place one song on the charts. **"Dirty Water"** went all the way to number 11 in 1966. Despite the song's boast, "Boston you're my home," The Standells were actually formed in Los Angeles in the early sixties. Comprised of drummer Dick Dodd (a former Mouseketeer), bassist Gary Lane, keyboardist Lawrence Tamblyn (brother of actor Russ Tamblyn), and guitarist Tony Valentino, the band got their most famous song from producer Ed Cobb. Cobb wrote "Dirty Water" while on vacation in Boston. When he presented it to the band, the response was less than enthusastic. "The group hated the record so much that they refused to do it," remembers Cobb. Eventually the band grudgingly relented, recording the song in a make-shift studio set up in a garage. "They fluffed through it every time," says Cobb. "Every week I got a phone call from Tony saying, 'Hey Eddie! My friends still don't like the song! I told you it was a turkey.'" Cobb had the last laugh. Nine months after the recording session the song entered the charts.

152. What Boston band had their only hit with a remake of Eddie Cochran's "Summertime Blues"?

A.)Boston's **Blue Cheer** only had one hit single, 1968's "Summertime Blues" (number 14, 1968), a revved-up version of Eddie Cochran's rock and roll classic. Sometimes called "the first truly American heavy-metal band," Blue Cheer were named after a strain of LSD. They were so loud and so wild their manager once boasted they could "play so hard and heavy they (made) cottage cheese out of the air." "Summertime Blues" was their only trip to the Top 20.

153. Which 1968 one-hit wonder went on to become head writer for "Saturday Night Live"?

A.) **Mason Williams** almost went all the way with his one hit. "Classical Gas," a song he described as "half flamenco, half Flatt and Scruggs, and half classical," reached number 2 in 1968. While the song was racing up the charts Mason was earning a living as head writer for the ill-fated "Smothers Brothers Comedy Hour." In 1980 he was once again head writer for a cutting-edge network comedy show, "Saturday Night Live." He only lasted six weeks at the helm of the show, forced out over creative differences. Mason was so burned out by the end of his time at "SNL" he left New York, moved to Oregon, and threw away his television set.

154. Who replaced Flo Ballard in The Supremes?

A.) Flo Ballard, one of the founding members of The Supremes, left the band in 1967. She was replaced by **Cindy Birdsong**, formerly of Patti LaBelle and the Bluebelles. Birdsong's first releases as a Supreme were the misguided attempt at psychedelia, "Reflections" (#2 8/19/67 *Billboard*), and "In and Out of Love" (#9 11/25/67 *Billboard*) a tin-pan-alley type pop song. Ballard died, penniless, in 1976.

155. In Gerry and the Pacemakers, what is Gerry's last name?

A.) Liverpudlians Gerry and the Pacemakers were lead by Gerry **Marsden,** a former British Railways employee. Inspired by his friend Paul McCartney's success Gerry gave up his railway job and delved into music. Like The Beatles, The Pacemakers perfected their sound in Hamburg, Germany, before landing a record deal. They became one of the frontrunners of the British Invasion, placing seven singles in America's Top 40 from '64 to late '66.

156. Who was the coat check girl at the Cavern Club in Liverpool, England?

A.) The coat check girl at Liverpool, England's Cavern Club was **Cilla White, who changed her name to Cilla Black** and became part of the British Invasion. White was signed to a management contract by Beatles overseer Brian Epstein after he saw her singing on stage with The Beatles at the Cavern. She changed her name after an editor at *Mersey Beat* forgot her name and guessed at the colour. He guessed wrong, and Cilla White became Cilla Black. Her only US hit was the love song "You're My World" (#26 7/25/64 *Billboard*).

157. Who were the main exponents of the "Tottenham Sound"?

A.) The main practitioners of the "Tottenham Sound" were **The Dave Clark Five.** The "Tottenham Sound" was more boisterous than the melodic "Liverpool Sound" typified by The Beatles and Gerry and the Pacemakers. The DC5 were one of the more successful of the British Invasion bands, and were the first British band to tour America in the spring of 1964. Appearances on "The Ed Sullivan Show" pushed seven of their singles to the Top 20 in 1964 alone. They disbanded in 1967 when Clark gave up the music business.

158. Who was known as "the Cool Boss with the Hot Sauce"?

A.) Apart from being "the Cool Boss with the Hot Sauce," **James Brown** might also be the most nicknamed man in music. As a child he was called "Crip" after he broke his leg playing football. Later, in prison, he was known as "Music Box." It wasn't until he started performing, though, that the nicknames came fast and furious. At different times he has been billed as "Mr. Dynamite," "The 'Please Please Please' Man," "The Hardest Working Man in Show Business," "The Sex Machine," "Soul Brother Number One," "His Bad Self," "The Godfather of Soul," and "The Minister of the New New Super Heavy Funk." He doesn't mind the nicknames, but as he writes in his 1986 autobiography, *James Brown: The Godfather of Soul*, he prefers to be called Mr. Brown.

159. How did Peter Noone earn the nickname Herman?

A.) Peter Noone was nicknamed Sherman because his of **resemblance to the cartoon character Sherman from the "Mr. Peabody" television show**. The "s" was eventually dropped and he adopted Herman as a stage name. When he was trying to think of a title for his band, he decided that the word "hermit" sounded good with his new stage name. Herman's Hermits peaked in 1965, scoring five Top 5 hits in America, and touring the world. The band broke up in the early seventies, and Peter Noone tried his hand at acting on British television. Noone resurfaced again in the eighties with an American new wave band that played the bars of southern California in an effort to recapture past glories.

160. Who are Levi Stubbs, Abdul "Duke" Fakir, Renaldo Benson, and Lawrence Payton known as?

A.) Levi Stubbs, Abdul "Duke" Fakir, Renaldo Benson, and Lawrence Payton have been singing together since the late fifties as **The Four Tops.** After several failed recordings for the Chess label in Chicago, The Four Tops relocated to Detroit and linked up with Berry Gordy Jr. of Motown. Under Gordy's guidance the band had a string of hits with Holland-Dozier-Holland penned songs like "Bernadette" (#4 3/18/67 *Billboard*), "Baby I Need Your Loving" (#11 8/29/64 *Billboard*), "I Can't Help Myself (Sugar Pie Honey Bunch)" (#1 5/22/65 *Billboard*), and "Reach Out I'll be There" (#1 9/17/66 *Billboard*). When Holland-Dozier-Holland left Motown in 1968 they took The Four Tops' magic with them. The singers were paired with several of Motown's staff producers, but they were unable to duplicate the H-D-H sound. The Four Tops abandoned Motown in 1972 for a contract with ABC. They scored a few hits, including "Are You Man Enough" (#15 7/28/73 *Billboard*) from the film *Shaft in Africa*. The Four Tops can still be seen on the nostalgia circuit, belting out their old hits.

161. Which "Groovin'" late sixties band turned down an appearance on "The Ed Sullivan Show" because of alleged "racist policies"?

A.) **The Rascals** turned down an appearance on "The Ed Sullivan Show" because of the alleged "racist policies" of the variety show. The band had once been known as The Young Rascals, and found great success with blue-eyed soul songs like "Good Lovin'" (#1 3/26/66 *Billboard*), and "I've Been Lonely Too Long" (#16 2/25/67 *Billboard*). As they matured, so did their music, which became sophisticated and socially aware. They dropped the prefix "Young" in 1967. The Rascals became very involved with the civil rights movement in the United States after the release of their hit "People Got to be Free" (#1 7/27/68 *Billboard*). The song was written after the band encountered some rednecks in Florida. From that point on they refused to appear in concert or on television on a bill that didn't involve at least one Afro-American act. They were forced to cancel many engagements as a result of this policy. They broke up in 1972 without duplicating the success of "People Got to be Free."

162. Which Sunday night variety show did Turtles' lead singer Howard Kaylan appear on, wearing a turtleneck sweater *and* a necktie?

A.) Howard Kaylan and his group The Turtles (featuring Mark Volman) appeared on **"The Ed Sullivan Show"** wearing a turtleneck sweater *and* a necktie. The Turtles were one of the few Los Angeles bands that weren't caught up in the pretension of folk-rock. They didn't take themselves seriously, and earned a reputation as fun-loving hipsters who made great singles. After The Turtles acrimoniously split in 1970, the duo of Howard Kaylan and Mark Volman became two of rock's most sought background singers. They appear on hundreds of records, including Bruce Springsteen's "Hungry Heart," and "Get It On" by T-Rex.

163. Which sixties television show put out a casting call for "4 insane boys aged 17 to 21"?

A.) Producers Bob Rafelson and Bert Schneider were casting **"The Monkees"** when they placed an ad in *The Hollywood Reporter* seeking "4 insane boys aged 17 to 21." The response was good — 437

109

BiBang! Baby

"Ben Franks-types" (including John Sebastian, Stephen Stills, Denny Hutton, Rodney Bingenheimer, and rumour has it Charles Manson) replied over the next few days. The producers chose thirty finalists, who were auditioned in a most bizarre manner. Rafelson and Schneider were searching for off-the-wall types, so they asked a series of questions like, "If you were on Mars, where would you go for a hamburger?" or "How would you like to be sitting in my chair?" The actors' suitability for the show was determined by their answers. The second step was a personality test, which would determine if they were compatible with the other actors, or if they would cause trouble on the set. After the auditions, the field was narrowed to eight. In the final cut it was Peter Tork, Mickey Dolenz, Michael Nesmith, and Davy Jones who were chosen. Of the eight finalists the four that didn't make it were Danny Hutton, who would later lead Three Dog Night; Don Scardino who has appeared on "The Guiding Light"; singer Miki, who won a contract (but no hits) from RCA; and Bill Chadwick, who became the show's roadie, sound-mixer, and sometimes songwriter.

164. Which Monkee was a child actor, and appeared on the show "Circus Boy"?

A.) At age 9 **Mickey Dolenz** (stage name: Mickey Braddock) played Corky, an orphan boy on the series "Circus Boy." Each week the show would focus on Corky's experiences as he travelled from town to town with a turn-of-the-century circus. Mickey's father, George Dolenz, was a well-known television character actor who played "The Count of Monte Cristo." Mickey didn't want to capitalize on his father's fame so he changed his surname to Braddock. When the series ended in 1957 he returned to school and pursued his love of acting in amateur plays. After graduation he returned to the small screen in "Peyton Place" as Kitch, and also had roles in "Mr.

Davy Jones in concert

Photo courtesy of Davy Jones

110

Novak" and "Playhouse 90." He was planning to leave Los Angeles and abandon his acting career when he landed the part on "The Monkees."

165. Where is Jimi Hendrix's Electric Ladyland Studio?

A.) Jimi Hendrix began building his dream studio Electric Ladyland in **New York City's Greenwich Village** in 1969. The building had been a rock bar since the fifties, having housed The Village Barn and The Generation Club. Construction of the studio was troubled by money restrictions and a high water table — Electric Ladyland sits directly over NYC's Minetta Creek, and has to constantly monitor the water level of the stream to avoid floods in the building. In planning Electric Ladyland Hendrix wanted state of the art equipment, but he also tried to make the surroundings as comfortable as possible. To this end he commissioned psychedelic murals, and erected lounges with theatrical lighting to make the artist feel at home. Electric Ladyland set the standard for modern recording studios. It is a shame that Hendrix never got to take full advantage of his dream, as he died before construction was completed. Since then many major artists (Stevie Wonder, The Rolling Stones, Billy Idol) have used this facility.

166. Who was married onstage at Madison Square Garden in 1974?

A.) **Sly Stone** (real name: Sylvester Stewart) married Kathy Silva onstage at New York's Madison Square Garden in June 1974. Silva filed for divorce the following October. In 1967 Sly and the Family Stone were rising stars, and forerunners in the "psychedelic soul" movement. In the next few years songs like "Dance to the Music" (#8 3/02/68 *Billboard*), "Everyday People" (#1 1/04/69 *Billboard*), and "Thank You (Falettinme Be Mice Elf Agin)" (#1 1/10/70 *Billboard*) did well on the charts, and showcased Sly's mastery of the recording studio. Unfortunately his erratic behaviour and no-show concerts were tarnishing his reputation, and the public was quickly losing interest in him and his music. By 1974 his star was dimmed, so the wedding at Madison Square Garden was arranged to supply some sensational publicity. The stunt didn't work. The marriage ended in disaster, his next single barely made it to the Top 40, and his record company dropped him a short time later.

167. Where is MacArthur Park?

A.) MacArthur Park, immortalized in song by Jimmy Webb, is located at **Alvarado and Wilshire in Los Angeles**. Webb and his girlfriend would meet at the park on her lunch breaks. The song inspired by those trysts was a number 2 hit for Richard Harris in 1968. MacArthur Park can be seen in some scenes from the 1976 David Bowie film *The Man Who Fell to Earth*.

168. Who played special-guest guitar on The Rolling Stones' hit "Play With Fire"?

A.) Legendary producer **Phil Spector** played guitar on The Rolling Stones' hit "Play With Fire." As well as his duties as producer, Spector popped up on many records as a musician/singer, including the Stones' "Little by Little" (maracas), The Drifters' "On Broadway" (guitar solo), George Harrison's "My Sweet Lord" (background vocals), John Lennon's "Oh Yoko," (background vocals), and several singles by The Coasters and Ben E. King (guitar).

169. Why did the government of Belgium take legal action against The Singing Nun?

A.) Belgian-born Jeanine Deckers, better known as The Singing Nun, spent four heady weeks at the top of the *Billboard* charts in 1963 with the insanely catchy "Dominique." "Dominique," a lilting song that eulogizes the founder of the Dominican order, was written by Deckers (known in the convent as Sister Luc-Gabrielle) for her Mother Superior's Saint's Day. The nuns at the convent enjoyed the song and encouraged Deckers to press some copies of the tune to give away as gifts. Phillips Records agreed to record an album's worth of original tunes for non-commercial purposes, but were so impressed with the results they released the album in Europe under the name *Soeur Sourire (Sister Smile)*. Sales were brisk, so brisk in fact that the decision was made to issue it stateside. Sales were sluggish until the single "Dominique" was released near the end of 1963. The song was an instant smash, rocketing to number 1, and in the process keeping "Louie Louie" by The Kingsmen out of the top spot. Nun-mania swept the nation. Deckers appeared on "The Ed Sullivan Show" (from the convent), and in 1965 Debbie Reynolds played Deckers in a movie about The Singing Nun's life. During this period of success Deckers stayed in her convent, donating all the song's earnings to the church. In 1967 she left the order, and resumed her recording career, releasing an unsuccessful pro-choice single about oral contraceptives. She also partnered with Annie Pescher to form a centre for autistic children. In the early 1980s the centre failed, and the Belgian government instituted legal action **to recover back taxes on all of Deckers' song earnings**. Despondent, she and Pescher killed themselves with an overdose of sleeping pills. In a note left at the scene the former nun said she had "lost all courage in the face of a losing battle with the tax people."

170. Who played French horn, piano, and organ on The Rolling Stones' hit "You Can't Always Get What You Want"?

A.) **Al Kooper** has had a career that has seen him involved with some of the greatest bands in history. Not only did he play French horn, piano, and organ on "You Can't Always Get What You Want," but he also discovered Lynyrd Skynyrd, and played rhythm guitar on Electric Ladyland. Perhaps his greatest performance was his organ noodling on Bob Dylan's "Like a Rolling Stone," made all the more intriguing given that he had never played organ before.

171. What is the most successful rock and roll single to originate in Holland?

A.) The most successful rock and roll single to emerge from Holland's small music industry was **"Venus" by Shocking Blue**. Although Shocking Blue's tune went all the way to the top of the charts in North

America, Belgium, France, Italy, Spain, and Germany, it only reached number 3 on the Dutch charts in 1969. "Venus" has actually gone to number 1 twice, once in its original form by Shocking Blue in February 1970, and again as a cover version by Bananarama in September 1986.

172. What film was the inspiration for Wayne Fontana's band name The Mind Benders?

A.) Wayne Fontana's (real name: Glyn Geoffrey Ellis) band The Mind Benders took their moniker from **a popular 1963 Dirk Bogarde movie**. In *The Mind Benders* Bogarde plays a scientist who suffers severe psychological damage after engaging in an experiment to test complete isolation from all normal senses. The band faired better than their movie namesake, placing two singles in the Top 5, "Game of Love" (number 1, 1965) and "A Groovy Kind of Love" (number 2, 1966).

173. Who lived at 710 Ashbury in San Francisco?

A.) **Several members of The Grateful Dead** lived communally in the house at 710 Ashbury from 1966 until March 1968. "The nice thing about Haight-Ashbury was the nice little Victorian houses," said guitarist Jerry Garcia, "these huge places and you'd get ten people in the place and everybody's rent was like fifty bucks a month or twenty bucks a month or something. It was cheap." The house was raided in October 1967, but police didn't find the large amount of pot hidden in the kitchen. A decade after the Dead moved out a San Francisco couple renovated the house. The results of their work can be seen in a 1980 issue of *Better Homes and Gardens*.

174. What is Big Pink?

A.) Big Pink is **an unassuming house (except that it is bright pink) in the woods near Woodstock, New York,** that served as home base for Bob Dylan and The Band in the summer and fall of 1967. The house is located at 2188 Stoll Road in West Saugerties, and is

114

the site of the recording sessions for The Band's *Music from Big Pink* and Dylan's *The Basement Tapes*. In residence at Big Pink for five months, it is estimated that the musicians committed 150 songs to tape, many of them still unreleased.

175. Which soul duo of the 1960s met at the King of Hearts nightclub in Miami?

A.) **Sam and Dave** met at Miami's King of Hearts nightclub in 1961. Sam Moore was working as the amateur night master of ceremonies, while Dave Prater was the club's short order cook. One night Dave, still dressed in his kitchen whites, jumped onstage to join Sam in song. The following year they recorded their first singles for Alston Records, but it was their singles for Stax that made them legends. "Hold On! I'm Comin'" (number 21, 1966), "Soul Man" (number 2, 1967), and "I Thank You" (number 9, 1968), featuring Prater's gritty delivery and Moore's tenor, are soul classics.

176. Whose father was the pastor at The New Bethel Baptist Church in Detroit?

A.) Aside from being a well-known recording artist for Chess Records, the Reverend C.L. Franklin is also known as **Aretha Franklin's** father. As a child Aretha frequently sang at The New Bethel Baptist Church (8450 C.L. Franklin Boulevard, Detroit).

177. Who is the subject of the 1992 biography *Love, Janis*?

A.) *Love, Janis* is a book written by Laura Joplin about her older sister **Janis**. The younger Joplin decided to write the book to provide a fully balanced look at a person who, Laura says, is often perceived as a "hedonist hippie." The book unveils a seldom seen side of the blues singer — someone who loved to knit, and on her father's advice read *Time* every week to keep abreast of current affairs. Laura Joplin saw the writing of the book as a way to heal the grief she felt over her sister's death, and says that she can now listen to Janis's records "with joy, instead of crying."

178. What incident got The Who banned from the Holiday Inn chain of hotels?

A.) **Out-of-control celebrations for Keith Moon's twentieth birthday** led to the Holiday Inn chain of hotels banning The Who for life. Following a sold-out show on August 23, 1967 (with Herman's Hermits), The Who returned to the Flint, Michigan, Holiday Inn (now a Days Inn at 2207 West Bristol Road) to throw a party for Moon. At midnight the hotel's manager asked them to keep the noise down. Moon took the simple request as a challenge, and proceeded to wreak as much havoc in the hotel as his drunken body would allow. He instigated a food fight, emptied a fire extinguisher onto cars in the parking lot, took off his clothes, ran through the halls, and fell and broke two teeth. Unconfirmed reports have Moon driving his rented Lincoln Continental into the hotel's swimming pool. The Who paid for all the damage and no charges were laid, but they were barred for life from the Holiday Inn chain.

179. On which lake did Otis Redding perish?

The Who in action in a still from *The Kids are Alright*, a 1979 rockumentary. Left to right: John Entwistle (bass), Roger Daltrey (vocals), Keith Moon (drums), and Pete Townshend (guitar/vocals).

Photo courtesy of New World Pictures

A.) On December 10, 1967, the plane carrying Otis Redding and his backup band The Bar-Kays crashed into **Lake Monona, near Madison, Wisconsin**. Redding and band were on their way to a performance in Madison, flying through poor weather conditions. The plane went down as it was preparing to land at Madison's airport. Only one person survived the wreck, Bar-Kay Ben Cauley. All the bodies were eventually recovered, and Redding is buried near Macon, Georgia.

180. Which band starred in the 1968 film *Mrs. Brown, You've Got a Lovely Daughter?*

A.) **Herman's Hermits** — Peter Noone, Karl Green, Keith Hopwood, Barry Whitwam, and Derek Leckenby — starred in the 1968 film *Mrs. Brown, You've Got a Lovely Daughter.* The movie was produced quickly to take advantage of the Hermits' popularity with British teenagers. Heart-throb Herman (Noone) inherits a greyhound racing dog named Mrs. Brown. He hatches a plan to get rich by running the dog in the National Derby. The dog, of course, wins. Herman's love interest is Judy Brown (Sarah Caldwell), a wealthy socialite, although a series of comedic mishaps keeps the two apart. The movie's highlights are the musical numbers, which include "There's a Kind of Hush" and "I'm Into Something Good."

181. Who designed the cover of Janis Joplin's *Cheap Thrills* album?

A.) Janis Joplin's *Cheap Thrills* album cover was designed by Bay Area artist **Robert Crumb.** In 1967 Crumb founded the Apex Novelty Company and began publishing Zap Comics. The magazines became instant cult classics, and led to the publishing of *Snatch*, which was deemed obscene by local authorities. Nearly all the issues of the premier edition were confiscated, which increased Crumb's reputation in the psychedelic underground. Crumb is responsible for some of the most famous underground comic characters of the sixties. His Felix the Cat was the inspiration for the first X-rated cartoon, and Mr. Natural put the phrase "Keep on Truckin'" on everybody's lips in the early seventies. Robert Crumb now lives in France.

117

Big Bang! Baby

182. Who was the voice of The Archies?

A.) The singing voice of The Archies was provided by session musician **Ron Dante**. Dante's first job for Don Kirshner (who produced The Archies) was as a demo singer. These demo versions would give the established stars an idea of what the song was supposed to sound like. Dante was also known as a backup singer, and one of New York's most popular commercial jingle vocalists. Through the use of studio trickery Dante performed the voices of all The Archies — he is Archie, and Jughead, Betty, and Veronica.

183. Who had hits with "1, 2, 3 Red Light," "May I Take a Giant Step," and "Simon Says"?

A.) **The 1910 Fruitgum Company** were the kings of bubblegum music. They produced records aimed squarely at the pre-teen market. Their songs were simplistic, and quite often were take-offs on nursery rhymes and children's games. The 1910 Fruitgum Company was the brainchild of producers Jerry Kasenetz and Jeff Katz, who guided the band to success with "Simon Says" (#4 2/10/68 *Billboard*), "1, 2, 3 Red Light" (#5 8/10/68 *Billboard*), and "Indian Giver" (#5 2/08/69 *Billboard*).

184. Which British soul singer was supported by The Grease Band?

A.) **Joe Cocker**'s backup band from the mid-sixties to 1970 was called The Grease Band. Featuring Chris Stainton (keyboards), Henry McCullough (guitars), Alan Spenner (bass), and Bruce Rowlands (drums), the band chose the name to reflect their working-class backgrounds. They rose to stardom with Cocker, playing on many of his biggest hits, including "With a Little Help from My Friends," and "Feeling Alright." The band toured relentlessly, appearing at the Woodstock Festival and on "The Ed Sullivan Show." Cocker dismissed the band in 1970, and put together a new ten-piece band with Leon Russell at the helm.

185. Who was the original leader of The Guess Who?

A.) The Guess Who began life as a high school combo called Allan and the Silvertones, led by **Chad Allan.** As they matured and started playing in night clubs, they changed their name to Chad Allan and the Reflections. The band changed their name again when they discovered another band had already released a record using the name The Reflections, and so they became Chad Allan and the Expressions. They changed their name a final time after recording the single "Shakin' All Over": hoping record buyers would mistake them for a British band, they put the words "Guess Who?" in place of the artists' name on the sleeve. The name stuck, and their cover of "Shakin' All Over" (#22 6/05/65 *Billboard*), featuring Allan's vocals, became a hit. They followed that success with "Tossin' and Turnin'," which didn't do as well. Chad decided that the world of rock and roll wasn't stable enough for him. He gave up his rock and roll lifestyle, enrolled in the University of Manitoba, and earned his master's degree in psychology. He was replaced by Burton Cummings, who led the band to the top of the charts. Allan was also associated with Brave Belt, Randy Bachman's band, which evolved into the chartmeisters Bachman-Turner Overdrive. He left that band just before they became popular. Allan's track record once led Burton Cummings to joke, "The guy is King Midas in reverse…. When he stops touching something, it turns to gold." In the early nineties Allan returned to music, releasing *Zoot Suit Monologue*, an album of contemporary Christian music.

186. Which band did Billy Corgan's father audition for, only to turn down the job?

A.) In 1965 Smashing Pumpkins front man Billy Corgan's father, Bill Corgan Sr., auditioned for the job as guitarist in **The Amboy Dukes**. He was given the job, but at the last minute decided that he preferred the more stable life of a nine-to-five job, and turned the band down. The guitarist's job was eventually filled by gonzo rocker Ted Nugent. The senior Corgan's dreams of being a rock star were briefly realized when he collaborated on a song with his son on a b-side called "The Last Song," recorded during the *Mellon Collie and the Infinite Sadness* sessions.

187. Who released the Beatles-themed novelty song "John, You Went Too Far This Time" in 1969?

A.) "John, You Went Too Far This Time," a Beatle-themed novelty tune, was sung by **Rainbo** in 1969. As a singer Rainbo was never heard of again, but she did find acting success under her real name, Sissy Spacek. The Beatles inspired a whole raft of tribute songs. In 1964 the Beagles — a group of Beatle-wigged dogs — barked their way through an album of Beatles tunes, while The Bon Bons issued "What's Wrong with Ringo" later that same year. The Bon Bons later became the Shangri-Las and scored a teen-angst hit with "Leader of the Pack" (#1 10/24/64 *Billboard*). Other artists who tried to cash in on The Beatles' popularity were Allen Sherman, Dickie Goodman, and The Chipmunks.

188. Which Beatles song features a high-pitched whistle that only dogs can hear?

A.) After the forty-two second fade-out on The Beatles' **"A Day in the Life"** from *Sgt. Pepper's Lonely Hearts Club Band* there is a high-pitched whistle, only audible to dogs. The Beatles may have borrowed the canine idea from The Beach Boys' *Pet Sounds* album, which features Brian Wilson's dogs barking at the end of "Caroline No" (#32 4/23/66 *Billboard*). The famous fade-out was performed by a forty-one piece orchestra that was directed by Paul to "freak out" during the twenty-four bar passage. Producer George Martin wrote forty-one individual scores for the orchestra, beginning with the lowest note capable by the instrument with a gentle slide upwards toward the highest note the instrument could reach. To create the proper atmosphere in the studio McCartney invited several of his friends, including Mick Jagger, Marianne Faithful, and the entire staff of the Apple Boutique. To lend a distinctive feel to the session, everyone was asked to wear formal dress, including the hired orchestra. The orchestra were also given false noses and party hats to wear, to add to

120

the unusual carnival atmosphere in the studio. The song's final dramatic piano chord was played on three pianos by four people — Ringo, Paul McCartney, John Lennon, and Mal Evans.

189. Which macabre British sixties singer claims that Winston Churchill once stubbed out a cigar on his palm?

A.) Singer **Screaming Lord Sutch** wrote in his autobiography that as a child he went to see Winston Churchill in a parade. A chance meeting with the British Prime Minister led to a conversation, at the end of which Churchill butted out his enormous cigar on young Sutch's "outstretched, pleading hand." In later years when Sutch entered politics, he writes that he realised that his scarred hand was his voting hand. He interpreted the mark as a brand that "passed on the torch of his destiny, and that of the British people, to little me." Screaming Lord Sutch is one of British rock's great eccentrics. While chart success eluded him on this side of the ocean, in the UK he enjoyed notoriety for his outlandish "rock'n'horror" stage show, and macabre hits like "Jack the Ripper," "My Black Coffin," "All Black and Hairy," and "'Til the Following Night." In the early days of his band he had a who's who of British rock backing him up. Nick Simper and Ritchie Blackmore played with him before leaving to form Deep Purple; bass player Noel Redding quit Sutch's band to join with Jimi Hendrix; Jeff Beck was in the band for a time; legendary British session player Nicky Hopkins tinkled the keys in the early days and was replaced by Matthew Fisher, who went on to play with Procol Harum. Now it is very common for actors and rock stars to get involved in politics; in the early sixties this was not so. Sutch distinguished himself by being the first rock star to run for Parliament in Britain. He ran (unsuccessfully) for almost three decades under the banner of the Raving Looney Party. His followers were familiar with slogans like "Parliament will be screaming if you vote Lord Sutch!", "Vote Sutch and gain much!", and "Vote for the Ghoul. He's No Fool!" His tongue-in-cheek campaigns earned him hundreds of column inches in the British newspapers, and thousands of votes over the years. On June 17, 1999, Screaming Lord Sutch was found dead in his home in South Harrow, London. Newspapers reported that he

121

had been suffering depression since the death of his mother two years previously, and had taken his own life. He was fifty-eight years old.

190. Who won more Grammy Awards — The Beatles or Elvis Presley?

A.) **The Beatles** beat out Elvis Presley in the Grammy race, but only by one. The Beatles had four Grammys to their credit, while Elvis only had three. Oddly, Elvis was never nominated for any of his rock recordings. His three Grammys were all for religious recordings (Best Sacred Performance – 1967, Best Inspirational Performance – 1972, and Best Inspirational Performance – 1974).

191. Who was the subject of The GTOs' 1969 song "Rodney"?

A.) The GTOs saluted **Rodney Bingenheimer**, "Sunset Strip's foremost male groupie," in the 1969 song "Rodney." Rodney is a legendary figure in the Los Angeles music world, without ever having lifted a musical instrument. In the sixties he hung out with rock stars, got beaten up by Brian Jones (who later apologised), doubled for Davy Jones on "The Monkees," meditated with George Harrison, and wrote about music for an L.A. newspaper. In the seventies Rodney owned the most happening club on the West Coast. For four or five years he presided over Rodney Bingenheimer's English Disco, which has been described as "a cathedral to David Bowie." The club attracted a who's who of rock and roll. Keith Moon liked the young girls the place attracted; Alice Cooper liked the beer; Elvis Presley stopped in to see what all the fuss was about; Marc Bolan, David Bowie, Iggy Pop, and Suzi Quatro were all regulars. The club closed in the late seventies. Rodney is now a highly rated disc jockey on "World Famous" KROQ-FM in Los Angeles.

The GTOs (Girls Together Outrageously) were a group of Los Angeles groupies who tried for pop stardom on their own with the help of Frank Zappa, who produced the album, and Jeff Beck, who lent his guitar wizardry. One of The GTOs, Pamela Des Barres, chronicled her life as a Los Angeles groupie in the sixties and seventies in the best-selling book

I'm With the Band.

192. Where did John Lennon meet Yoko Ono for the first time?

A. John Lennon met Yoko Ono for the first time at the **Indica Gallery in London's West End.** Yoko was mounting a show of her avant garde art, which had not been opened to the public yet when John walked into the gallery. Legend has it that Yoko did not recognize Lennon on their first meeting. They began talking, and Yoko told John that he could pound a nail into one of her performance art pieces for five shillings. Lennon replied that instead he would give her an imaginary five shillings and pound in an imaginary nail. Thus began one of the most publicized relationships of the 1960s.

WHAT'S GOIN' ON?
The 1970s

1. Who was "Shine on You Crazy Diamond" from Pink Floyd's *Wish You Were Here* album written for?

A.) "Shine on You Crazy Diamond" from Pink Floyd's *Wish You Were Here* album was written for **Syd Barrett** (real name: Roger Keith Barrett). As childhood friends Barrett and future bandmate Roger Waters discovered a mutual interest in American blues and R&B. They formed a band to play blues and rock standards like "Louie Louie" and "Road Runner," although Barrett embellished them with his off-the-wall guitar stylings. Barrett combined the names of two of his favourite Georgia-based blues men, Pink Anderson and Floyd Council, to create the band's original name, The Pink Floyd Sound. It was also Barrett's influence that moved the band away from its original R&B sound to the more psychedelic sounds of San Francisco's Bay Area bands. After penning the bulk of the band's first album and their initial singles, Barrett started to behave erratically. He became unreliable both in the studio and on the stage, taking time off to recuperate from "nervous exhaustion" during the band's first tour, costing the band almost four thousand pounds in cancelled dates. The British music papers began detailing accounts of Barrett's bizarre behaviour. One story found Barrett locked in a bathroom during the recording of the band's debut album. After repeated attempts to get him to come out, the other band members broke down the door, only to find the bathroom empty and demolished. Syd had crawled out a window, quietly disappearing for the rest of the day. Later, during a taping of Dick Clark's "American Bandstand" Syd refused to lip-sync their latest

124

single, "See Emily Play," because he didn't "feel like moving his lips" that day. Syd remained a full-fledged member of Pink Floyd for a short while after that, although he didn't play live with the band. He was relegated to the studio, where the band felt they could control his mood swings. When even this proved impossible he was permanently replaced (by Dave Gilmour) both on stage and in the studio. After an uneven recording career he dropped out of sight.

2. In 1973 The Rolling Stones released "Angie" (#1 9/22/73 *Billboard*), a single from the *Goat's Head Soup* album. Who was the subject of the song?

A.) The Rolling Stones' single "Angie" (#1 9/22/73 *Billboard*) was written about **David Bowie's then-wife Angela**. Angela is the mother of Bowie's only child, Zowie, and the author of two books about her life with Bowie. Angie made headlines in 1993 with the release of her second book, *Backstage Passes: Life on the Wild Side With David Bowie*. In this book the ex-Mrs. Bowie claims that David is a member of an alien race known as "the Light People." Angie is convinced that David is one of the Light People because he shares so many of their characteristics, including great musical talent. Mr. Bowie refuses to comment on the book.

3. Who was the subject of Carly Simon's 1972 hit "You're So Vain" (#1 12/16/72 *Billboard*)?

A.) Carly Simon's 1972 hit "You're So Vain" (#1 12/16/72 *Billboard*) was originally written about a fictitious man named Ben. The song was called "Bless You Ben," and told the story of a happy romance and young love. Simon retooled the song, replacing its saccharine lyrics with more pointed words. Today, Carly Simon claims that the words to "You're So Vain" were inspired by several men, although **Warren Beatty** was the main inspiration. She refuses to name any other names because she wants to keep people guessing, and she feels listeners would lose interest in the song if they knew too much about it.

BiBang! Baby

4. What was the first platinum single?

A.) The first platinum singles were not issued until 1976. Originally this certification level required a minimum sale of two million units. On January 1, 1989, the platinum-single requirements were dropped to a minimum sale of one million units. Johnnie Taylor was the first person to receive a platinum disc for the song **"Disco Lady"** (#1 3/06/76 *Billboard*). The song also garnered two Grammy nominations that year for Best R&B Song (songwriter's award) and Best R&B Male Vocal. In spite of "Disco Lady"'s huge commercial success, Taylor left the Grammys empty-handed. Boz Scaggs took Best Songwriter award for "Lowdown" (#3 8/07/76 *Billboard*), while Stevie Wonder took Best R&B Male Vocal for "I Wish" (#1 12/04/76 *Billboard*). Taylor had several other hits, most notably "Who's Makin' Love" (#5 11/02/68 *Billboard*).

5. What was the name of the first record released by The Police?

A.) The Police's first vinyl outing was 1977's **"Fall Out"** on Illegal Records, and sold about two thousand copies. (Illegal Records was founded by drummer Stewart Copeland's brother Miles.) This single featured The Police's original guitarist Henri Padovani, who was later replaced by Andy Summers. Once Summers joined the band they moved away from the hard-edged punk of their early tunes and incorporated reggae stylings into their sound. Their new "white reggae" sound led to a major recording contract. With a major record deal, and their sound intact, they now dyed their hair blond (for a Wrigley's gum ad), strengthening their image, and turning Sting into the object of many a teeny-bopper's passion. Their first single, "Roxanne" (#32 4/07/79 *Billboard*), broke into the Top 40 in the US, although it sank without a trace in Britain. It wasn't until their next single, "Can't Stand Losing You," generated more interest in the band in the UK that "Roxanne" was re-released, and broke into the Top 40. By 1980 they were the biggest act in Britain, a position they held until their split in 1985.

6. What was The Sex Pistols' first record?

A.) The Sex Pistols unleashed **"Anarchy in the UK"** in 1976 for EMI. The BBC banned the record after only five plays, but nonetheless the record sold 55,000 copies and made the charts. EMI terminated the Pistols' contract amid a storm of controversy while they were on tour in Holland, paying their manager Malcolm McLaren a severance fee of twenty thousand pounds.

7. In 1974 Telly Savalas (TV's Kojak) released an album on MCA called *Telly*. What was the name of the single released from that album?

A.) Telly Savalas released a remake of The Righteous Brothers' classic **"You've Lost That Lovin' Feelin.'"** Telly's hopes of a long-term singing career were dashed when nobody bought the record.

8. What was Chuck Berry's first number 1 hit on both sides of the Atlantic?

A.) After seventeen years of making records, and helping to define the sound of rock and roll, Chuck Berry's first international number 1 hit was 1972's novelty **"My Ding-A-Ling"** (#1 9/09/72 *Billboard*) from *The London Sessions* double album. The song is a sing-a-long ode to penises and masturbation, which was subtle enough (or stupid enough) to garner huge amounts of airplay on both sides of the Atlantic. Even Chuck realized it wasn't up to his usual standards — he introduced the song to the live audience at the Lancaster Arts Festival in Coventry, England, as a "fourth-grade ditty."

9. Who were the first rock artists to have all their records in the Top 150 at the same time?

A.) **Led Zeppelin** had all their six albums in the Top 150 in 1975. Zeppelin were known primarily as an album band, rarely releasing singles. In eleven years they managed to place only six singles in

Billboard's Top 40 — "Whole Lotta Love," "Immigrant Song," "Black Dog," "D'yer Maker," "Trampled Under Foot," and "Fool in the Rain." Oddly, their most popular song, "Stairway to Heaven," was never released as a single, and never appeared on the *Billboard* charts.

10. Where was the cover photograph for Joe Walsh's 1978 LP *But Seriously Folks* taken?

A.) The cover photo for Joe Walsh's *But Seriously Folks* was snapped **underwater, on the bottom of a pool.** The photo shows Joe sitting under a Ciao umbrella, having a bite to eat completely underwater. This record produced the Top 20 hit "Life's Been Good" (#12 7/01/78 *Billboard*).

11. Who did the cover art for Long John Baldry's 1972 release *Everything Stops for Tea*?

The six-foot, seven-inch Long John Baldry. His strong, deep voice can be heard on many recordings, including the 1967 UK number 1 hit "Let the Heartaches Begin." In the early 90s his voice was used as Captain Robotnik on the *Sonic the Hedgehog* computer game.

A.) The cover art for Long John Baldry's *Everything Stops for Tea* shows Long John having tea with the march hare and a sleeping door mouse, and was drawn by Rolling Stones guitarist **Ronnie Wood.** Wood has had a lifelong interest in art, having studied at Ealing College of Art in London. Wood's renderings of his friends and colleagues, like Mick Jagger, Keith Richards, Jimi Hendrix, and Marvin Gaye, give the viewer an up-close and personal view of the subject. In 1987 Wood collaborated with writer Bill German on a collection of his

128

sketches, paintings, and doodles called *Ron Wood by Ron Wood: The Works*. He has had exhibitions of his work in the United States, Japan, Europe, and Scandinavia. In 1992 he designed the cover for his solo album *Slide on This*.

12. On the cover of The Who's *Who Are You?* album, what does the chair Keith Moon is sitting in have written on it?

A.) 1978's *Who Are You?* was The Who's last album before the death of drummer/insane person Keith Moon. The chair he sits in is ironically inscribed **"Not to be taken away."** Moon died in 1978 when he overdosed on the pills he was using to combat his alcoholism. The Who continued on with ex-Faces drummer Kenney Jones.

13. Who appears with David Bowie on the cover of 1973's *Pinups* album?

A.) Model and actress **Twiggy** is David Bowie's partner on the *Pinups* album cover. The photo was taken during a *Vogue* shoot, although the magazine chose not to run the picture. The album was Bowie's tribute to all his favourite bands of the 1960s, including The Easybeats, The Merseybeats, and The Who. The album was not well-received by the music press, who felt that Bowie had done nothing new with the songs. The critics charged that by faithfully interpreting the sixties classics, Bowie was no longer challenging his audience, and perhaps losing his edge. He proved the critics wrong by bouncing back the following year with *Diamond Dogs*, an ambitious work that drew from George Orwell's *1984* for inspiration.

14. How much did Bruce Springsteen pay for his first guitar?

A.) Bruce Springsteen bought his first guitar from a pawnshop in Freehold, New Jersey, for **eighteen dollars.** He had his eye on a set of drums but couldn't afford them, so he settled on a guitar instead.

15. What was the first sound recorded on a machine?

A.) The first sound recorded on a machine was Thomas Edison singing **"Mary Had a Little Lamb"** on December 6, 1877. Ninety-five years later Paul McCartney and Wings scored a Top 30 hit with the children's favourite ("Mary Had a Little Lamb": #28 7/08/72 *Billboard*).

16. Who designed the cover of The Cars' 1979 platinum album *Candy-O*?

A.) Well-known pinup artist **Alberto Vargas** designed the cover for the album. The Vargas Girls, a series of pinups created for *Esquire* between 1940 and 1946, are among the most reproduced images in popular culture.

17. What is floating between the smokestacks of the Battersea Power Station on the cover of Pink Floyd's *Animals*?

A.) A **giant pig** floats between the smoke stacks of the Battersea Power Station on the cover of Pink Floyd's *Animals*. The cover, designed by Hipgnosis, was shot in early 1977 using a forty-foot zeppelin pig. The big pig broke free of its moorings during one photo shoot, drifting from London to Kent, before settling down on a farm pasture.

18. Which Pink Floyd album pictures a burning man shaking hands with a man in a business suit?

A.) Pink Floyd's **Wish You Were Here** (1975) features a man engulfed in flames shaking hands with a suited man.

19. What was Eric Clapton's musical address in August 1974?

A.) Eric Clapton released **461 Ocean Boulevard** in August 1974. The album yielded one major hit, "I Shot the Sheriff" (#1 8/03/74 *Billboard*), a cover of the Bob Marley hit. Clapton is generally given credit for exposing reggae music to the general record-buying public, although he feels the song was done with "too much of a white feel." 461 Ocean Boulevard (Golden Beach, Florida) was the rented house that Eric Clapton stayed in during the recording of the record, his first solo album. He posed for the jacket photographs in the house's backyard, which backs onto the beach.

20. Which band was named the top-selling band of the twentieth century?

A.) **The Beatles** were named the top-selling band of the twentieth century by the Recording Industry Association of America, racking up sales of more than 106 million records in the United States alone. The Mop Tops are the only band in history to garner five diamond albums, signifying sales of greater than ten million copies. Three of those albums, *The Beatles (White Album)* (17 million), *Sgt. Pepper's Lonely Hearts Club Band* (11 million), and *Abbey Road* (11 million) were the top-selling albums of the 1960s. The remaining two, *The Beatles/1967–1970* and *The Beatles/1962–1966,* have sold a combined total of 27 million copies.

21. Who did Ray Davies meet in a club in "old Soho"?

A.) Ray Davies claims that his song **"Lola"** (#9 9/12/70 *Billboard*) is based on a true story. In interviews over the years his story has changed, but it does seem clear that he was drinking in a pub when his fancy turned to a young woman at the bar. It wasn't until the light stubble on the "woman's" face became apparent that the inspiration for this song was born. "Lola" was banned in Australia because of its unusual subject matter. It was almost banned in Britain as well, but not for its sexual imagery. The BBC has a very strict policy about advertisements — they don't run them. The line in "Lola" that mentions Coca-Cola constituted an ad, and would have to be changed if the song was to find airplay in Britain. The band re-recorded the offending line, replacing the brand name with the acceptable "cherry cola."

22. Who, according to Randy Newman's 1977 hit, have no reason to live?

Big Bang! Baby

A.)**"Short People"** (#2 12/10/77 *Billboard*) have no reason to live, according to Randy Newman's 1977 satirical attack on prejudice. Newman originally made his name as the songwriter in residence at Metric Music, a division of Liberty Records. His tunes were recorded by a wide variety of artists including The Fleetwoods, Gene McDaniels, Gene Pitney, Judy Collins, and Jerry Butler. His greatest success in those days was the Cilla Black rendering of his tune "I've Been Wrong Before," which reached the British Top 20 in 1967. Later that same year ex-Animals organist Alan Price scored a Top 10 hit with Newman's ode to circus life "Simon Smith and His Amazing Dancing Bear." He began his solo recording career in 1970 with an eponymous release that failed to make a dent in the charts. Newman has continued to release high quality solo recordings and movie soundtracks (*Ragtime*, *The Natural*, *The Three Amigos*, *Avalon*, *A Bug's Life*, *Toy Story*, and *Toy Story 2*), but he remains best known as a writer of other people's hits.

23. The first Blondie album (1977) was not Debbie Harry's vinyl debut. What was her first album titled?

A.)Debbie Harry's debut was 1968's ***The Wind in the Willows***. Debbie was not yet blonde, nor was she much of a singer. This album was a misguided attempt to cash in on the "summer of love" hippy movement that was generating big sales for bands like the Quicksilver Messenger Service and The Steve Miller Band. The credits even include a thanks to "Freddy," their spiritual advisor. According to British writer Muck Raker, this album was so unpopular that unsold album returns actually exceeded the number of copies sold. It was discovered that even reviewers were returning their promotional discs, which meant that when all the numbers were added up, the record company received more rejected copies of the album than they had actually offered for sale. The album was re-released in 1978 as *The Wind in the Willows featuring Debbie Harry* after the success of Blondie's *Parallel Lines* album.

24. Which 1976 hit has the distinction of being the chart-topper with the most repeated words in its title?

A.) According to the people who monitor the *Billboard* charts, the song with the most repeated words in its title ever to make number 1 was K.C. and the Sunshine Band's **"(Shake, Shake, Shake) Shake Your Booty"** (#1 7/31/76 *Billboard*). Singer Harry Wayne Casey said that this hit had a deeper meaning than people realized, and urged people to look beneath the surface. He said he used dancing as a metaphor for everyday life. If you can shake your booty on the dance floor, then why not shake your booty in everyday life and achieve your goals.

25. How much does Brian Eno claim to have spent on the recording of the *(no pussyfooting)* album with Robert Fripp?

A.) Brian Eno claims that his 1974 collaboration with Robert Fripp, *(no pussyfooting)* cost only **fourteen dollars** — the price of the tape. Recorded in Eno's home studio in late 1972, it features two long jams by Eno and Fripp. The record was released by Island in 1974. *Village Voice* critic Robert Christgau gave *(no pussyfooting)* a rating of B+, noting "these two twenty-minute duets ... are the most enjoyable pop electronics since Terry Riley's *A Rainbow in Curved Air*, achieving their goal with admirable formal concision."

26. In 1976 Hall and Oates re-released *Abandoned Luncheonette*, which produced the Top 10 single "She's Gone." What was the song written about?

A.) "She's Gone" (#7 8/14/76 *Billboard*) was written about **Daryl Hall's divorce from Bryna Lublin, and John Oates' experience of being stood up on New Year's Eve.** When the single was originally released in 1974, it didn't get much airplay, only reaching number 60 on the charts. The second try at success for "She's Gone" earned it a gold record, and kick-started the careers of Daryl Hall and John Oates.

27. Who played keyboards on Prince's first album, *For You* ?

BiBang! Baby

A.) **Prince** played keyboards, and all other instruments, on his debut album, *For You*. That album was the result of his contract with Warner Brothers. He signed his major label deal in 1977, and received well over one million dollars, probably the biggest contract ever for an unknown.

28. Who was the 1977 number 1 Hall and Oates single "Rich Girl" written about?

A.) Hall and Oates' "Rich Girl" (#1 2/05/77 *Billboard*) was actually written about a man, an **ex-boyfriend of Sara Allen** (Daryl Hall's girlfriend). The gender was changed to avoid confusion. Taken from the *Bigger Than the Both of Us* album, it was Hall and Oates' biggest hit up to that time, spending fourteen weeks on the charts, two of those at number 1.

29. Who provided the background moans on Rod Stewart's hit "Tonight's the Night"?

A.) The background moaning for Rod the Mod's "Tonight's the Night (Gonna Be Alright)" (#1 10/23/76 *Billboard*) was provided by his then-girlfriend **Britt Ekland.** Her moans helped keep the song at number 1 for eight weeks.

30. Who is thought to be the "jester" mentioned in Don McLean's "American Pie"?

A.) Don McLean's "American Pie" (#1 12/04/71 *Billboard*) has cryptic references to several music legends. It is thought that **Bob Dylan** is the jester, and The Beatles are the marching band, although McLean has never confirmed these suspicions. He does concede though that "the day the music died" was February 3, 1959, when Buddy Holly, Ritchie Valens, and The Big Bopper were killed in a plane crash. The tune is interesting for another reason: a careful listen will reveal that the song begins in mono and gradually moves to stereo during its nine-minute length. McLean wanted to symbolize the history of the sound of rock and roll, and so the song begins with mono, representing early rock, then gradually works through to today's modern stereo sound.

31. Who was the singer who sang the background "doot-de-doots" on Lou Reed's "Walk on the Wild Side" ?

A.) **Helen Terry** provided the background "doot-de-doots" for Lou Reed's "Walk on the Wild Side" (#16 3/31/73 *Billboard*). Her voice is often compared to Aretha Franklin, for its power and soulfulness. When Terry worked with Culture Club (on 1983's *Colour by Numbers*), drummer Jon Moss had nothing but praise for her. "To find a woman singer who could fit in with the band is incredible, and Helen's heaven-sent. She's perfect, she's a bit eccentric, she's not exactly what we call a 'dolly bird,' and she's got a great personality. She's fantastic, y'know, she's actually got her type of sex appeal."

32. In 1978 Nick Lowe released *Jesus of Cool* in the UK. For its US release the album was retitled. What was the North American title?

A.) For its US release Nick Lowe was forced to change the title of *Jesus of Cool* to the less controversial **Pure Pop for Now People**. The album added several popular songs to Lowe's repertoire ("I Love the Sound of Breaking Glass," "Little Hitler," and "36 Inches High"), but failed to find any significant chart action in America. The following year Lowe hit the Top 20 with "Cruel to be Kind" (#12 8/18/79 *Billboard*), and married Johnny Cash's daughter Carlene.

33. What was the name of Charlie Manson's 1970 release?

A.) **LIE** was Charles Manson's album, released to help finance his defence in the Sharon Tate murder trial. The cover art shows a *Life* magazine cover with the "F" removed.

34. What album has the longest run on the *Billboard* album charts?

A.) Pink Floyd's **Dark Side of the Moon** was in the Top 200 of the *Billboard* album charts for over a decade. It has far surpassed other long-running records, such as *Johnny Mathis' Greatest Hits* and Carole King's *Tapestry. Dark Side of the Moon* was the first Pink Floyd release to earn a gold record.

35. What was the biggest-selling UK single of the 1970s?

A.) According to the British Market Research Bureau (BMRB) the biggest-selling single of the seventies was Paul McCartney and Wings' **"Mull of Kintyre" b/w "Girls' School."** This double a-sided single stayed atop the *New Musical Express* charts for nine weeks, and sold over 100,000 copies a week during that period (selling 300,000 copies from Dec 10–Dec 17, 1977). "Mull of Kintyre" was inspired by the town of Kintyre, located near Paul's farm. The flip side, "Girls' School," was inspired by newspaper advertisements for pornographic movies.

36. What year did The Bee Gees top the American Top Selling Singles charts with "Night Fever" and "Stayin' Alive"?

A.) The Bee Gees topped the American Top Selling Singles charts with "Night Fever" and "Stayin' Alive" in **1978.** Both songs appeared on the soundtrack for *Saturday Night Fever,* which became the top-selling record up to that time, heading the album charts in the US for twenty-four weeks. 1978 was also a good year for the youngest Gibb sibling, Andy. His hit "Shadow Dancing" stayed alive at number 1 for seven weeks, while "An Everlasting Love" and "(Our Love) Don't Throw It Away" both broke into the Top 10.

37. How long did it take Van Morrison's critically acclaimed *Moondance* album to go gold in the US?

A.) Van Morrison (real name: George Ivan Morrison) was presented with a gold record for *Moondance* in November 1976, **six years** after its initial pressing. 1970's Moondance was the beginning of a hectic

136

and prolific period in Morrison's career. In the next four years he would release five single albums and one double live album, which contained the most commercially successful and accessible work of his career. With the backing of The Caledonia Soul Orchestra he pumped out *Moondance* (1970), then *His Band and the Street Choir* (1970) — which spawned the single "Domino" (#9 12/05/70 *Billboard*) — followed by *Tupelo Honey* (1971), *St. Dominic's Preview* (1972), and *Hard Nose the Highway* (1973). In 1974 he capped off this extraordinary burst of creativity with the fine live album *It's Too Late to Sleep Now*. In 1974 a compilation album of material recorded in the 1960s for the Bang label was also released under the title *T.B. Sheets*. Morrison has continued to issue superior quality albums, although not with the frequency or the commercial success of his early seventies output.

38. What Harry Nilsson song topped the charts on both sides of the Atlantic in 1972?

A.) In 1972 Harry Nilsson topped the charts on both sides of the Atlantic with **"Without You"** from the album *Nilsson Schmilsson*. Harry admits to being quite drunk the night he heard the song for the first time, and by the next morning he couldn't remember much about the tune, except that he knew he wanted to record it. He couldn't place the name of the original band — he thought they were called "Grapefruit or something." Some time later, he finally realized it was a song written by Pete Ham and Tom Evans of Badfinger. Nilsson took the song to producer Richard Perry, who turned it into a worldwide number 1 hit.

39. Name the independent English record company whose slogan was "We Came, We Saw, We Left."

A.) "We Came, We Saw, We Left" was the slogan of **Stiff Records,** founded by Jake Riviera. Over the years Stiff has used a variety of catch phrases to promote their records, and themselves. A partial list includes: "If it ain't Stiff, It ain't worth a fuck," "Surfing the New Wave," and "Be Stiff." Stiff Records left behind a rich legacy of British new wave, including Lene Lovich's albums *Stateless* (1979) and *Flex* (1980), and Ian Gomm's *Gomm With the Wind* (1979), which produced the US hit single "Hold On" (#18 10/06/79 *Billboard*). The label's biggest-selling artists were Ian (*New Boots and Panties*) Dury, Elvis (*My Aim is True*) Costello, and the ska band Madness (*One Step Beyond*). Stiff Records can also claim credit for releasing the first punk single to make the charts, The Damned's "New Rose."

40. Who wrote: "I saw rock and roll's future and its name is Bruce Springsteen"?

A.) On May 9, 1974, *Real Paper* rock critic **Jon Landau** saw Bruce Springsteen in concert for the first time. The show, at The Harvard Square Theatre in Cambridge, Massachusetts (on the eve of Landau's twenty-seventh birthday), impressed him so much he went home and wrote, "I saw rock and roll's future and its name is Bruce Springsteen." The quote appeared in Landau's May 22, 1974, column in *The Real Paper*, and has gone on to become one of the most famous rock-critic quotes of all time.

41. Who said: "Rock journalism is people who can't write, interviewing people who can't talk, for people who can't read"?

A.) **Frank Zappa**, whose hatred of the musical press is quite plain, made this statement.

42. Where did David Bowie announce his retirement in 1973?

A.) David Bowie announced his retirement on the stage of the **Hammersmith–Odeon in London** on July 3, 1973. Bowie (as Ziggy Stardust) announced, "This night shall always be special in my memory. Not only is it the last show of my British tour, but it is the last show I will ever do." The stunned audience (including Ringo Starr, Mick and Bianca Jagger, Tony Curtis, and Barbra Streisand) didn't realize that

Bowie would be seen almost a year to the day later with *The 1980 Floor Show* in 1974.

43. What did Robert Fripp say was a political movement that votes with its feet?

A.) Robert Fripp made this comment about **disco.**

44. Who said "The sicker you kids get, the greater shows we'll have for you"?

A.) "The sicker you kids get," said **Alice Cooper** in 1973, "the greater shows we'll have for you." At the time Alice Cooper's stage show was second to none, featuring mock decapitations, hangings, and baby doll mutilations. Steve Demorest's 1974 book *Alice Cooper* provides a partial list of stage props from 1973's *Billion Dollar Babies* tour that will give you some idea of the scope and size of the shows: To prepare for the tour Alice had two semi-ton trucks carrying 40 tons of equipment, including the sound systems, the dentist's drill, the surgical table for the sawing-in-half machine, 4 whips, 6 hatchets, 22,000 sparklers, 33,000 program books, 1,000 patches, 300 baby dolls, 58 manikins, 14 bubble machines, 28 gallons of bubble juice, 280 spare light bulbs, 6000 mirror parts, and 250,000 packages of bubble bath.

45. Who said that the second most important event of the 1970s was, "My solo on 'Wang Dang Sweet Poontang' in Detroit, September 3, 1979"?

A.) In the March 1980 issue of *Musician (Player and Listener)* **Ted Nugent** said that, "My solo on 'Wang Dang Sweet Poontang' in Detroit, September 3, 1979" was the second most important event of the 1970s. He went on to say that, "eighties rock is heading to room 1415 of the Hyatt Regency Hotel in Atlanta, Ga. (My Room!!!)."

Big Bang! Baby

46. What was the name of the first band Holly Johnson of Frankie Goes to Hollywood was involved in?

A.) Before Frankie Goes to Hollywood's huge success, Holly Johnson was the singer in the Liverpool cult band **Big in Japan**. Also in this band were Budgie, who went on to play with Siouxsie and the Banshees and The Creatures; Ian Broudie, who produced Echo and the Bunnymen; and Bill Drummond, manager of Echo and the Bunnymen.

47. Who were The Spiders From Mars?

A.) The Spiders From Mars were David Bowie's backup band on two albums, *The Rise and Fall of Ziggy Stardust* and *The Man Who Sold the World.* They consisted of **Mick Ronson (guitar, piano, vocal), Trevor Bolder (bass), and Mick "Woody" Woodmansey (drums).**

48. What was the name of David Byrne's first band in high school?

A.) David Byrne's first band in high school was known as **Revelation**, and they did Beatles and Rolling Stones covers. Later, after Revelation broke up, he played solo in coffee houses. He played rock and roll, but with a twist. Byrne became locally famous for his version of "Summertime Blues" picked out on a ukulele.

49. Dave Stewart, Annie Lennox, and Pete Coombes released three albums together in the late seventies. What was the name of their band?

A.) The trio released three albums under the name **The Tourists.** The first album, produced by Connie Plank on the independent label Logo was called *The Tourists*, and fared poorly. Their second album was released on Epic, a division of CBS in England. Epic then combined the first two albums into one streamlined package released in the US under the name *Reality Effect*. This album charted in both the UK and the US. Their third release, *Luminous Basement,* fared badly,

140

and The Tourists broke up in 1980.

50. Who was the backup band on Cheech and Chong's "Basketball Jones" from their 1973 LP *Los Cochinos* ?

A.) The backup band on Cheech and Chong's tune "Basketball Jones" from the *Los Cochinos* album was **George Harrison, Billy Preston, Carole King, Klaus Voormann, and Nicky Hopkins.** (By the way, "Los Cochinos" is Mexican slang for "nasty guys.")

51. Why did Jermaine stay behind when The Jackson 5 changed labels from Motown to Philadelphia International?

A.) Jermaine Jackson didn't leave Motown with his siblings when they moved over to Philadelphia International because **he was married to Motown president Berry Gordy Jr.'s daughter.** The Jackson 5 became The Jacksons, and enjoyed chart success without Jermaine. Jermaine scored several hits on his own, including 1982's "Let Me Tickle Your Fancy" (#18 8/21/82 *Billboard*) featuring background vocals by Devo.

52. Who was Eric Clapton's backup band at his 1973 comeback concert at The London Rainbow Theatre?

A.) Eric Clapton was supported by Scotland's **Average White Band** for his comeback concert at The London Rainbow Theatre. They released their first album on MCA in 1973, but didn't meet with much success until 1974's *Average White Band* album for Atlantic. Clapton's comeback concert was arranged by Pete Townshend, Stevie Winwood, and Ron Wood.

53. Name the members of ABBA.

A.) ABBA is an acronym for the first names of the band members. They are: **Anni-Frid Lyngstad (vocals), Bjorn Ulvaeus**

141

biBang! Baby

(guitar, vocals), **Benny Andersson (keyboards, vocals), and Agnetha Faltskog (vocals).** ABBA was the first non-English-speaking rock act to achieve superstar status.

54. Who played guitar for both The James Gang and Deep Purple?

A.) **Tommy Bolin** joined The James Gang after the departure of Joe Walsh in 1973, and recorded two albums with them before splitting in 1974 to record his first solo album *Teaser.* In 1975 he joined Deep Purple, replacing the recently departed Ritchie Blackmore. When Deep Purple broke up in 1976, Bolin went solo again and recorded one more album, *Private Eyes,* before his death in December 1976.

55. Who sang the lead vocal on Pink Floyd's "Have a Cigar" from 1975's *Wish You Were Here* album?

A.) **Roy Harper,** the semi-legendary British folk singer, contributed the lead vocal to Pink Floyd's "Have a Cigar." Harper is probably best known for a tribute track on *Led Zeppelin III* called "Hats Off to Harper." His own catalogue includes upwards of ten albums, and he has appeared as an actor in 1972's movie *Made.*

56. Which founding member of Sha Na Na wrote the Top 10 hit "Shannon" in 1976?

A.) In 1969 **Henry Gross** was a Political Science and Speech major at Brooklyn College. Friends at nearby Columbia University enlisted him to help put together a new fifties-style band. Gross sang lead and played guitar with Sha Na Na at many high-profile gigs, including the Fillmore East, the Fillmore West, and Woodstock before leaving the band to pursue a solo career. He wrote "Shannon" in 1976 after hearing a story about an Irish setter named Shannon that had been killed by a car. Originally he had hoped The Beach Boys would record the song. When they didn't, he cut the track himself, releasing it on the Lifesong label. "There were a lot of people who thought it was a love song," Gross said.

142

"And in a way they're right. It was about the love of a dog." "Shannon" reached gold status with sales in excess of 1.5 million.

57. When did The Doors officially break up?

A.) The Doors didn't officially break up until **1973,** two years after Jim Morrison's death. They struggled on without Morrison for two albums, *Other Voices* and *Full Circle,* before calling it quits. The albums met with tepid response from critics. Robert Christgau sarcastically noted, "Anyone can sing rock, but that doesn't mean just anyone. Richard Nixon can't, and neither can Barbra Streisand, and I bet Peter Fonda can't either. Well, neither can Ray Manzarek or Robbie Krieger."

58. Who wrote "James Dean" for The Eagles, "Doctor My Eyes" for The Jackson 5, "Jamaica Say You Will" for Joe Cocker, "These Days" for Tom Rush, and "Fountain of Sorrow" for Joan Baez?

A.) "James Dean," "Doctor My Eyes," "Jamaica Say You Will," "These Days," and "Fountain of Sorrow" were all written by **Jackson Browne,** who in addition to his own recording output has also written songs for Nico, Johnny Rivers, and The Nitty Gritty Dirt Band. He has also tried his hand at producing, manning the boards for Warren Zevon's debut on Island Records.

59. When were the Concerts for Bangladesh held?

A.) The Concerts for Bangladesh were held on **August 1, 1971**, at Madison Square Garden, New York City. The concerts were arranged by George Harrison, and featured Ringo Starr, Eric Clapton, Leon Russell, Billy Preston, Badfinger, and Bob Dylan. The concerts were initiated after Ravi Shankar appealed to George Harrison to arrange a benefit concert to assist UNICEF in their efforts to help the refugee children in Bangladesh. In six weeks George rounded up several of his superstar friends, and booked Madison Square Garden in New York for the biggest rock event of the early seventies. The concerts raised $243,418.50 in two shows — one in the afternoon and one in the evening. Both shows were filmed for theatrical release, with Phil Spector producing the album of the event. The total proceeds exceeded fifteen million dollars, although because of legal difficulties with the IRS very little of the money actually made it to Bangladesh. As a reward for their efforts, George Harrison and Ravi Shankar were awarded UNICEF's The Child is the Father of Man Award in 1972.

60. Who starred in the ill-fated 1979 disco flick *Roller Boogie?*

A.) **Linda Blair** (of the *Exorcist*) starred in *Roller Boogie* (1979), which tried to combine the public's fascination with roller skating and disco music. It quickly skidded off the track into disco oblivion. *Roller Boogie* was not alone though. In 1978 Jeff Goldblum and Donna Summer starred in *T.G.I.F.*, an adventure set to the pulsating rhythms of disco, while The Village People stopped the people from going to the movie theatre with *Can't Stop the Music* (1980). In a review for *Can't Stop the Music, Time Out Magazine* commented that "the (movie's) pervasive tackiness is unrelieved." In 1991 seventies icons David Cassidy and Leif Garrett sent up the disco movie genre with *The Spirit of '76*, which combined space adventure with every garish cliché from the dark disco era.

61. Why was the majority of The Sex Pistols' first UK tour cancelled in 1976?

A.) The majority of The Sex Pistols' first UK tour was cancelled in a storm of controversy after they **appeared on Bill Grundy's "Today Show."** It was shortly after the release of "Anarchy in the UK," and Grundy repeatedly asked questions about their nasty image, egging Glen Matlock on to saying "fuck" on the air. As a result of the public outrage most of their UK tour was axed by promoters.

62. Who is the only major rock star to perform a benefit concert for the Canadian National Institute for the Blind?

144

A.) Rolling Stones' guitarist **Keith Richards** (with backup band The New Barbarians) is the only major rock and roll star to ever perform a benefit concert for the Canadian National Institute for the Blind. He was commanded by the court to perform the April 1979 concert to satisfy his sentence in a 1977 drug bust in Toronto.

63. Where did Talking Heads pinch their name from?

A.) Talking Heads pinched their name **from an article in *TV Guide*** while they were students at the Rhode Island School of Design. Looking to expand their audience, they moved to New York in 1974. Soon, they found a regular gig and following at CBGB, New York's premier new music club. Their brand of minimal art-school punk (with a liberal mix of original songs and sixties covers), coupled with David Byrne's off-the-wall lyrics, landed them a recording deal in 1977. Their debut, *Talking Heads '77,* garnered considerable critical praise, although it failed to break into the Top 100 album chart. Brian Eno took over the production chores for their next two albums, texturing their music with more percussion, and guiding the band to the Top 30 with "Take Me to the River" (#26 12/23/78 *Billboard*). In 1981 the band fragmented, with Byrne releasing a solo album with the help of Eno, and scoring *The Catherine Wheel* for choreographer Twyla Tharp. Other band members released solo ventures, with Chris Franz and Tina Weymouth finding chart success with the reggae influenced "Genius of Love" (#31 4/10/82 *Billboard*). In 1983 the band regrouped, and enjoyed their commercial peak with *Speaking in Tongues*, which produced the Top 10 hit "Burning Down the House" (#9 9/03/83 *Billboard*). A well-received concert film (*Stop Making Sense*) and two albums (*Little Creatures* and *True Stories*) later the group quietly disbanded, although no official announcement was ever released.

64. What were the names of the original members of KISS?

A.) The original line-up of KISS was: **bassist Gene Simmons (real name: Gene Klein), guitarist and singer Paul Stanley (real** name: Stanley Eisen), drummer Peter Criss (real name: Peter Crisscoula), and guitarist Ace Frehley (real name: Paul Frehley).

65. Sting's real name is Gordon Sumner. How did he acquire his nickname?

A.) Gordon Sumner acquired the nickname Sting when he was playing in a trad-jazz band called Phoenix. His bandmates came up with the name because he **always wore a black and yellow striped sweater** that reminded them of a bee.

66. What is "Devo" short for? Who is Devo's mascot?

Devo — the self-described "spud boys" from Akron, Ohio. Left to right are: Mark Mothersbaugh (vocals/keyboard/guitar), Alan Myers (drums), Jerry Casale (bass/vocals), Bob Casale (guitar/vocals), and Bob Mothersbaugh (guitar/vocals).

Photo courtesy of Mark Mothersbaugh

A.) "Devo" is short for **devolution**, the process by which organisms degenerate from complex to simple forms. Their cover of "Satisfaction" is a fine example of devolution. They have stripped the song down to its bare minimum — rhythm and clipped, mechanical vocals.

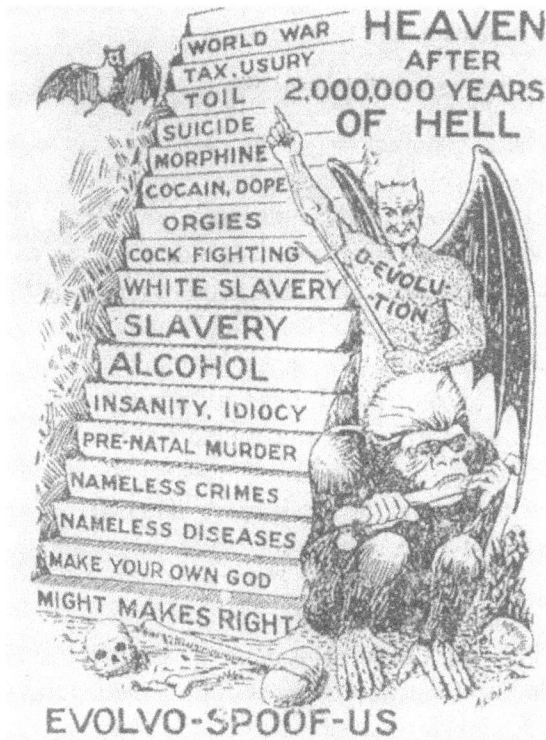

EVOLVO-SPOOF-US

Their robotic rock only made the Top 40 once, with "Whip It" (#14 10/04/80). Their mascot is **Booji Boy**, who is the infantile spirit of devolution.

67. Who was the inspiration for David Bowie's character Ziggy Stardust?

A.) David Bowie's inspiration for Ziggy Stardust was **The Legendary Stardust Cowboy.** He was a one-man band who used to stand on the hood of his car and "perform" in front of a hamburger joint in Texas. His vinyl legacy consists of two notoriously bad singles for Mercury.

This unusual illustration from a 1920s religious tract titled "Jocko-Homo Heavenbound" inspired Devo Leader Mark Mothersbaugh to pen one of his band's best-known songs, "Jocko Homo."

68. 10CC enjoyed Top 10 success in the seventies with such hits as "I'm Not in Love" and "The Things We Do for Love." What does "10CC" refer to?

A.) "10CC" is the **average amount of a male ejaculation.** After considerable chart success in the seventies, founding members Lol Creme and Kevin Godley left the band to pursue other interests. Their guitar synthesizer "The Gizmo" failed to stir up any real excitement, but it was as video directors that they would make their mark. They produced two of the most striking videos of the eighties — Herbie Hancock's

147

BigBang! Baby

"Rockit" and Frankie Goes to Hollywood's "Two Tribes."

69. Who punched out a very drunk Elvis Costello in a bar because he referred to Ray Charles as "a blind, ignorant nigger" in 1979?

A.) **Bonnie Bramlett**, (ex of Delaney and Bonnie), punched Elvis Costello because of the slur. The much-publicized incident occurred in Columbus, during Elvis's 1979 American tour. Elvis (who has appeared at Rock Against Racism concerts and recorded Nick Lowe's anthem to harmony, "What's So Funny 'Bout Peace, Love and Understanding") was involved in a verbal one-upmanship game with Bonnie and some members of The Stephen Stills Band. He was very drunk and tried to end the argument by saying "the most outrageous thing I could possibly say to them." The whole thing was written up in the newspapers, and even made it to *People*, before Elvis held a press conference to apologize and try to explain his actions.

70. On January 25, 1971, Grace Slick and Paul Kantner's baby girl was born at the French Hospital in San Francisco. They eventually named the baby China Wing Kantner, but not before causing a stir in the press because of Grace's first choice for a name. What did Grace want to call her child?

A.) After the birth of her first child on January 25, 1971, Grace Slick told a nurse in the hospital that the baby's name was going to be "**god**," "with a small g, we want her to be humble." The item was leaked to the press, and carried by newspapers all over the country.

71. Declan McManus was born in London in 1955. In 1977 he changed his name to Elvis Costello. Who suggested the switch?

A.) Declan McManus's name change to Elvis Costello was suggested by Stiff Records' co-founder, **Jake Riviera**. Riviera thought of the name as a marketing ploy. They wanted a distinctive, different name (in 1977 everyone was calling themselves Johnny Rotten, Johnny Snot, etc.), so they borrowed from the past and came up with Elvis Costello. (The source of "Elvis" is obvious, while "Costello" came from Declan's old stage name: he had played in an unsuccessful country rock band called Flip City using the name C.P. Costello.)

72. From 1974 to 1977 what well-known band played in the Boston area under the name Cap N Swing?

A.) **The Cars** played under the name Cap N Swing for several years with a line-up that included Ric Ocasek, Benjamin Orr, Greg Hawkes, and Elliot Easton. In 1977 drummer David Robinson joined the band, and they recorded a demo tape under the name The Cars.

73. Chrissie Hynde (of The Pretenders) and Steve Strange (of Visage) once performed in a band together. What was the name of this band?

A.) Before The Pretenders and Visage, Chrissie Hynde and Steve Strange played in a band called **The Moors Murderers.** They borrowed the name from the moniker the British press gave to Myra Hindley and Ian Brady. They murdered people (with a preference for small children) and buried their bodies on the Moorland in the Midlands near their home. The band was made up of Steve Brady (Strange), Vince and John Kay, and Christine Hindley (Hynde).

74. What is the origin of the name Three Dog Night?

A.) According to legend, the term "three dog night" comes from an **Australian Aboriginal term.** Aborigines sleep with their dogs, and the colder it gets the more dogs they sleep with. A "three dog night" is a very cold night. Danny Hutton, Chuck Negron, and Cory Wells formed the hit-making trio Three Dog Night, who enjoyed success (nine million-selling singles in five years) until 1976, when personnel problems caused a split. Their best-known song, "Joy to the World" was number 1 for six weeks in 1971.

Big Bang! Baby

75. What was the origin of the name Alice Cooper?

A.) Legend has it that Vince Furnier discovered through a Ouija board that he was the reincarnation of a **seventeenth-century witch, Alice Cooper**. Under the name Alice Cooper, Vincent would go on to become a pioneer in rock and roll theatrics, staging outrageous shows featuring electric chairs, buckets of raw meat, and snakes. "The sicker you kids get," said Alice in 1973, "the greater shows we'll have for you."

76. Who thought of the name Led Zeppelin?

A.) The Who's **Keith Moon** is credited with coming up with the name for Led Zeppelin. Moon made a joke to Jimmy Page, saying that Page's new band would be as popular as "the world's largest lead balloon — lead zeppelin." Moon was wrong, of course, as Led Zeppelin went on to release a slew of platinum records with their mix of blues and heavy metal. The band was forced to play several gigs under the name The Nobs in 1970 when members of the von Zeppelin family threatened to sue over the use of their family name. The case was settled out of court, with Led Zeppelin winning the right to use the name.

Othello (Richie Havens, left) urges Iago (actor Lance Le Gault) to renounce Satan in a scene from *Catch My Soul*, a pop-music version of Shakespeare's *Othello*.

77. What was the rock and roll version of Shakespeare's *Othello* called? Who starred as Othello?

A.) The rock and roll version of *Othello* by William Shakespeare was called **Catch My Soul**. The title was taken from Othello's line, "Perdition,

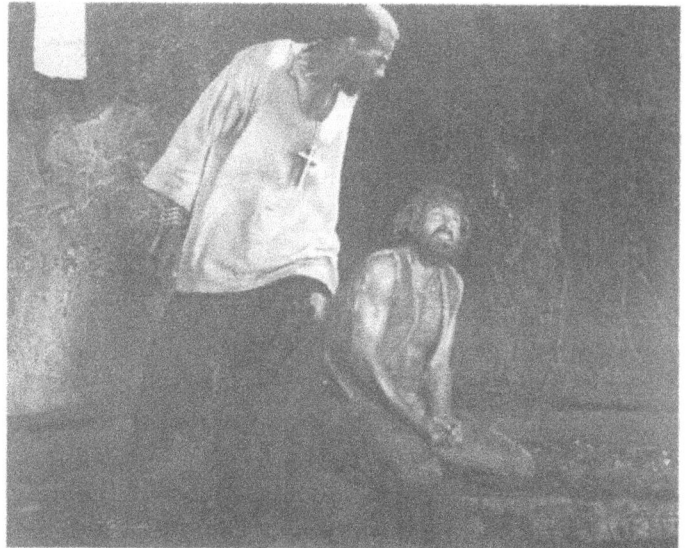

150

catch my soul, but I do love thee." Richie Havens played Othello. Directed by Patrick McGoohan (best remembered as No. 6 on television's "The Prisoner") and written and produced by Jack ("Shindig!") Good III in 1974, the film is sometimes called *Santa Fe Satan*. Besides Havens, other notable musicians in the cast include Tony Joe White, Bonnie Bramlett, Delaney Bramlett, and Billy Joe Royal.

78. What is the origin of Southern rockers Lynyrd Skynyrd's name?

A.) The members of Lynyrd Skynyrd adapted their name from their high school gym teacher's name, **Leonard Skinner.** Mr. Skinner strictly enforced the school's dress code, which cited long hair as a punishable offence. He tormented the future bandmates, and made gym class unpleasant for them, but they still refused to cut their hair. After high school the nucleus of the band, Ronnie Van Zant, Allen Collins, and Gary Rossington formed the band that was destined to become the main practitioners of the Southern boogie tradition begun by The Allman Brothers Band. Lynyrd Skynyrd was discovered in 1972 by Al Kooper (ex-Blood, Sweat and Tears keyboardist) after a performance in a small bar in Atlanta. The band released six hit albums in the next five years before their careers where tragically cut short by a plane crash that claimed the lives of their manager and three band members, including singer Ronnie Van Zant. The surviving members went on to form the Rossington-Collins Band and .38 Special.

79. Who played Leather Tuscadero on the 1977 season of "Happy Days"?

A.) During the 1977 season of "Happy Days" **Suzi Quatro** played Leather Tuscadero, leader of the hard rock band Leather and the Suedes. Quatro had been performing music since the age of 8, when she would play bongos with her father's jazz trio. At age 15 she quit high school to pursue a career in music with her all-girl band Suzi Soul and the Pleasure Seekers. It wasn't until she moved to England in the early seventies, hooked up with producer Mickie Most, and started playing

151

Big Bang! Baby

glitter rock that her career took off. A string of British hits followed, including "Can the Can" (#1 UK, over two million sold), "48 Crash" (#3 UK), "Devil's Gate Drive" (#1 UK, over a million sold), and "The Wild One" (#7 UK). Trying to replicate her British success in the United States proved difficult, although she soon gained a reputation as a female rock icon. Joan Jett idolized her, and modeled her career after Quatro's. The "Happy Days" appearances revitalized her recording career, leading to a record deal with RSO and the number 4 hit "Stumblin' In," a duet with Chris Norman.

80. Which future rock star was one of the founding members of The Cramps' fan club?

A.) The Legion of the Cramped, a fan club for Cramps fans, was formed in 1977. **Morrissey**, who would later take The Smiths on to worldwide fame, was one of the founding members.

81. Who was the inspiration for Rickie Lee Jones's hit "Chuck E.'s in Love"?

A.) Singer-songwriter Rickie Lee Jones penned her hit "Chuck E.'s in Love" with gruff-voiced singer **Chuck E. Weiss** in mind. The Denver-raised Weiss learned to play drums by hanging around local clubs at age 10. Shortly after, he earned a spot in The Lightin' Hopkins Band, and soon was playing with blues legends like Muddy Waters, Willie Dixon, and Dr. John. In 1973 Weiss was working in the kitchen of the famous Troubador Club in Hollywood, while Jones would often perform on the club's stage. They had a mutual friend in Tom Waits, who invited them to room with him at an L.A. hotel. The three became very close. In 1979 Jones said, "Chuck E. and Tom have been my family for a while now. We love each other very much." The anonymous woman that Chuck E. was in love with was actually his cousin, according to Jones. "I mean, that's what I heard. There was a telephone call from Denver one day and it was Chuck E. And Waits hung up the phone and said, 'Chuck E.'s in love!' I just made the rest of the song up." Weiss has only released a handful of records in the last twenty years — 1981's *The Other Side of Town*, some movie soundtracks, and *Extremely Cool* in 1999. Weiss is also co-owner (with Johnny Depp) of the infamous Viper Club in Los Angeles.

82. Who did the female vocals on Meat Loaf's "Paradise by the Dashboard Light"?

A.) Female vocal duties on Meat Loaf's "Paradise by the Dashboard Light" were performed by singer/actress **Ellen Foley**. Foley went on to co-star on the 1984–85 season of the sitcom "Night Court." The voice behind the famous mid-song baseball play-by-play was Phil Rizzuto, former New York Yankees shortstop and radio voice of the team. "Paradise" writer Jim Steinman described the over-the-top song as "sardonic, operatic, desperate, extreme and really passionate — there's something dangerous to it. It's an anthem to that moment when you feel like you're on the head of a match."

83. Bad Company was formed in late 1973, and was first seen in public on March 9, 1974. All the members of the band were originally in other well-known groups. Who were they, and what groups spawned them?

A.) Bad Company was a "supergroup" of sorts, having been formed from the ashes of several other well-known bands. Singer **Paul Rodgers** and drummer **Simon Kirke** made their name with **Free**, while guitarist **Mick Ralphs** was a founding member of **Mott the Hoople,** and bass player **Boz Burrell** was with **King Crimson**. Signed to Led Zeppelin's Swan Song label, they hit the charts with several power-pop singles, "Can't Get Enough"(#5 8/31/74 *Billboard*), "Feel Like Makin' Love" (#10 7/26/75 *Billboard*), and "Rock 'N' Roll Fantasy" (#13 4/14/79 *Billboard*).

84. Before becoming successful as Gary Glitter, what other names did Gary record under?

153

A.) Before finding success with Gary Glitter (real name: Paul Gadd), he had a minor hit in 1961 with "Walk On By" under the alias **Paul Raven.** In 1971 he released "Here Comes the Sun," using the stage name **Paul Monday**. It wasn't until he changed his name to Gary Glitter and shamelessly exploited the glitter fad that he made any headway.

85. Name all five of the original Jackson 5.

A.) The original Jackson 5 were: the oldest brother **Jackie** on lead vocals and guitar; **Tito** on guitar and vocals; **Jermaine** on bass and vocals; **Marlon** and **Michael** on vocals. The youngest brother **Randy** (born 1962) joined in 1975 after Jermaine left the band when they switched record companies.

86. What was the name of the record company Elton John started in 1973?

A.) Elton John and John Reid formed **Rocket Records** in 1973. They enjoyed chart success with Neil Sedaka ("Laughter in the Rain," "Bad Blood") and Kiki Dee ("I've Got the Music in Me").

87. What album marked the first time that The Jefferson Airplane used the name The Jefferson Starship?

A.) The first time The Jefferson Airplane used the name The Jefferson Starship was 1970's ***Blows Against the Empire***, with the name listed as Paul Kantner and the Jefferson Starship. At this point the Starship was made up of session men. The band with Grace Slick continued to record under the Airplane moniker until the release of *Dragon Fly* in the early 1970s.

88. Who is the backup band on Chuck Berry's 1972 number 1 hit "My Ding-A-Ling"?

154

A.) Chuck Berry's "My Ding-A-Ling" was recorded live at the 1972 Arts Festival in Lancaster, England, with the **Average White Band** on backup. Three years later the AWB would hit gold for themselves with the release of "Pick Up the Pieces," a jazz-tinged soul stew so infectious it hit number 1 on the *Billboard* charts in February 1975.

89. Who appeared on the covers of both *Time* and *Newsweek* in October 1975?

A.) **Bruce Springsteen** appeared on the covers of both *Time* and *Newsweek* in October 1975. He was riding his first wave of popularity, boosted by Jon Landau's often-quoted remark, "I saw rock and roll's future, and its name is Bruce Springsteen."

90. What was The Bromley Contingent?

A.) The Bromley Contingent was a group of **rabid fans of The Sex Pistols** from the London suburb of Bromley. Among them were Siouxsie (later of The Banshees) and William Broad (who went on to become the sneering Billy Idol).

91. Bruce Springsteen's *Darkness on the Edge of Town* was based on what famous American novel by John Steinbeck?

A.) Bruce Springsteen turned to John Steinbeck's ***The Grapes of Wrath*** for the inspiration for 1977's *Darkness on the Edge of Town*. *Darkness* was Springsteen's follow-up to the mega-hit *Born to Run*, emerging after two years of legal hassles with his former manager. The Top 40 hit "Prove It All Night" (#33 7/15/78 *Billboard*) was culled from this album.

92. Who was Billy Preston's famous mother?

A.) Billy Preston's famous mother was **Ernesta Wade,** an actress best known as Saffire on radio and television's "Amos 'N' Andy." In addition to impeccable credits as a session musician (The Beatles and The Rolling Stones) Billy enjoyed a successful solo career in the seventies. He cracked the Top 10 four times in two years, with the instrumental "Outa-Space" (#2 5/13/72 *Billboard*), "Will It Go Round in Circles" (#1 5/19/73 *Billboard*), "Space Race" (#4 10/13/73 *Billboard*), and "Nothing From Nothing" (#1 8/03/74 *Billboard*).

93. Did Elvis Presley drink alcohol?

A.) Elvis Presley **did not drink alcohol**, although after his death a wine was marketed under his name. "Always Elvis" (Blanc D'Oro) was sold by the Frontenac Vineyards of Raw Paw, Michigan. A company spokesman for "Always Elvis" said, "We feel that this is the kind of wine Elvis would have drunk if he did drink wine."

94. How much did Alice Cooper's accountants estimate he spent on beer in 1972?

A.) Alice Cooper's accountants estimated he spent **between $30,000 and $32,000** on Budweiser beer in 1972. While Bud was his favourite beer, he also had a passion for Seagrams VO. There was a clause in his contract that there must be two sealed bottles of VO and six cases of Bud in his dressing room at every show. "At least with booze you know you have 30 years before you go, but with drugs you can go in one night," Alice reasoned in 1972. He has since given up drinking.

95. What did Sting do for a living before joining The Police?

A.) Before joining The Police, Sting studied at the Northern Counties Teacher Training College in Newcastle were he earned a Teachers Certificate in English and Music, and actually **taught school** for a time. Later he said that the difference between being a music star and a teacher isn't so great — in both cases you have to entertain delinquents. Sting also tried his hand at modelling, and did quite well. He appeared in ads for Brutus jeans, Triumph bras, and Wrigley's gum (the latter with the other members of The Police).

96. Which country/folk singer of the 1970s has found a second career writing gritty detective novels set in Greenwich Village?

A.) Alternative country singer **Kinky Friedman** has virtually retired from performing to concentrate on writing detective novels — *Greenwich Killing Time; A Case of Lone Star; Elvis, Jesus and Coca-Cola; The Love Song of J. Edgar Hoover; God Bless John Wayne; Armadillos and Old Lace; Musical Chairs; Frequent Flyer; When the Cat's Away; Blast From the Past;* and *Roadkill* — in which he is a private eye working New York's Greenwich Village. Friedman first achieved semi-legendary status with his band The Texas Jewboys, which he says was a country band with a social conscience. But songs like "They Ain't Makin' Jews Like Jesus Anymore," and "Get Your Biscuits in the Oven and Your Buns in Bed" offended many, and aren't the stuff of which Top 10 hits are made. After the disappointing sales of his first five albums, he turned to penning novels, and found success right away. Mystery fans now enjoy Friedman's wry sense of humour, and have grown fond of his literary character (based on himself), who solves murders and performs valiant acts. At press time there were plans for a Kinky Friedman detective movie, starring Willie Nelson, Friedman, and Ruth Buzzi.

97. What year did Ken Russell's film *Lisztomania*, starring Roger Daltrey, open?

A.) Ken Russell's *Lisztomania* opened in theatres in **1975**. It tells the story of Franz Liszt (Roger Daltrey), with the premise that Liszt was music's first superstar. The film displays decadent nineteenth-century culture, and features some truly bad music. Songs like "Chopsticks Fantasia" and "Rape, Pillage, and Burn" didn't exactly burn up the charts, and neither did this film do much business. Music fans might be interested in Ringo Starr's portrayal of The Pope, and former Yes keyboardist Rick Wakeman's study of an Aryan Superman, but this film has very little to offer.

98. Which 1979 film marked Sting's debut on celluloid?

A.) Sting's motion picture debut came in 1979's rock opera *Quadrophenia.* He played a Mod called Ace Face. He later called it the perfect role for him, "Long enough to make an impression, but not long enough to blow it."

99. Who played Jesus in the 1973 film adaptation of *Jesus Christ Superstar?*

A.) The lead in *Jesus Christ Superstar* was given to an unknown singer from Ranger, Texas. After considering Mick Jagger, David Cassidy, and John Lennon, **Ted Neeley** was given the prize role. His performance was panned by most major critics, with *Playboy*'s Bruce Williamson saying that Neeley's performance of Christ "ought to fix him permanently in public memory as the Screamin' Jesus."

100. What is the name of the 1978 made-for-TV movie starring KISS?

A.) The 1978 KISS made-for-TV movie was titled ***KISS Meets the Phantom of the Park.*** In the film KISS tries to outdo a mad scientist who hides out in an amusement park. They have secret powers, which eventually overcome the evil doctor. "Doing a film was obviously the next logical step for our career," said guitarist Paul Stanley in 1978. "Our whole idea with television was to go for the largest audience possible. If we did this on a larger scale, like with a regular theatre movie, the only people who would see it would be KISS fans. Here though, it will be everyone from little children to grandmothers."

101. Who played The Scarecrow in the 1978 film musical *The Wiz?*

A.) **Michael Jackson** played The Scarecrow in the 1978 film *The Wiz.* The movie, a retelling of *The Wizard of Oz*, tells the story of a twenty-four-year-old Dorothy (Diana Ross) who lives in Harlem. She finds Michael in a vacant lot next to a burned-out tenement. Together with the Tinman (Nipsey Russell) and the Cowardly Lion (Ted Ross), they try to find Oz, which is New York City south of 125th Street. The film fared poorly in the theatres and with critics. In defence Michael Jackson released a statement saying, "I don't think it could have been any better, I really don't."

102. Who scored the 1971 Paramount film *Friends*?

A.) The film *Friends* was scored by **Elton John and Bernie Taupin**. Elton's career was just beginning to take off, so Paramount insisted on releasing a soundtrack album to cash in on his newfound fame. "I don't want them to release a soundtrack with three songs on it and fill it out with the sounds of garbage being dumped and motorists peeing by the sides of lakes," said Elton to *Rolling Stone* at the time. He and Taupin added two more songs to the soundtrack ("Can I Put You On?" and "Honeyroll") to flesh out the album.

103. Who did Bob Dylan play in the 1973 MGM film *Pat Garrett and Billy the Kid*?

A.) Bob Dylan portrayed **Alias**, Billy the Kid's partner. After being denied final editing rights on this gory Sam Peckinpah western, Dylan disassociated himself from the project.

104. Where were the musical sequences for the black and white rockumentary *The Blank Generation* shot?

A.) The musical sequences for the film were shot at **CBGB,** a seminal New York punk/new wave club. CBGB gave birth to a whole generation of performers, including The Ramones, Talking Heads, Blondie, and Television. *The Blank Generation* showcases Blondie performing "He Left Me," Talking Heads with "Psycho Killer," and Patti Smith covering "Gloria."

105. Who are the bands that appear in the 1970 rockumentary

Big Bang! Baby

Gimme Shelter?

A. The 1970 rock film *Gimme Shelter* is made up of concert footage from the American tour of 1969. The film's capper is a show at the Altamont Speedway, near San Francisco, where a young man was beaten to death by the Hell's Angels, who had been hired to act as security. The headliners of the show are **The Rolling Stones,** who sing "Jumpin' Jack Flash," "Satisfaction," "You Gotta Move," "Wild Horses," "Brown Sugar," and "Sympathy for the Devil." Also appearing are **Ike and Tina Turner, The Jefferson Airplane, The Grateful Dead, and The Flying Burrito Brothers.**

106. Who played Eddie the biker in the cult classic *The Rocky Horror Picture Show?*

A. *The Rocky Horror Picture Show's* Eddie the biker was played by rock singer **Meat Loaf.** Mr. Loaf (real name: Marvin Lee Aday) was a struggling vocalist who sang with a great many bands (including Ted Nugent and The Amboy Dukes) before landing this role. He went on to even bigger success in 1977 with the release of *Bat out of Hell.* This album produced three Top 40 hits, "Two out of Three Ain't Bad" (#11 4/29/78 *Billboard*), "You Took the Words Right Out of My Mouth" (#39 1/20/79 *Billboard*), and "Paradise by the Dashboard Light" (#39 9/16/78 *Billboard*). The latter song featured a female vocal by Ellen Foley, and a double entendre baseball play-by-play by announcer Phil Rizzuto.

107. Who played The Acid Queen in Ken Russell's 1975 screen version of The Who's *Tommy?*

A. **Tina Turner** played The Acid Queen in *Tommy.* This rock opera tells the story of a "deaf, dumb, and blind kid, who sure plays a mean pinball," and features a cast of superstars. Roger Daltrey stars as Tommy, the "deaf, dumb, and blind kid," with Ann-Margret and Oliver Reed as his mother and stepfather, and Jack Nicholson as The Doctor.

160

Many rockers make appearances; Eric Clapton is The Preacher, Keith Moon is Uncle Ernie, and Elton John is The Pinball Wizard. The film met with mixed critical response, but director Ken Russell proclaimed *Tommy* "the greatest work of art the twentieth century has produced." He went on to say that it is greater than "any painting, opera, piece of music, ballet, dramatic work, or what you will of the century."

108. What was the name of the 1973 film Ringo Starr directed that documented the T-Rex phenomenon?

A.) Ringo Starr filmed a March 18, 1972, T-Rex concert at England's Wembley Stadium for his rockumentary **Born to Boogie.** The movie tried to document the T-Rex phenomenon, and also featured Elton John.

109. What was the name of the character David Essex played in *That'll be the Day* and its sequel, *Stardust*?

A.) David Essex played **Jim McLean** in both *That'll be the Day* and the sequel, *Stardust*. The two films follow the fictional McLean's career from his modest beginnings to superstar status. Two of rock's most

A scene from the rock-drama *That'll be the Day* featuring Keith Moon (as drummer J.D. Clover on left) and David Essex (as singer Jim McLean, centre).

Photo courtesy of Columbia Pictures Industries

BiBang! Baby

David Essex (first from left) in another scene from *That'll be the Day*.

Photo courtesy of Columbia Pictures Industries

famous drummers appear in the original movie. Ringo Starr plays a co-worker and friend of McLean, who he ends up betraying, while Who drummer Keith Moon is one of the stars, and the music co-ordinator of the film. The success of *That'll be the Day* revitalized Essex's singing career, and in 1974 he scored his biggest American hit, "Rock On" (#5 1/12/74 *Billboard*).

110. Who directed *Monterey Pop*, Bob Dylan's *Don't Look Back*, and David Bowie's *Ziggy Stardust and the Spiders From Mars: The Motion Picture*?

A.) All were directed by **D.A. Pennebaker**. As the leading rock filmmaker of the sixties, Pennebaker's films aren't the slick MTV-style music films that have become popular in the last few years. His work is characterised by shaky, hand-held camera work, and direct-to-the-board audio tracks. A Pennebaker concert film offers an analytical documentary-style view of the subject, with no high-tech embellishments. By today's standards the films look under-produced and sloppy, but they do offer a documentarian's perspective of rock's history.

111. Who portrayed Buddy Holly in 1978's *The Buddy Holly Story*?

A.) **Gary Busey** was already a well-known session drummer (using the name Teddy Jack Eddy) when he won the lead role in 1978's *The Buddy Holly Story*. Reviewing Busey's Academy Award-nominated performance, critic Vincent Canby said, "Mr. Busey's performance is tremendous, full of drive, eccentric life, and the sort of idiosyncrasy that

162

creates a screen personality that the public will remember." Busey lost the Oscar to Jon Voight (for his performance in *Coming Home*), but has continued to have a thriving screen career, appearing in films such as *Point Break* and *Under Siege*.

112. What was the original theme song for ABC's "Happy Days"?

A.) The original theme for ABC's popular sitcom "Happy Days" was Bill Haley and the Comets' **"Rock Around the Clock."** In the second season the theme was changed to "Happy Days" (#5 4/24/76 *Billboard*) by one-hit wonders Pratt and McClain. The theme song was the sole new song included on an album of fifties hits titled *Fonzie's Greatest Hits*.

113. What was the name of the 1978 Beatles satire starring Eric Idle and Neil Innes?

A.) ***The Rutles*** was a 1978 Beatles satire, starring Eric Idle as Dirk McQuigley (the Paul McCartney figure), and Neil Innes as Ron Nasty (the John Lennon type). The movie is a take-off of *The Complete Beatles*, and features original Innes-penned satirical songs like "Let It Rot," "Hold My Hand," and "Cheese and Onions." Innes received his musical background as a member of The Bonzo Dog Band. *The Rutles* features a star-studded cast, with cameos by Mick and Bianca Jagger, John Belushi, Gilda Radner, Bill Murray, Ron Wood, Paul Simon, and ex-Beatle George Harrison.

114. What year saw The Edgar Winter Group hit the top of the charts with the instrumental "Frankenstein"?

A.) The Edgar Winter Group topped the charts in **1973** with the instrumental "Frankenstein" (#1 4/21/73 *Billboard*). Edgar Winter is the Texas-born younger brother of blues guitarist Johnny Winter. The Edgar Winter Group featured Rick "Rock and Roll Hoochie Coo" Derringer, Ronnie "Open Fire" Montrose, and Dan "I Can Dream About

163

You" Hartman. The group broke up in 1974.

115. Which popular rock band released a comic book, allegedly printed with real blood?

A.) Marvel Comics released two **KISS** comic books in the mid-seventies. Blood from the band members was alleged to have been mixed in with the red ink used for printing the books. Each issue sold in excess of 700,000 copies, which was double the usual print runs for Marvel comics. KISS ended their professional relationship with the comic book makers when Marvel wanted to buy the rights to the KISS characters.

116. Who collaborated with KISS on *Music From the Elder*?

A.) **Lou Reed** co-wrote the songs on KISS's concept album *Music From the Elder*. The album stiffed, peaking well outside the Top 40, although it was favourably reviewed. Ten years after the release of this ill-fated collaboration Gene Simmons said that the album suffered because KISS got too creative, and stopped being a rock band. He goes on to say that the album wasn't typically KISS, but "it sure was an interesting Genesis record."

117. What was the name of the cartoon spin-off series to "The Partridge Family"?

A.) The cartoon spin-off of "The Partridge Family" was called "**The Partridge Family: 2200 A.D.**," and aired from September 1974 to March 1975. All major cast members returned to do the voice work, with the exception of David Cassidy and Shirley Jones, whose voices were replaced by Chuck McLennan and Sherry Alberoni. The plots were essentially updates of the live-action series, with the colourful Partridge bus replaced by a spaceship that transported them from planet to planet.

118. Who provided the voices for "The Jackson 5 Cartoon" series?

A.) The **original Jackson 5** supplied their own voices for the cartoon series based on their lives. The show ran for two years, starting September 1971, and put the Jacksons in many unusual situations. The first episode detailed how Diana Ross discovered them after their pet snake got loose in her dressing room. Other episodes featured such storylines as Michael and the Jacksons performing a Royal Command Performance in London, and re-enactments of *Cinderella* (retitled "CinderJackson") and *The Wizard of Oz* ("The Wizard of Soul"), where Michael is carried off by a storm and must find his way back to Las Vegas. The show always featured lots of music, and is occasionally re-run on Saturday mornings.

119. Which seventies television show introduced teeny-boppers to Shaun Cassidy?

A.) Shaun Cassidy became a heart-throb via the ABC television show **"The Hardy Boys Mysteries."** He played Joe Hardy, who, with his brother, would solve crimes each week. Once Cassidy's singing career took off, Joe became a detective who would solve crimes and sing each week. His first three albums (*Shaun Cassidy, Born Late*, and *Under Wraps*) were certified platinum, and spawned several big hits. In real life his half brother is Partridge Family heartbreaker David Cassidy.

120. Which late seventies musical-comedy television series featured a pre-"Late Night" David Letterman?

A.) David Letterman was a regular on CBS TV's short-lived **"The Starlight Vocal Band Television Show"** (July 31, 1977–September 2, 1977). The Starlight Vocal Band was given their own show after "Afternoon Delight" (#1 6/05/76 *Billboard*) topped the charts. The show featured a generous mix of music from The Starlight Vocal Band, interspersed with political comedy sketches performed by David Letterman, Mark Russell, and Jeff Altman. The show vanished after

165

six episodes, and The Starlight Vocal Band dissolved shortly after.

121. Who were Martin Lee, Sandra Stevens, Nicky Stevens, and Lee Sheridan better known as?

A.) Martin Lee, Sandra Stevens, Nicky Stevens, and Lee Sheridan were better known as **The Brotherhood of Man.** This British group only hit the US charts twice, once in 1970 with "United We Stand" (#13 5/23/70 *Billboard*), and again in 1976 with "Save Your Kisses for Me" (#27 6/19/76 *Billboard*). They were always more popular at home, where they graced the UK Top 40 frequently with ABBAesque tunes like "Angelo" and "Figaro." The band retired from recording in 1982, but still plays the occasional live date.

122. Who enjoyed a string of hits in 1974 with "Billy Don't Be a Hero," "The Night Chicago Died," and "Black Eyed Boys"?

A.) **Paper Lace** scored worldwide hits in 1974 with "Billy Don't Be a Hero" and "The Night Chicago Died." The song "Black Eyed Boys" signalled the end of their chart success, as it only reached number 11 on the UK charts. The band — Peter Vaughn (drums and lead vocals), Cliff Fish (bass), Mick Vaughn, Carlo Santana, and Chris Morris (guitars) — were catapulted to fame when they appeared on Britain's televised talent show "Opportunity Knocks." Their clean-cut image and bubble-gum music were immediately accepted by the public and the British press. *The Daily Mirror* said they were much preferable to "those rowdy groups like Slade and Sweet."

123. Whose recorded output includes: *Free Your Mind.... And Your Ass Will Follow, Some of My Best Jokes are Friends,* and *Lunchmeataphobia (Think! It Ain't Illegal Yet!)*?

A.) As leader of Parliament-Funkadelic, **George Clinton** released records with some of the wildest names to ever hit the charts. *Free Your Mind.... And Your Ass Will Follow,* was recorded in one day —

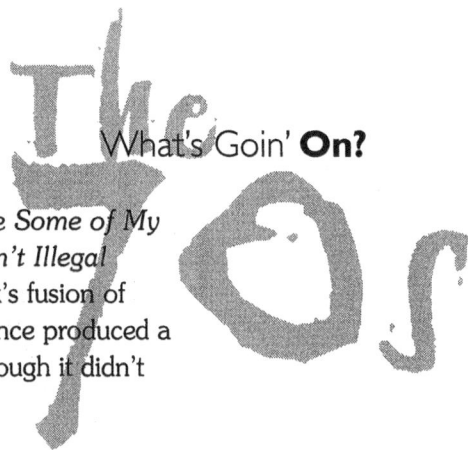

while the whole band was stoned on acid. Other albums like *Some of My Best Friends are Jokes, Lunchmeataphobia (Think! It Ain't Illegal Yet!)*, and *One Nation Under a Groove* showcased P-Funk's fusion of doo-wop, soul, psychedelic, comedy, and funk. In 1989 Prince produced a comeback album, *The Cinderella Theory,* for P-Funk, although it didn't chart nationally.

124. What was Simon and Garfunkel's final studio duet?

A.) Simon and Garfunkel teamed up in the studio for the last time for the recording of **"My Little Town"** (#9 11/01/75 *Billboard*). They recorded together for the last time ever during their farewell tour of 1981. Their final chart entry as a team was "Wake Up Little Susie" (#27 5/01/82 *Billboard*), recorded live in concert at New York's Central Park on September 19, 1981.

125. What was ABBA's biggest worldwide hit?

A.) ABBA's highest-charting single worldwide was 1977's **"Dancing Queen"** (#1 1/22/77 *Billboard*). The song was written for and performed at the wedding of the king and queen of Sweden. ABBA was formed as a supergroup of Swedish musicians. Each of the members had obtained some prominence in their native country — Agnetha Faltskog and Anni-Frid Lyngstad were solo artists, while Bjorn Ulvaeus and Benny Andersson were members of popular Swedish pop bands. Andersson had been a member of The Hep Stars, who were known as the Swedish Beatles. ABBA first gained worldwide attention when their song "Waterloo" (#6 6/22/74 *Billboard*) won the Eurovision Song Contest in 1974. Their bouncy Mamas and Papas-style pop, enhanced with sweet harmonies, became a fixture on the world stage for the next ten years, until the pressures of life on the road took their toll on their professional and personal lives. Each of the members of ABBA went into semi-retirement after the break-up of the band. Anni-Frid and Agnetha released occasional solo albums, but none equalled the success of their work with ABBA. Benny and Bjorn came out of retirement in the mid-eighties to

BiBang! Baby

collaborate with Tim Rice on the musical *Chess*.

126. Who teamed with Jeff Beck in 1973 to form the short-lived supergroup BBandA?

A.) After the dissolution of The Jeff Beck Group, Beck joined forces with ex-Vanilla Fudge members **Carmine Appice** and **Tim Bogert** to form BBandA (Beck, Bogert, and Appice). They only released one eponymous album (featuring the single "Superstition") and a live album that was only issued in Japan. After the break-up of BBandA Beck decided to only release instrumental albums.

127. Which Canadian band opened the show for The Rolling Stones at the El Mocambo in 1977?

A.) Canadian rockers **April Wine** supported The Rolling Stones at their club dates at Toronto's El Mocambo in 1977. The Rolling Stones recorded one side of their *Love You Live* at these dates, while April Wine culled a live album (produced by Eddie Kramer) from their set. April Wine earned the coveted spot opening for the Stones in a rather unusual way. A bomb had destroyed some of The Rolling Stones' sound equipment during a 1973 concert in Montreal. Hearing the news, April Wine offered their equipment as a replacement, although they didn't have all the gear the Stones required. The closest place to get the extra sound apparatus was Los Angeles, which wasn't a problem, except that the only available flight was already booked — carrying a cargo of Alaska King Crab. April Wine's quick-thinking promoter bought the entire shipment of crab, bounced it from the flight, and had the necessary equipment airlifted in. Four years later April Wine was repaid by being given the prime job of opening for The Rolling Stones' first club dates in fifteen years.

128. What record label was Rush's first album released on?

A.) Rush's first album was released on **Moon Records**. The eponymous record was released in 1974, and featured the concert favourites "In the Mood" and "Working Man." Reviewing the album, *The Ottawa Citizen* said the music was "loud, proud and take-it-or-leave-it, played with shrieking energy and some musical skill."

129. What was the name of Rush's original drummer?

A.) Rush's original drummer was named **John Rutsey.** After playing on their first album, 1974's *Rush*, he left the band due to health problems. Neil Peart joined the trio on June 29, 1974, just in time to do a major American tour opening for Uriah Heep. Peart's influence on the band was immediate. His drumming prowess drove their sound into new territory, setting them a cut above every other Canadian heavy metal band. As the band's wordsmith Peart introduced imaginative lyrics (inspired by the writings of Ayn Rand) that avoided the usual boy-meets-girl clichés, and focused instead on space travel and mythological figures. Rush has never been a singles band, but through constant touring and a steady output of fine albums they have built up a diehard following that is entranced by their musical tales of swords and sorcery.

130. In 1970 who did *Cashbox Magazine* say had sold more singles than any other group in the world that year?

A.) In 1970 *Cashbox Magazine* reported that Winnipeg's own **The Guess Who** had outsold everyone that year, including The Beatles and The Rolling Stones. Their output that year included "No Time" (#5 1/17/70 *Billboard*), "American Woman" b/w "No Sugar Tonight" (#1 3/28/70 *Billboard*), "Hand Me Down World" (#17 8/08/70 *Billboard*), and "Share the Land" (#10 11/07/70 *Billboard*).

131. What was Randy Bachman's first recording after leaving The Guess Who?

A.) When Randy Bachman left The Guess Who he formed Brave Belt, who released two unsuccessful records on the Reprise label in 1971 and 1972. After a change in musical policy, Brave Belt became

169

BTO and started recording for Mercury Records in 1972. BTO enjoyed a string of hits, and topped the *Billboard* charts in 1974 with **"You Ain't Seen Nothin' Yet"** (#1 10/05/74 *Billboard*).

132. Who had a Top 5 with "Indiana Wants Me" in 1970?

A.) Toronto-born singer **R. Dean Taylor** broke into the *Billboard* Top 5 with "Indiana Wants Me" (#5 9/19/70 *Billboard*) in 1970. Taylor had been a producer for Motown, and co-wrote "I'll Turn to Stone" for The Four Tops, and "Love Child" (#1 10/26/68 *Billboard*) and "I'm Living in Shame" (#10 2/01/69 *Billboard*), which were picked up by The Supremes. "Indiana Wants Me" was the first single released on Berry Gordy Jr.'s Rare Earth label.

133. Which Deep Purple studio album featured Whitesnake's David Coverdale on vocals and Tommy Bolin on guitar?

A.) Deep Purple's ***Come Taste the Band*** featured David Coverdale on vocals and Tommy Bolin on guitar. Coverdale had replaced original vocalist Ian Gillan, while Bolin was filling in for Ritchie Blackmore, who quit the band in 1974. Coverdale left after Bolin's drug habit began to inhibit the band's performance. Bolin died of a heroin overdose in 1976, while Coverdale and several other Deep Purple veterans formed the popular Whitesnake.

134. What is Malcolm "Mac" Rebennack better known as?

A.) Malcolm "Mac" Rebennack is better known to the record-buying public as **Dr. John.** Rebennack is known today primarily as a pianist, but he started his musical career as a guitar player. His guitar can be heard on Art Neville's "What's Going On" and Johnny Adams' "Losing Battle." A gunshot wound to the hand ended his guitar strumming days, and forced him to switch to piano. His greatest solo chart success came in 1973 with "Right Place Wrong Time" (#9 5/12/73 *Billboard*), although as a session player he can be heard on hundreds of albums.

135. Which Eagles' song was used as the theme for television's "The Hitchhiker's Guide to the Galaxy"?

A.) The cult television show "The Hitchhiker's Guide to the Galaxy" borrowed **"Journey of the Sorcerer"** from the Eagles album *One of These Nights* as its theme. This 1975 album spawned three Top 5 singles, "One of These Nights" (#1 6/14/75 *Billboard*), "Lyin' Eyes" (#2 9/27/75 *Billboard*) and "Take It to the Limit" (#4 1/17/76 *Billboard*). *One of These Nights* was the last album featuring founding Eagle Bernie Leadon, who departed in 1975 for The Nitty Gritty Dirt Band.

136. What was Peter Gabriel's last record as lead singer for Genesis?

A.) Peter Gabriel's last record as lead singer of Genesis was 1974's ***The Lamb Lies Down on Broadway.*** Gabriel had been one of the founding members of the band, which was composed of school friends from England's Charterhouse school. Genesis had released six unsuccessful albums before placing one single on the UK charts. "I Know What I Like (In Your Wardrobe)" was popular in Britain, but made no impact in North America. *The Lamb Lies Down on Broadway* was a conceptual double album that broke the band in the United States. After a ground-breaking theatrical North American tour Peter Gabriel left for a solo career. In 1976 Gabriel sound-alike Phil Collins stepped out from behind his drum kit to take over lead vocals.

137. Who sang the role of Jesus on the original double album of *Jesus Christ Superstar*?

A.) **Ian Gillan**, the former lead singer for Deep Purple, essayed the role of Jesus on the original 1971 version of *Jesus Christ Superstar*. After unsuccessfully fronting his own bands for most of the seventies, he joined Black Sabbath for a time, before joining the reformed Deep Purple in 1984. Gillan recorded three albums with this line-up before returning to his solo career in 1986.

171

Big Bang! Baby

138. What was Queen's first chart entry in the US?

A.) Queen's first appearance on the *Billboard* charts was 1975's **"Killer Queen"** (#12 3/29/75 *Billboard*) from the album *Sheer Heart Attack*. They followed this single with a UK Top 20 release, "Now I'm Here." Their reputation was solidified with *A Night at the Opera*, the album that spawned the operatic "Bohemian Rhapsody" (#9 2/07/76 *Billboard*), which *Rolling Stone* called a "classical hodge podge." The next fifteen years saw Queen's fortunes in the United States wane, while their popularity rose in Britain and the rest of the world. In the 1980s their albums barely made an impact in the US, but they were still a major concert draw in Europe. A stateside Queen resurgence was under way at the time of Freddy Mercury's death of AIDS in 1991.

139. What are "The Troggs' Tapes"?

A.) The Troggs' Tapes are recordings of one of the **last studio sessions** The Troggs would do as a band. They had enjoyed some success in the mid-sixties with "Wild Thing" (#1 7/09/66 *Billboard*), and "Love is All Around" (#7 3/23/68 *Billboard*), but by 1970 their chart success was well behind them. The Troggs gathered at Dick James Music Studios in London to record a single called "Tranquility." The session fell apart quickly, and the song never did get recorded. The producer of the session kept a tape running and preserved for posterity the rude language and in-fighting of The Troggs. Since then the hilarious Troggs' Tapes have been bootlegged and passed around the music community as a good example on how NOT to run a recording session. The Spinal Tap-esque Troggs' Tapes can be heard in their entirety on the 1993 Polygram Chronicles' CD box set *The Troggs Anthology 1966–76*.

140. What did Carl Douglas find "a little bit frightening" in 1974?

A.) One-hit wonder Carl Douglas found **"Kung Fu Fighting"** (#1 11/09/74 *Billboard*) "a little bit frightening" in November 1974. The song was originally slated to be the b-side of "I Want to Give You My

Everything," but after hearing both tunes record company executives insisted on flipping the record and promoting "Kung Fu Fighting." They were banking that the novelty song might catch on with people who were already fans of Bruce Lee and David Carradine. They were right. "Kung Fu Fighting" topped the charts for two weeks, but unfortunately it was Carl Douglas's last appearance in the Top 40.

141. Who is the youngest member of the Jackson family?

A.) The youngest Jackson is sister **Janet,** who was born in Gary, Indiana, in 1966. Janet performed with her brothers in 1973–74, doing a charming Mae West impression in their Las Vegas stage show. After several well-received acting roles in the sitcoms "Good Times" and "Diff'rent Strokes" and the musical-drama series "Fame," she turned to a recording career. While still in her teens she released two unsuccessful albums of adult contemporary R&B. At age 20 she hit the top of the charts with the dance-oriented *Control* album.

142. Who did Nils Lofgren dedicate "Keith Don't Go" to in 1975?

A.) After leaving Crazy Horse and recording four albums with the band Grin, Nils Lofgren released his eponymous solo album in 1975. A long-time **Keith Richards** fan, he wrote and recorded "Keith Don't Go" as a tribute to the Rolling Stone. Lofgren's solo albums have generally fared poorly, and he is best known as a sideman to rock superstars like Neil Young, Bruce Springsteen, and Ringo Starr.

143. What building is pictured on the cover of The Eagles' *Hotel California*?

A.) The building on the cover of The Eagles' *Hotel California* is **The Beverly Hills Hotel** on Sunset Boulevard. Photographer David Alexander shot the moody cover photo from a sixty-foot fire department cherry picker dangling over Sunset Boulevard. The hotel was built in 1912, and is home to the world famous Polo Lounge. The title track from

Bang! Baby

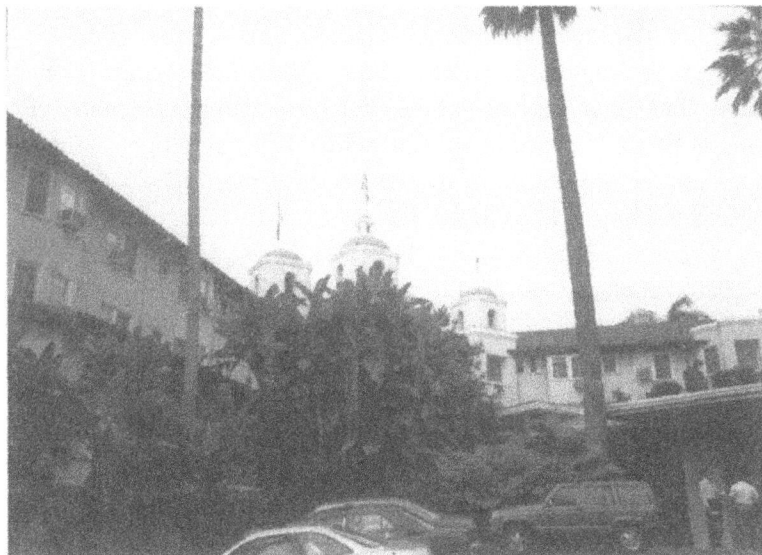

Hotel California (#1 3/12/77 *Billboard*) topped the charts in 1977.

144. Where did Sid Vicious allegedly murder his girlfriend Nancy Spungen?

A.) Sex Pistol Sid Vicious allegedly stabbed Nancy Spungen to death in Room 100 of **The Chelsea Hotel** in New York City. The Chelsea has since renumbered their rooms to discourage Vicious's fans from visiting the scene of the crime. The hotel has a long and varied history. The structure was built in the 1880s as a co-op apartment building, becoming a hotel in 1905. Since then it has been a stopover for many of this century's biggest names. A glance at the guest book for the last century will reveal that everyone from Mark Twain to The Mamas and the Papas has stayed there. Many writers have lodged at the Chelsea. William S. Burroughs wrote *Naked Lunch* here, and Arthur C. Clarke penned the screenplay for *2001: A Space Odyssey* while in residence. Rock and rollers have long favoured the Chelsea. Bob Dylan composed "Sad Eyed Lady of the Lowlands" during one of his many stays here; Alice Cooper's pet python escaped in the lobby of the

Chelsea during an FBI raid some years ago; and Janis Joplin and The Jefferson Airplane partied the nights away, as did The Red Hot Chili Peppers, who apparently skateboarded up and down the halls. Jimi Hendrix, The Grateful Dead, Patti Smith, and Bob Marley all spent time here. The Chelsea has been immortalized by several generations of artists. Poet Edgar Lee Masters penned "The Hotel Chelsea" shortly before his death, while Leonard Cohen wrote one of his most famous songs in tribute to the hotel. Andy Warhol directed his most renowned film, *The Chelsea Girls,* within these walls, and, in reference to the Chelsea, Keith Richards once commented that you had to be "a certified drug dealer to get a job as a bellboy."

The Chelsea Hotel (222 West 23rd Street, New York). This hotel's guest book includes a who's who of writers, musicians, and artists, including Mark Twain, Arthur Miller, O. Henry, Eugene O'Neill, Tennessee Williams, Jimi Hendrix, Janis Joplin, The Grateful Dead, The Mamas and the Papas, The Jefferson Airplane, The Red Hot Chili Peppers, Jackson Pollack, and Willem de Kooning.

Photo by Greg Jones

145. What are CBGB and OMFUG acronyms for?

A.) The famous New York City club name CBGB is an acronym for **Country, BlueGrass and Blues,** while OMFUG stands for **Other Music For Uplifting Gormandizers.** In the late seventies CBGB and OMFUG were the breeding grounds for punk and new wave

175

Big Bang! Baby

music. Several of the eighties' biggest bands came from this scene, including Blondie, Talking Heads, The Ramones, Patti Smith, and The Dead Kennedys. Many of these artists got signed to record deals because of the support they received at CBGB and their Festival of Unsigned Bands. CBGB and OMFUG is still open on New York's Bowery, and still presents cutting edge music every week. Call (212) 982-4052 for details.

The fabled CBGB (313 Bowery) in New York City. As punk rock's premier showcase club, this lower-Manhattan nightclub has been described as "the archetypal dive — dark, warm, graffitied, and odorous of beer."

Photo by Greg Jones

146. Which 1971 Top 40 single described an airplane crash in graphic detail?

A.) The band Bloodrock described an airplane crash in gut-wrenching detail in their 1971 Top 40 single **"D.O.A."** (#36 2/27/71 *Billboard*). This Fort Worth, Texas, band followed in the dubious teen tragedy tradition pioneered by Ray Peterson and his Top 10 death disc "Tell Laura I Love Her" (#7 6/27/60 *Billboard*). In "D.O.A." Bloodrock vocalist Jim Rutledge recounts the horrors of an airplane disaster and its human toll. He sings, "I try to move my arm and there's no feeling, and when I look, I see there's nothing there." Later he intones "Life is flowing out of my body, the sheets are red and moist where I'm lying." The song fades out as the singer's heart stops beating, and the wail of an ambulance siren moves into the distance. Bloodrock were never heard from again (on the charts, anyway).

147. Who plays Mr. Kite in the 1978 film adaptation of *Sgt. Pepper's Lonely Hearts Club Band*?

A.) **George Burns** plays Mr. Kite in the 1978 film adaptation of *Sgt. Pepper's Lonely Hearts Club Band*. Responding to criticism of the film, George Burns said, "If I can play God I can certainly sing a Beatles song." Also starring in this misbegotten epic were The Bee Gees, Peter Frampton, Billy Preston, and Alice Cooper. Very few films have been savaged so widely and thoroughly as this Robert Stigwood piece of kitsch. Typical of the bad taste that surrounded this film are George Burns' take on "Fixing a Hole" and Steve Martin's rendition of "Maxwell's Silver Hammer." 1978 was a big year for music films with *FM*, Bob Dylan's *Renaldo and Clara*, *The Buddy Holly Story*, and *Thank God It's Friday* all opening in theatres.

148. Which two rock acts released live albums recorded at Japan's Budokan in the 1978/79 season?

A.) **Cheap Trick (*Cheap Trick at Budokan*) and Bob Dylan (*Live at Budokan*)** both released live albums recorded at Japan's Budokan Theatre during the 1978/79 season. Dylan's 1978 album was not greeted kindly by critics. Several critics dubbed him "Vegas Bob" after listening to his onstage patter: "I wrote this about fifteen years ago," Bob warmly tells the audience as he introduces "The Times They are A-Changin'." "It still means a lot to me. I know it means a lot to you too." Cheap Trick fared better with their release, which was originally available only in Japan. US import sales of the live disc were so strong that the band issued it domestically. A live single, "I Want You to Want Me," (#7 5/26/79 *Billboard*), gave Cheap Trick their biggest hit to date.

149. About which of his albums did Lou Reed comment, "No one I know has listened to it all the way through, including myself"?

A.) On the liner notes to 1975's ***Metal Machine Music*** Lou Reed writes, "No one I know has listened to it all the way through, including myself. It is not meant to be." This album's title says it all — it is 64:04 of ear-splitting, industrial clatter that *Rolling Stone* says is "guaranteed to clear any room of humans in record time." Opinions on why Reed chose to release this aural pandemonium vary. Some think that it was a brave (though very flawed) attempt at modern electronic music. Most rock critics, though, agree that it was Reed's contractual obligation album, and a cynical joke at the expense of his record company. Needless to say, this album did not chart.

150. What did Elvis Presley refer to as his "Flying Graceland"?

A.) Officially Elvis Presley's **Convair 880 plane** was known as "The Lisa Marie" after his only daughter, although he often referred to it as his "Flying Graceland" or "Hound Dog One, the pride of Presley Airways." He purchased the ninety-six seat commercial plane in 1975 for $250,000, and promptly spent $850,000 to turn it into his home away from home. Elvis tore out most of the seats and installed twenty-four carat gold seat belt buckles, booths of velvet, green leather-topped tables, telephones, a private bedroom, and a large stereo system. Today the plane is on display across from Graceland on Elvis Presley Boulevard.

151. Why did The Beatles' music publishers sue the producers of "Sesame Street"?

A.) The Beatles' music publishers took the producers of "Sesame Street" to court **over the use of two songs — "Letter B" ("Let it Be") and "Hey Food" ("Hey Jude") — that appeared on the show and were released on a children's album**. The Fab Four's representatives objected to the comical use of the classic rock songs.

178

152. What is the claim to fame of the 2001 Odyssey nightclub in Brooklyn, New York?

A.) The 2001 Odyssey disco was the nightclub where the famous dance scenes in **"Saturday Night Fever"** were filmed. The club is located at 64th Street and 3rd Avenue (near the Verrazano-Narrows Bridge) in Brooklyn, New York. The famous white suit John Travolta wore in the dance scenes was purchased off the rack (by Travolta) at the Leading Man haberdashery in Brooklyn. The suit was part of the late movie critic Gene Siskel's memorabilia collection.

153. Which Fleetwood Mac single (and video) featured the USC Trojan Marching Band?

A.) The Fleetwood Mac single and video **"Tusk"** (#8 10/13/79 *Billboard*) featured the USC Trojan Marching Band. The song was the title track to Fleetwood Mac's follow-up album to the phenomenally successful *Rumors*. The tune "Tusk" was recorded live with the marching band at Dodger Stadium. *Tusk* had a much more experimental feel than the visceral *Rumors*, which led *Rolling Stone* to say that they had "succumbed to artiness."

154. Who was the mysterious orchestra leader on the 1977 album *Thrillington*?

A.) The mysterious orchestra leader on 1977's *Thrillington* was **Percy "Thrills" Thrillington,** although the name may have been a pseudonym for Paul McCartney. The album was an orchestral rendering of McCartney's *Ram* album, which was recorded at Abbey Road Studios. Originally intended for a 1972 release, it was delayed until 1977 because of legal difficulties. The startling cover art, which depicted a ram, dressed in formal clothing, playing the violin, was designed by Hipgnosis, while the fictitious back cover liner notes were penned by Clint Harrigan. This album fell out of print very quickly, and has become a sought-after collector's item.

Big Bang! Baby

155. What classic science fiction movie inspired the cover for Ringo Starr's 1974 album *Goodnight Vienna*?

A.) The cover illustration for Ringo Starr's 1974 album *Goodnight Vienna* was a doctored still from the classic 1951 science fiction movie **The Day the Earth Stood Still,** which starred Michael Rennie as Klaatu. The cover shows the nine-foot-tall robot Gort exiting a spaceship, with Klaatu (with Ringo's head superimposed on Rennie's body) in the doorway of the craft. The album features a collection of Ringo's superstar friends, including John Lennon, Dr. John, Elton John, and Robbie Robertson. Despite the impressive list of players, the album was not well received (*Rolling Stone* only gave it two stars) and only produced one hit, the Hoyt Axton-penned novelty number "No No Song" (#3 2/22/75 *Billboard*).

156. Who made his recording debut with *Chestnut Street Incident* in 1976?

A.) **John Mellencamp** was given the stage name of **Johnny Cougar** for the release of *Chestnut Street Incident* in 1976. His manager, Tony De Fries (ex-manager of David Bowie), suggested the name change to give him a more catchy name than the cumbersome Mellencamp. The album (with ex-Bowie guitarist Mick Ronson), was a glam-rock collection of Roy Orbison, Elvis Presley, Lovin' Spoonful, and Doors covers. The album stiffed, and years later John Mellencamp (having dropped De Fries and "Cougar") disowned it.

157. What speed metal guitarist was once a roadie for Jimi Hendrix?

A.) **Lemmy Kilminster** of Motorhead was once a roadie for Jimi Hendrix. He left Hendrix to join Hawkwind, a legendary British heavy metal band. In 1975 he was dismissed by the band after a drug bust in Canada made it difficult for Lemmy to get visas for travel. He rebounded by forming Bastard, the power trio that eventually became Motorhead. Their albums, a mix of heavy metal and speed thrash, have consistently charted in the United Kingdom, but have been slow to catch on stateside. Although they remain a strong live draw, their best showing on the US album charts was 1982's *Iron Fist*, which reached number 172.

158. Which EMI Abbey Road studio engineer found greater fame as a recording artist, reinterpreting the works of Edgar Allen Poe?

A.) **Alan Parsons** worked as a producer/engineer at EMI's Abbey Road studio (he was nominated for a Grammy for his work on Pink Floyd's *Dark Side of the Moon*) before forming The Alan Parsons Project with songwriting partner Eric Woolfson. The Project featured a floating cast of singers and musicians, including Gary (Procol Harum) Brooker and Steve Harley. Their first collaboration was a concept album based on the work of macabre writer Edgar Allen Poe's work. *Tales of Mystery and Imagination* featured British rock stars Arthur (The Crazy World of ...) Brown and David Pack. One single, "(The System of) Doctor Tarr and Professor Fether" (#37 9/11/76 *Billboard*) reached the American Top 40. A 1987 reissue of the album added narration by Orson Welles. Following the success of that album, they embarked on a series of theme albums — *Eve* (1979) dealt with the battle of the sexes, while *The Turn of a Friendly Card* (1980) examined gambling and *The Eye in the Sky* (1982) told the story of a police state.

159. How did The Edgar Winter Group's number 1 hit single "Frankenstein" get its name?

A.) "Frankenstein" was originally written as a show-stopping musical tour de force to showcase Edgar Winter's multi-instrument talent. While he was playing with his younger brother, guitarist Johnny Winter, Edgar was given a solo spot in the show. He conceived a song called "The Double Drum Solo," a raucous jazz number in which he played saxophone, drums, and keyboards. It brought the house down every night. When Edgar left his brother's band to form The Edgar Winter Project, he recorded the still-untitled instrumental song for the album *They Only Come Out at Night*. The problem was it was way too long. After a series of edits by producer Rick Derringer, the tune was dubbed "Frankenstein"

181

because of all the cuts and splices that had been made to the master tape. "Frankenstein" spent one week at number 1 on the *Billboard* charts in May 1973.

160. Peter Gabriel released four albums, with the same name. What were they called?

A.) Peter Gabriel's first four solo albums released between the years 1977 and 1982, were all simply called **Peter Gabriel**. The fourth album was called *Security*, but only in America, at the insistence of the record company. "I originally thought I would avoid titles and make my records like magazines," Gabriel explained to Timothy White in *Spin*. "When you look at home at a pile of magazines, you remember them usually by the picture on the cover; I wanted it to look like a body of work." Gabriel changed his stance on eponymously titled albums with the release of 1986's *So*.

161. What film inspired the band name Bad Company?

A.) Bad Company were one of the first rock supergroups, formed from the ashes of three successful British bands of the sixties and seventies. Singer Paul Rodgers and drummer Simon Kirke came from Free, guitarist Mick Ralphs was formerly a member of Mott the Hoople, and Boz Burrell had played bass for King Crimson. They scored five Top 20 singles from 1974 to 1979 — "Can't Get Enough" (number 5, 1974), "Movin' On" (number 19, 1975), "Feel Like Makin' Love" (number 10, 1975), "Young Blood" (number 20, 1976), and "Rock 'N' Roll Fantasy" (number 13, 1979). The band took their name from **Jeff Bridges' 1972 Civil War drama *Bad Company***, directed by Robert Benton.

162. Which blues song inspired the name of the band Badfinger?

A.) The name Badfinger was suggested by Neil Aspinal, the head of Apple Records, inspired by **an old blues track titled "Badfinger Boogie."** Formed in mid-sixties Swansea, Wales, the band

182

was originally called The Iveys. When they were signed to Apple in 1968 it was decided that the name was not contemporary enough and a change was in order. Under the name Badfinger the band placed three songs in the American Top 10, "Come and Get It" (number 7, 1970), "No Matter What" (number 8, 1970), and "Day After Day" (number 4, 1971). The group disbanded in 1975 after the suicide of founding member Pete Ham, briefly reuniting in 1978 with former Yes keyboardist Tony Kaye.

163. What was the inspiration for the band name Big Star?

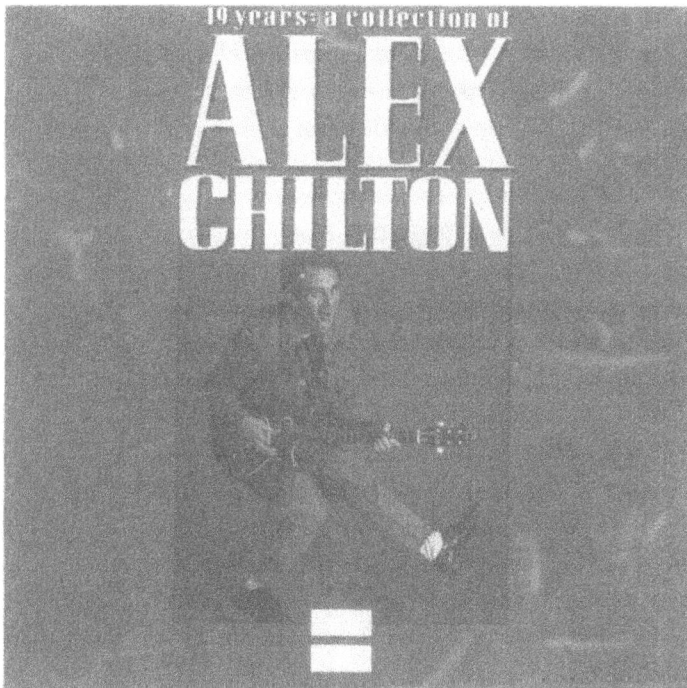

A.) Big Star formed in Memphis in 1971. Former Box Tops singer Alex Chilton joined ranks with a local band called Ice Water (guitarist Chris Bell, bassist Andy Hummel, and drummer Jody Stevens). The nameless band began recording bed tracks at Ardent Studios, preparing for their first album. After one long night of recording, they left the studio and noticed **a supermarket kitty corner to the studio. It was called Big Star Foodmarkets,** and thus Big Star was born. Their skillful fusion of British pop with mid-sixties Los Angeles-styled harmonies failed to yield any hits, but made them a well-loved cult band.

Former Box Tops lead vocalist Alex Chilton. Commenting on Big Star's records Chilton once said, "The music is sometimes maudlin and stupid, but inspired nonetheless."

Photo courtesy of Rhino Records

183

164. What inspired the band name Cabaret Voltaire?

A.) Formed in 1974, the members of Cabaret Voltaire took their name from **the Zurich café that served as a meeting place for the Swiss dadaists** in the years before World War I.

165. What was the inspiration for the band name Durutti Column?

A.) Manchester, England, guitarist Vini Reilly named his band Durutti Column after **a cartoon strip used by the SI in Strasbourg in the 1960s**. The trio came together in 1978, combining elements of jazz, electronic, and folk in their eclectic music. A series of interesting albums established a solid cult following for the group, but they have been unable to capitalize on that success, as Reilly has an eating disorder and is frequently too ill to tour.

166. Which railroad inspired the name Grand Funk Railroad?

A.) The Flint, Michigan, band Terry and the Pack almost had a Top 40 hit with a single called "I (Who Have Nothing)" in 1967. The song reached number 46, making the band local stars, but failing to generate any national interest. Disappointed by the relative failure of the song, the group's leader, Terry Knight, resigned from performing, instead taking up the position of The Pack's manager. With Knight gone, it seemed a good time for the remaining members — guitarist Mark Farner, bassist Mel Schacher (The Mysterians), and drummer Don Brewer — to change their name, re-establishing themselves as a heavy metal band. It was Knight who suggested the name Grand Funk Railroad — a take-off on **Michigan's Grand Trunk Railroad**. Under this name they charted three Top 40 singles, "Closer to Home" (number 22, 1970), "Footstompin' Music" (number 29, 1972), and "Rock 'N' Roll Soul" (number 29, 1972). After an acrimonious split with Knight in 1972 the band streamlined their name to Grand Funk, and placed six more singles in the Top 20.

167. What inspired the band name Rainbow?

A.) Guitarist Ritchie Blackmore split with Deep Purple in May 1975, forming Rainbow later that same year. He named his new band after **the Rainbow Bar and Grill (9001 Sunset Strip, Los Angeles),** an infamous rock and roll hangout. Opened in 1973, the Rainbow originally attracted music business executives, but by 1974 when Led Zeppelin started hanging out there, the whole complexion of the place changed. Gone were the conservative guys in suits, in were the wild long-haired musicians. In a previous incarnation the building was a restaurant called The Villanova, where Marilyn Monroe first met Joe Dimaggio on a blind date.

The Rainbow (9001 Sunset Strip, Los Angeles). Opened in 1973, it became an instant favourite of touring rock bands, including Led Zeppelin, who frequented the club during the seventies. In a previous incarnation as The Villanova, it was where Joe Dimaggio first met Marilyn Monroe on a blind date.

Photo by Richard Crouse

168. What Los Angeles hotel was nicknamed The Riot House?

A.) **The Continental Hyatt House (now called Hyatt on Sunset)** at 8401 Sunset Strip in Los Angeles was nicknamed The Riot House. The hotel has a rich rock and roll history. In the 1960s Doors singer Jim Morrison lived at The Riot House, causing a traffic jam one afternoon when he hung out a window by his fingertips. He wasn't evicted for his behaviour — he was simply moved to the other side of the hotel to a room facing away from the street. In the 1970s it was Led Zeppelin's home away from home. Renting as many as six floors at a time, the band would stage motorcycle races in the halls, have orgies, and generally break up the place. Their business was always welcome, as long as they were willing to pay a $50,000 damage deposit each time they stayed there. Lemmy, of Hawkwind, wrote the song "Motorhead" while in residence,

185

and in the 1980s Little Richard lived at the hotel for most of the decade. Bands flocked to the hotel, seeing it as a place where they could pretty much do whatever the hell they wanted without interference from the management. The hotel's owners catered to the rock bands. Behind the front desk was a picture of a long-haired musician with the message "Treat This Man With Respect, He May Have Just Sold a Million Records."

169. What was the only Top 10 hit for Commander Cody and His Lost Planet Airmen?

A.) Despite selling lots of albums, Commander Cody and His Lost Planet Airmen only placed one single in the Top 10, 1972's **"Hot Rod Lincoln."** The tune was a cover of the 1960 novelty hit by country artists Johnny Bond and Charlie Ryan. Subsequent singles, "Beat Me Daddy Eight to the Bar" (number 81, 1972 *Billboard*), "Smoke! Smoke! Smoke! (That Cigarette)" (number 94, 1973 *Billboard*), and "Don't Let Go" (number 56, 1975 *Billboard*) failed to establish them on the charts, and the band split in 1976.

170. Under what name is George Frayne IV better known?

A.) George Frayne IV is known to record buyers as **Commander Cody**. With his band, The Lost Planet Airmen, Cody released several popular albums in the 1970s, including *Lost in the Ozone* (1971), *Hot Licks, Cold Steel, and Truckers' Favorites* (1972), and *Country Casonova* (1973). The Commander took his unusual name from a 1940s Republic Pictures serial, *Commando Cody*, while his band's name was derived from a line in Coleridge's *The Rime of the Ancient Mariner*.

171. Who scored his only Top 10 hit with 1972's "Popcorn"?

A.) The 1972 number 9 hit "Popcorn" was the brainchild of **Stan Free, a session musician, who played under the name Hot Butter**. As a freelance session player, Free had added Moog synthesizers and keyboards to records by a variety of artists, including John Denver,

186

Arlo Guthrie, and Arthur Fiedler's Boston Pops. Subsequent singles — his "Moog-ized" versions of "Tequila," "Percolator," "Pipeline," and "Apache" — failed to match the success of "Popcorn." In fact, not one of them charted.

172. What two one-hit wonder bands did Bill Bartlett play guitar for?

A.) Bill Bartlett's first run at chart success was with **The Lemon Pipers**. They hit number 1 with "Green Tambourine" in 1968. When that band broke up Bartlett went into semi-retirement, moving to a farm in Ohio. He listened to American roots music, eventually coming across a song by Leadbelly called "Black Betty." He recorded a demo version of the song, which found its way to Buddah Records in New York City. Sensing the hit potential of the song, an album was hastily recorded with a pick-up band dubbed **Ram Jam**. The single performed well, hitting number 18 on the charts in 1977, despite a boycott by the NAACP. "(They say that) 'Black Betty' is considered an insult to black womanhood, but that's a lot of hogwash," complained Bartlett in the *Illinois Entertainer*. "Leadbelly was black, and he wrote all of the lyrics. No blacks that I have talked to find the song offensive." Ram Jam recorded two albums, *Ram Jam* (1974) and *Portrait of an Artist as a Young Ram* (1975), but failed to produce another hit single.

173. What was Norman Greenbaum's only hit?

A.) Norman Greenbaum's sole entry in the Top 10 was 1970's number 3 hit **"Spirit in the Sky,"** a quasi-religious tune recorded for Reprise Records. When his next two singles, the bizarre "Canned Ham" and "California Earthquake," didn't burn up the charts, Greenbaum moved to a farm in northern California, starting a dairy business. "I got money — fuck it," he told *Creem* in 1972. Briefly returning to the music business, he sporadically released several acoustic and country-styled albums in the late seventies and early eighties.

174. What was Daddy Dewdrop's sole Top 40 hit?

187

Big Bang! Baby 1989

A.) Daddy Dewdrop (real name: Dick Monda) was a songwriter/producer for the Saturday morning CBS cartoon show "Sabrina and the Groovy Ghoulies." **"Chick-A-Boom (Don't Ya Jes' Love It)"** was written for the show by songwriters Janis Lee Guin and Linda Martin. Sensing the tune had hit potential, Monda quickly inked a deal with Sunflower Records, put together a band of session musicians, and recorded the song. "Chick-A-Boom (Don't Ya Jes' Love It)," went to number 9 in May 1971. It was Daddy Dewdrop's last visit to the Top 40. In the late 1970s another singer using the name Daddy Dewdrop tried (and failed) to crack the Top 40 with another television-inspired hit, "Nanu Nanu (I Wanna Get Funky With You)," which attempted to capitalize on the success of the "Mork and Mindy" TV series.

175. What 1972 Top 10 hit is credited to songwriter J.S. Bach?

A.) Tom Parker's band Apollo 100's February 1972 hit **"Joy"** was an electronic adaptation of J.S. Bach's "Jesu, Joy of Man's Desiring." Their next single, a re-working of "Mendelssohn's 4th (2nd Movement)," squeaked into the Top 100 later that year. Parker moved on after Apollo 100 split, enjoying success as keyboardist for Doggerel Bank and record producer for Gerry Rafferty, Chris White, and Status Quo.

176. Which Scottish pipe-and-drum band hit the Top 20 with "Amazing Grace" in 1972?

A.) **The Royal Scots Dragoon Guards** had a fluke number 11 hit in 1972 with "Amazing Grace." Their version of the 1779 John Newton classic is the first record to ever sell one million copies with bagpipes as the predominant instrument. The song featured twenty pipers and ten drummers, and eventually sold upwards of seven million copies.

177. What was KISS guitarist Ace Frehley's only solo hit?

A.) KISS guitarist Ace Frehley only had one hit outside of the group, 1979's **"New York Groove."** After leaving KISS in 1983 he released

188

three hitless albums (*Frehley's Comet, Live + 1,* and *Second Sighting*) with his own band Frehley's Comet.

178. Which Clash hit song has never been included on the track listings for *London Calling*?

A.) The track listing for the Clash's *London Calling* only lists eighteen songs, although there are nineteen songs on the double album. After the artwork was completed, The Clash decided to add another song to the record. It was too late to add **"Train in Vain"** to the artwork, and in subsequent releases (including the CD remastering) the song has been left off the track listing.

179. What was The Pipkins' only hit?

A.) The Pipkins had one hit, 1970's **"Gimme Dat Ding,"** a novelty song commissioned for a British kid's show. Technically they weren't a band, just a group of British session players headed by singer Tony Burrows. Burrows was a busy session singer, having provided vocals on Edison Lighthouse's "Love Grows (Where My Rosemary Goes)" (number 12, 1970), the Brotherhood of Man's "United We Stand" (number 13, 1970), and First Class's "Beach Baby" (number 4, 1973). One of the song's writers, Albert Hammond, would go on to have considerable success as a solo artist, taking "It Never Rains in Southern California" to number 5 in 1972.

180. In the song "Ain't No Sunshine," how many times does Bill Withers repeat the phrase "I know"?

A.) Bill Withers holds the record for the most consecutively repeated phrase in a Top 5 hit. During the course of "Ain't No Sunshine" (number 3, 1971), Withers uses the phrase "I know" **twenty-six times**. Another Withers hit, "Lovely Day" (number 30, 1978), holds the record for non-consecutive repeating of a phrase. He takes fifty-eight seconds to get to the title of this hit, but in the remaining three minutes and sixteen seconds he repeats the title 105 times.

181. Which small Texas town has a statue honouring Buddy Holly?

A.) Buddy Holly lived in **Lubbock, Texas**, for most of his life. In 1979 the town unveiled a 2,500-pound bronze statue in honour of its favourite son. Created by sculptor Grant Speed, the eight-and-a-half-foot likeness of Holly stands at the entrance to Lubbock's Civic Center. Surrounding the statue is a West Texas Walk of Fame with plaques commemorating The Crickets, Waylon Jennings, Mac Davis, Joe Ely, Bob Wills, Tanya Tucker, The Gatlin Brothers, and Roy Orbison.

182. Which letter on the famous "HOLLYWOOD" sign was paid for by Alice Cooper?

A.) The Hollywood sign on Mt. Lee in Los Angeles originally read "HOLLYWOODLAND" and was an advertisement for a housing development. By the 1970s the sign had fallen into such disrepair the City Council was considering demolishing the landmark. In 1978 a group of wealthy entertainers donated $27,000 each to restore the sign. Rocker Alice Cooper donated **the last "O"** on behalf of his friend Groucho Marx.

183. Who founded The Raspberries in 1971?

A.) Singer/guitarist **Eric Carmen** founded The Raspberries in 1971. Over the next four years they enjoyed some Top 40 success with tunes like "Go All the Way" (#5 8/19/72 *Billboard*), "I Wanna Be with You" (#16 12/09/72 *Billboard*), and "Overnight Sensation (Hit Record)" (#18 10/12/74 *Billboard*). The band's repertoire featured an equal mix of rockers and ballads, although Carmen's voice was best suited to slick, romantic ballads. Carmen dissolved the band in 1975 and headed out for a solo career. Since then, his output has been uneven, but he has placed a few songs on the charts. He took the number 2 spot for three weeks in 1976 with the ballad "All By Myself" (#2 1/17/76 *Billboard*), and contributed music to the hugely successful *Dirty Dancing* soundtrack.

190

Carmen is also a prolific songwriter, having penned tunes for Shaun Cassidy, Olivia Newton-John, and Frankie Valli.

184. Who led The Silver Bullet band to fame?

A.) **Bob Seger** formed The Silver Bullet Band in 1976 after the break-up of his former backing unit The System. The Bullets' line-up in 1976 was: Alto Reed (horns), Robyn Robbins (keyboards), Drew Abbott (guitar), Chris Campbell (bass), and Charlie Allen Martin (drums). The gruelling touring schedule took its toll on the members the band, and there have been several personnel changes. Seger enjoyed the pinnacle of his success while recording with this band. The blue-collar rock of "Night Moves" (#4 1/15/77 *Billboard*) and "Tryin' to Live My Life Without You" (#5 9/26/81 *Billboard*) drew favour from the public and critics alike.

185. What were Victor Willis, Alex Briley, David Hodo, Glenn Hughes, Randy Jones, and Felipe Rose better known as?

A.) The sextet was better known as **The Village People.** They were brought together by producer Jacques Morali, who wanted to put together a group embodying six male stereotypes — the motorcycle cop, the cowboy, the Indian chief, the construction worker, the soldier, and the biker. They drew their name from New York City's Greenwich Village. Their best year was 1979 when the album *Cruisin'* produced two Top 5 singles, "Y.M.C.A." (#2 11/11/78 *Billboard*) and "In the Navy" (#3 3/31/79 *Billboard*). The shine was beginning to fade as they played themselves in the ill-fated movie *Can't Stop the Music*, and released a live double album, *Live and Sleazy*, which would be their last gold album.

186. Which illiterate band released a string of British chart-toppers in the early seventies with names like, "Coz I Love You," "Mama Weer All Crazee Now," "Gudbuy T'Jane," "Cum On Feel the Noize," and "Skweeze Me Pleeze Me"?

191

Big Bang! Baby

A.) **Slade** (who apparently titled their songs without the aid of Webster's) topped the British charts with a series of misspelt tunes from 1971 to 1973. The trend began with "Coz I Love You," which reached number 1 on the British Top 40 and paved the way for a string of illiterate hit singles ("Mama Weer All Crazee Now," "Gudbuy T'Jane," "Cum On Feel the Noize," "Skweeze Me Pleeze Me," and "Merry Xmas Everybody"). In 1983 Los Angeles rockers Quiet Riot tried to bring illiteracy back to the charts when they covered two of Slade's tunes. The revamped version of "Cum On Feel the Noize" (#5 10/15/83 *Billboard*) broke into the Top 5, while "Mama Weer All Crazee Now" failed to make an impression, to the relief of spelling teachers everywhere.

187. What 1979 song is generally credited with being the first rap hit?

A.) The first hit rap song is generally thought to be **The Sugar Hill Gang's "Rapper's Delight"** (#36 1/05/80 *Billboard*). The Harlem-based rappers were discovered by Sylvia Robinson, a legendary figure in hip-hop circles, and the founder of Sugar Hill Records, a company devoted to producing rap records. Up until this time, rap was a strictly underground movement, performed mainly in New York City dance clubs, and was perceived as a passing fad with no commercial appeal. "Rapper's Delight" (its rhythm track was borrowed from the Chic record "Good Times") sold two million copies. The myth that rap was not viable was dismissed, and the floodgates opened for a style of music that would grow in the eighties and prosper in the nineties.

WHO'S ZOOMIN' WHO?
The 1980s

1. What was Tina Turner's first number 1 hit?

A.) **"What's Love Got to Do With It"** (#1 6/23/84 *Billboard*) stayed atop the charts for three weeks, giving Tina Turner her first ever number 1 hit, and launching her hugely successful comeback. Tina was married to Ike Turner from 1958 to 1976. They enjoyed success as an R&B act, managing to place six singles in *Billboard*'s Top 40 from 1960 to 1973.

2. What was the first Culture Club single to be released?

A.) Culture Club debuted with **"White Boy"** and **"I'm Afraid"** on the Virgin label. While the songs garnered some play in London's dance clubs, neither made the charts. The band's run at the charts started with their third release, "Do You Really Want to Hurt Me" (#2 1/15/83 *Billboard*). Their first Top 10 was a critical success as well as a financial one. *The New Musical Express* raved about the single, adding that the band was very talented, as well as being trendy and accessible. The band scored several more hits in the next twelve months before falling apart, in part due to Boy George's well-publicized problems with heroin.

3. What was Duran Duran's first single?

A.) Duran Duran found success with their first single, **"Planet Earth,"** on EMI records. The song reached number 12 on the

BiBang! Baby

British charts, though it failed to crack the Top 40 in America. Duran Duran spearheaded the "New Romantic" movement in Britain, which was the antithesis of punk rock. New Romantics (or Blitz Kids as they were sometimes known) favoured neatly coiffed hair, make-up on boys, and exotic tailored clothing. Writer Tom Hibbert (in his book *Rockspeak: The Dictionary of Rock Terms*) commented that New Romantics would "show off their style by affecting an air of poise whilst standing around without smiling as futurist music or funk is played in some hygienic disco club." Home base to the New Romantics was London's trendy Blitz Club.

4. Why was the cover of Bronski Beat's debut album *Age of Consent* rejected by their American record company?

A.) The cover of Bronski Beat's debut, *Age of Consent* (which spawned the mega-single "Smalltown Boy"), was turned down because it **listed the age of consent for gay sex in European countries.**

5. What book is Sting reading on the cover of the Police's 1983 hit album *Synchronicity*?

A.) On the cover of *Synchronicity*, the well-read Mr. Sting (real name: Gordon Sumner) is reading **Jung's *Synchronicity.*** The centrepiece of this album is Sting's ode to jealousy and obsession, "Every Breath You Take" (#1 6/04/83 *Billboard*), which topped the *Billboard* charts for eight weeks in the summer of 1983. The pressures of superstardom and infighting in the band forced an early end to The Police's run at the top of the charts. In 1984 Sting left for a successful solo career, producing several hit albums, while drummer Stewart Copeland formed the arty Animal Logic in 1989. The Police last played together at an Amnesty International concert in 1986.

6. Which Blondie album showed Debbie Harry sporting a lion's mane haircut?

A.) Debbie Harry wore her lion's mane hairdo on the cover of 1980's *The Hunter*. The album produced one hit, "The Tide is High" (#1 11/29/80 *Billboard*), which sat on the charts for seventeen weeks.

7. Which Van Halen album cover depicts an angel smoking a cigarette?

A.) There is an angel smoking a cigarette on the cover of Van Halen's album *1984 (MCMLXXXIV)*. The album produced their biggest hit, "Jump" (#1 1/21/84 *Billboard*), which rode the top of the charts for five weeks. The album was kept out of the top spot by Michael Jackson's *Thriller*, which ironically featured Eddie Van Halen on guitar on one track.

8. What instrument did Annie Lennox study at the Royal Academy of Music?

A.) Annie Lennox studied the **flute** (which she still plays on stage) at London's Royal Academy of Music. She entered the Academy in 1971 on a scholarship to study flute, piano, and harpsichord. While she loved classical music, and became an accomplished flautist, she hated the school and the pretentious attitude of many of the students. She studied at the Academy for three years, only to leave three days before her final exams. Joe Jackson also enrolled in the same year as Lennox. In a *Rolling Stone* interview Lennox commented that she always felt sorry for Jackson because he had such bad skin.

9. On the cover of The Police's 1983 hit album *Synchronicity,* what is unusual about the piano that Andy Summers is playing?

A.) Andy Summers' *Synchronicity* cover shot features him playing a piano with **eggs resting on the keys.**

10. Who produced the hit single "Too Shy" for Kajagoogoo?

195

Big Bang! Baby

A.)One-hit wonders Kajagoogoo found success with "Too Shy" (#35 5/21/83 *Billboard*), produced by Duran Duran's **Nick Rhodes.** Shortly after the success of "Too Shy," lead singer Chris Hamill left the band for a solo career, under the name Limahl (an anagram of his last name). His one and only solo hit was the title track to the film *Neverending Story* (#17 5/04/85 *Billboard*).

11. Who played the guitar break on Michael Jackson's "Beat It"?

A.)**Eddie Van Halen** guested on guitar on Michael Jackson's "Beat It" (#1 3/19/83 *Billboard*), which stayed in the number 1 spot for three weeks. Ironically Jackson's *Thriller* album kept Van Halen's *1984 (MCMLXXXIV)* album out of the top spot, allowing them a chart high of only number 2.

12. Which teeny-bopper chanteuse made her Broadway debut in 1992 in *Les Miserables*?

A.)Teeny-bopper star **Debbie Gibson** received positive reviews for her Broadway debut in *Les Miserables*. While many were cynical about her chances on the Broadway stage, Debbie praised her co-stars: "They realized that positive energy goes further than cynicism." The Long Island native has been playing piano since age 5, and wrote her first tune at age 6. At age 16 she broke into the Top 5 with "Only in My Dreams" (#4 6/27/87 *Billboard*) and followed that success with a string of Top 30 singles like "Shake Your Love" (#4 10/24/87 *Billboard*), "Out of the Blue" (#3 2/06/88 *Billboard*), "Foolish Heart" (#1 5/07/88 *Billboard*), and "Lost in Your Eyes" (#1 1/28/89 *Billboard*).

13. How many songs did Michael Jackson consider before settling on the tracks that appear on *Thriller*?

A.)Michael Jackson and producer Quincy Jones recorded **three hundred songs** while working on the *Thriller* album. Of those they chose the winning tracks that appear on the disc. It is a long, expensive process to record that many tunes, but in this case it paid off, as *Thriller* sold forty million copies worldwide, won a record eight Grammys, and contained seven Top 10 singles.

14. Which Styx concept album features the characters Jonathan Chance and Dr. Everett Righteous?

A.) Jonathan Chance, Dr. Everett Righteous, and Kilroy are characters in Styx's mini rock opera *Kilroy was Here*. The 1983 album tells the story of the battles between bad guy Righteous and Kilroy, a rock star, and produced the Top 5 hit "Mr. Roboto" (#3 2/12/83 *Billboard*).

15. How many versions of 1984's "The War Song" did Culture Club release?

A.) Culture Club released **five** versions of "The War Song" (#17 10/20/84 *Billboard*). Versions in English, French, German, Spanish, and Japanese were intended to spread the message the world over. Too bad the single didn't sell.

16. Who recorded an acoustic version of Van Halen's "Jump" in 1984?

A.) **Aztec Camera** released a kinder, gentler "Jump" in 1984. The song's writer David Lee Roth says he was inspired to write the tune after watching a news item about a man who threatened to jump from a skyscraper in New York City. In the newscast he heard someone in the background yelling, "Go ahead and jump!!" at the hapless fellow on the window ledge. When it came time to write the song, that phrase stuck in his head. In January 1984 Van Halen's version of "Jump" sat in the number 1 position on the *Billboard* charts for five weeks.

17. Whose boisterous cry of "Science!" appears on Thomas Dolby's 1983 hit "She Blinded Me With Science"?

Big Bang! Baby

A.) Thomas Dolby sampled famous British chemist **Dr. Magnus Pyke** for the boisterous cry of "Science!" that appears on "She Blinded Me With Science" (#5 3/19/83 *Billboard*). The Cairo, Egypt-born Dolby was a leader in computer-generated music, and actually designed and built many of the electronic instruments heard on his albums. Before finding success as a solo artist, Dolby was a session player who wrote and produced hits for many artists, including Lene Lovich ("New Toy"). His session credits include backup on the fourth Foreigner album and the Joan Armatrading hit "Walk Under Ladders." In the early eighties, his live shows were a one-man affair, and incorporated a multi-media presentation that accompanied his computer-driven music. The proceeds from his solo recordings and one-man shows were donated to a fund dedicated to preserving the cultural artifacts of Venice. Other projects included the soundtrack to the ill-fated *Howard the Duck* film, and a band project titled Dolby's Cube.

18. What was the title of Paul McCartney's follow-up to *Tug of War*?

A.) Paul McCartney followed-up his *Tug of War* success with an album called **Pipes of Peace**. *Tug of War* topped the *Billboard* album charts for three weeks, and produced the Top 10 hit, "Take It Away" (#10 7/17/82 *Billboard*). *Tug of War* features a who's who of musicians spread out over its twelve tracks. Eric Stewart of 10CC fame lends his electric guitar to the title track, while ex-Beatles mate Ringo Starr bangs out the beat on "Take It Away," which also features producer George Martin on piano. Bass whiz Stanley Clarke checks in on two cuts, while Stevie Wonder contributes synthesizer and vocals to "Ebony and Ivory" (#1 4/10/82 *Billboard*). One of Paul's heroes, Carl Perkins, adds electric guitar and vocals to "Get It." At the end of this track Perkins can be heard laughing in response to a joke. Paul had told him a rude joke while they were recording the song, but it was considered too racy, and was edited out of the song, leaving only Perkins' strange disembodied laugh. McCartney himself displays his musical prowess, playing acoustic, electric, and Spanish guitars, bass, piano, synthesizers, drums, and vocoder on the record.

198

19. What song was Weird Al Yankovic parodying when he sang, "Another One Rides the Bus"?

A.) Weird Al Yankovic poked fun at Queen's **"Another One Bites the Dust"** with his take-off "Another One Rides the Bus." Al's parody failed to make the charts, but Queen's version was their biggest American hit to date, and won them *Billboard*'s award for Top Crossover Single of 1980.

20. Who sang the Valley Girl voice on Frank Zappa's 1982 hit "Valley Girl"?

A.) The irritating voice in Frank Zappa's hit "Valley Girl" (#32 9/04/82 *Billboard*) belonged to his fourteen-year-old daughter **Moon Unit.** The song that introduced the term "grody to the max" to the lips of millions of teenagers was a spoof of the spoiled, rich children of television and film executives who live in the San Fernando Valley. Questioned about his daughter's unusual name, Zappa explained that when she was born in 1967 he was on a European tour. The last instructions he left with his wife Gail were in regards to acceptable names for the baby: Moon for a girl, and Motorhead for a boy. Zappa has other children; a son named Dweezil (named after his mother Gail's "funny looking toe," which Frank had nicknamed a "dweezil"), and Diva, who was so named because she was the loudest baby in the hospital.

21. Who wrote and produced Diana Ross's 1982 hit "Muscles"?

A.) Diana Ross's 1982 hit "Muscles" (#10 10/16/82 *Billboard*) was written and produced by **Michael Jackson.** The inspiration for the tune came from Jackson's eight-foot boa constrictor, appropriately named "Muscle." Jackson often joked that the snake was "trained to eat interviewers."

22. In 1981 Virgin Records released a single featuring The Sex Pistols and British train robber Ronald Biggs. What was the single called?

Big Bang! Baby

A.) The Sex Pistols/Ronnie Biggs collaboration was titled **"Ronnie Biggs (He was Only the Tea Boy)."** Biggs was in exile to avoid serving a thirty-year jail term for his part in the Great Train Robbery. The proceeds from the song were to benefit Biggs's son, however the boy never saw a penny from the release.

23. Who said: "My speaking voice is ridiculous"?

A.) **Cyndi Lauper** feels that her speaking voice "is ridiculous." Her heavy Queens accent is the result of a youth spent in Ozone Park, New York. Lauper's multi-octave voice and her unusual wardrobe, gleaned from Salvation Army thrift bins, helped win a record deal for her band Blue Angel in 1980. Their only album bombed, leaving Lauper deeply in debt. In 1981 she declared bankruptcy, and sang part-time in bars. She was re-discovered by David Wolff, who became her manager, and won her a second chance with a major record company. With the release of her first solo album, *She's So Unusual,* in 1983, Cyndi became the first artist in rock and roll to garner four Top 10 singles from a debut album.

24. Who released this statement to the press in 1984? "NO! I've never taken hormones to maintain my high voice. NO! I've never had my cheekbones altered in any way. NO! I've never had cosmetic surgery on my eyes. YES! One day in the future I plan to get married and have a family."

A.) **Michael Jackson** released a tersely worded statement to the press in 1984 to put an end to several rumours that had been circulating for years about his personal life. "NO! I've never taken hormones to maintain my high voice," reads the first line of the statement, referring to the rumour that alleged that Joe Jackson had his son Michael injected with female hormones as a child to keep his voice in the upper registers. "NO! I've never had my cheekbones altered in any way": Michael admits that he has had plastic surgery; he owns up to two nose jobs and the cleft in his chin, but absolutely denies any cheekbone implants. While it is possible to achieve high cheekbones by tooth extraction, several experts have stated that that doesn't seem to be the case here. Examination of pre-1980s photos and recent snaps would imply that there is some difference. "NO! I've never had cosmetic surgery on my eyes": Michael denies any cosmetic surgery on his eyes, although he has admitted to tweezing his eyebrows. "YES! One day in the future I plan to get married and have a family": this final clause in the press release would apparently be his way of ending the annoying rumours that questioned his sexual preference. In 1979 an unfounded rumour linked Michael with actor Clifton Davis, leading Michael to announce that he was not gay, and couldn't understand why people thought he was. Coming from a strict Jehovah's Witness background, homosexuality would be seen as a sin by his family. Before his short-lived marriage to Lisa Marie Presley in 1994 he was spotted dating Brooke Shields and was seen in public with Madonna. In 1996, just two months after his divorce from Presley, he married Debbie Rowe, whom he met while she was working at the office of Dr. Arnold Klein, "skin doctor to the stars." At the time of their wedding Jackson announced to the press: "I fell for the beautiful, unpretentious, giving person that she is." Rowe filed for divorce in October 1999 after bearing Jackson's two children — son Prince, born in February 1997, and daughter Paris, born in April 1998.

25. On the 1983 Grammys, who said: "Thanks a lot, America. You've got taste, you've got style, and you know a good drag queen when you see one"?

A. **Boy George** threw a kiss to the camera, and thanked America for having taste, style, and knowing "a good drag queen when you see one" at the 1983 Grammys as he accepted the award for Best New Band of the Year. Later, on British television, he was asked why he referred to himself as a drag queen, when in interviews he usually denies that part of his sexuality. "I don't see myself as a drag queen," he replied. "No one laughs at priests because they wear dresses. Their clothes are accepted. I'd eventually like society to accept the way I look that easily too. I'm not a woman. I'm a man. When I go to the bathroom every morning, I look at myself, and I'm in no doubt of that."

26. Who did *Billboard* magazine call "the most successful duo in the history of the recording industry" in 1984?

A.) According to *Billboard* magazine circa 1984, **Hall and Oates** were "the most successful duo in the history of the recording industry." Singles like "Kiss on My List," which sat at number 1 for three weeks, and "Private Eyes," which held the top spot for two weeks, helped this dynamic duo outsell both The Everly Brothers and Simon and Garfunkel.

27. Who says: "WAR! Hide Yourself"?

A.) "WAR! Hide Yourself" was just one of the many sloganeering "Frankie Says" t-shirts designed by Katherine Hamnett for **Frankie Goes to Hollywood**. Frankie made a big splash in 1983 with the release of the singles "Relax" and "Two Tribes." In 1988 Frankie would experience the same trouble that would soon plague Milli Vanilli. A London court determined that Frankie Goes to Hollywood did not play on their hits, and relied on the studio brilliance of producer Trevor Horn and session players to form the distinctive Frankie sound.

28. Who did *Rolling Stone* say had cultivated "the Bulgarian bag lady look"?

A.) In 1982 *Rolling Stone* said that **Boy George** had cultivated "the Bulgarian bag lady look." George's baggy, multi-layered look caused a stir at the time, earning features in many magazines, including *Vogue, Women's Wear Daily,* and *Mademoiselle.* The clothes caught on with kids in Britain because they were fun, and, as writer Merle Ginsberg noted, "every little fat girl in Britain was forever grateful to Boy George for giving her enough fabric to hide her girlish pulchritude." Veteran fashion designer Betsey Johnson praised George's look: "It's always nice when someone comes along and picks up the fashion industry. He's an inspiration to wear what you want, how you want it."

29. What was the first Eurythmics album called?

A.) The first Eurythmics album was 1981's **In the Garden** on RCA. It was an experimental album that *Rolling Stone* called, "a minor masterpiece of pop songwriting." The album was recorded in Germany at Conny Plank's studio. Plank advised the band to keep the project small, and exercise control over every aspect of the record — from the music, to the album graphics, to the marketing strategy of the record company. They took her advice, and hired some of Germany's best avant-garde musicians: from the band Can they borrowed Holger Czukay and Jaki Liebezeit; Robert Gorl of Deutsche Americanische Freundschaft was enlisted as was Marcus Stockhausen, the son of Germany's best known avant-garde composer; and American Clem Burke, of the band Blondie, was brought in to play drums. The record sold poorly, and was not widely released in the United States.

30. Where did the name "The Honeydrippers" come from?

A.) The Honeydrippers scored a Top 5 hit in 1984 with "Sea of Love" (#3 10/27/84 *Billboard*). The supergroup, with front man Robert Plant (and, rumour has it Nile Rodgers, Jimmy Page, and Jeff Beck on guitars), borrowed their name from **Joe Liggins' 1945 hit instrumental "The Honeydripper."**

31. "Dance Hall Days" was a 1984 hit single for a band called Wang Chung. What does their unusual name mean?

A.) Wang Chung is Chinese for **"perfect cosmic pitch."** The British pop/rock trio (previously known as Huang Chung) featured Jack Hues (lead vocals, guitar, keyboards), Nick Feldman (bass, keyboards), and Darren Costin (drums). Drummer Costin left the band before their biggest hit, "Everybody Have Fun Tonight" (#2 10/25/86 *Billboard*), reached number 2, where it sat for two weeks. Another single, "Let's Go" (#9 2/14/87 *Billboard*), managed Top 10 success for the band, though their subsequent releases weren't as popular. "Hypnotize Me" (#36 7/25/87

203

Billboard) from the motion picture *Innerspace* was Wang Chung's last chart entry.

32. What was the first band Boy George was involved in?

A.) Boy George's first experience with a band was as a member of **In Praise of Lemmings.** He formed the band with his roommate, bassist Kirk Brandon, with Suede on guitar and a friend named Luke on drums. The music was heavy, political, sexual, and not very good. This led to George meeting with punk rock entrepreneur Malcolm McLaren about singing with a new band Malcolm was putting together — Bow Wow Wow. George played one gig with the newly formed band, under the name Lieutenant Lush, before being fired by McLaren.

33. Who is the only member of ZZ Top without a beard?

A.) The only member of ZZ Top without a beard is their drummer **Frank Beard.** Frank Beard and ZZ Top bassist Dusty Hill played together in the Texas-based American Blues Band (the two can be heard on the LP's *American Blues is Here* (1967) and *American Blues Do Their Thing* (1969) while guitarist Billy Gibbons was a member of the legendary psychedelic band The Moving Sidewalks. The three joined forces in 1970, and produced an album of derivative Jimi Hendrix-styled blues. Their second album, *Rio Grande Mud*, featured more of the Sante Fe Tabasco-flavoured guitar boogie they would become famous for. Their reputation as a major touring act was cemented in 1976 during the *Worldwide Texas Tour*. The show featured a host of animals on stage, and reportedly out-grossed every other show that year en route to breaking existing attendance records set by Elvis Presley and The Beatles. Top 40 hits like "Gimme All Your Lovin'" (#37 5/07/83 *Billboard*), "Legs" (#8 6/02/84 *Billboard*), "Sleeping Bag" (#8 10/26/85 *Billboard*), and a series of humorous "beard and boiler suit" videos turned ZZ Top into one of the biggest acts of the 1980s.

34. What was the original name Boy George had in mind for Culture Club?

A.) Boy George originally wanted to call Culture Club **The Sex Gang Children**, but backed down before they ever played live. The moniker was eventually used by another band. Boy George decided his band needed an inviting sounding name, one that allowed them to "be all things to all people." The "culture" half of their name implied that they would be borrowing from different facets of world music for their sound, while the "club" reference paid homage to Boy George's roots as the king of the London nightclub scene.

35. In late 1981 The Tom Tom Club released an album on Island Records that sold 600,000 copies. Two members of the Tom Tom Club were key members in another successful group. Who were they, and what was the group?

A.) The Tom Tom Club was the brainchild of **Tina Weymouth and Chris Frantz** of **Talking Heads**. Frantz called The Tom Tom Club album "one of the sillier records of a silly time in musical history." The album produced one hit, "Genius of Love" (#31 4/10/82 *Billboard*), which got heavy play in clubs.

36. Who did drummer Jon Moss play with before joining Culture Club?

A.) Culture Club drummer Jon Moss had played drums for **The Clash**, but was forced to quit because of personality conflicts with Mick Jones and Joe Strummer. Then there was his own band called **London**, who actually made records and toured, but no hits were forthcoming so they broke up. His next job was with **The Damned**. Things were going well, until he got into a car crash and had to quit that band as well. For a time he toured with **Adam Ant**, but didn't like the music and resigned before Adam had his first big hit with "Antmusic."

37. What two well-known bands merged in 1980 to produce one album, *Drama*, before splitting up?

205

Big Bang! Baby

A.) In 1980 **The Buggles** and **Yes** merged to record one album, *Drama*. Trevor Horn and Geoff Downes of The Buggles replaced Jon Anderson and Rick Wakeman in Yes for one album and one tour. After the tour Horn became a very hot record producer, masterminding works by ABC and Frankie Goes to Hollywood. Downes and Steve Howe enjoyed some success with Asia.

38. What movie did Duran Duran borrow their name from?

A.) Duran Duran pinched their name from the campy Jane Fonda flick *Barbarella* (1968). Duran Duran was the villain in this sci-fi sex story, which was based on a popular French comic strip. From 1982 to 1986 Duran Duran placed ten singles in the Top 20 on the *Billboard* charts, among them, "Hungry Like the Wolf" (#3 1/22/83 *Billboard*), "Is There Something I Should Know?" (#4 6/18/83 *Billboard*), "Union of the Snake" (#3 11/19/83 *Billboard*), "New Moon on Monday" (#10 1/28/84 *Billboard*), "The Reflex" (#1 4/28/84 *Billboard*), "The Wild Boys" (#2 11/03/84 *Billboard*), "A View to a Kill" (#1 5/25/85 *Billboard*), and "Notorious" (#2 11/15/86 *Billboard*).

39. What inspired the name "Frankie Goes to Hollywood"?

A.) The inspiration for the name "Frankie Goes to Hollywood" came from a movie poster for **Frank Sinatra's film debut, *Las Vegas Nights*** (1941). This Liverpool-based quintet created a huge sensation in Europe, but only managed to place one song in the US Top 10. "Relax" (#10 2/02/85 *Billboard*) was originally issued in 1984, when it only reached number 67 in the United States. It wasn't until MTV picked up on the song's controversial video that Frankie saw any chart action at all.

40. What was the first band Cyndi Lauper made a record with?

A.) Cyndi Lauper made her vinyl debut with a band called **Blue Angel.** The album, Cyndi says, "went lead," and as a result she filed for bankruptcy in 1981 because of debts incurred during the recording and promotion of the unsuccessful album.

41. What does the name "Eurythmics" mean?

A.) The band name "Eurythmics" is a Greek word that means, roughly, **"moving in rhythm."** Guitarist Dave Stewart explains that they chose the name because his partner, Annie Lennox, had studied Eurythmy at the London Academy of Music. "It was invented by a nineteenth-century Frenchman," says Stewart, who goes on to explain that this French composer was the first to marry music with rhythm and dance. It was his theory that music was meant to be spirited, and move the listener — a concept Stewart and Lennox regarded highly. They also liked the name for the sum of its parts: Dave and Annie liked that "Eurythmics" has "rhythm" in the middle of the name, and begins in "Eu," which they believed hinted at their European sound. The Eurythmics made a big splash in 1983 with the release of the "Sweet Dreams (are Made of This)," which was a US number 1 hit.

42. UB40 emerged in the 1980 British Ska revival. Where did they get their name?

A.) UB40 are a Birmingham, England-based multi-racial reggae group who took their unusual name from the number on a **British Unemployment Benefit Attendance card.** A friend suggested they name themselves after the governmental paperwork because all the members of the band were on the dole. "We didn't realize it at the time," said Robin Campbell, "but it was a stroke of genius. It meant we had three million fans automatically. But it wasn't a calculated political move. We set out to play reggae and make money." They were regular visitors to the top of the charts in the UK, but failed to duplicate that success in North America. UB40's highest chart position in the US came in 1988 with the re-release of their 1983 cover of the Neil Diamond chestnut "Red Red Wine" (#1 9/03/88 *Billboard*).

Big Bang! Baby

43. Who was Captain Lou Albano, and what was his claim to fame?

A.) "Captain" Lou Albano was a **pro wrestler,** and part of Cyndi Lauper's entourage. He made his video debut in "Girls Just Want to Have Fun," playing Cyndi's dad. Cyndi met Lou during her days as lead vocalist for Blue Angel, and he travelled with her until late 1984 when they had a falling out after Albano said to the press, "Women belong in the kitchen getting pregnant."

44. Who was Jamie Starr?

A.) "Jamie Starr" was an alias that (The Artist Formerly Known as) **Prince** sometimes used when writing songs for other people. The American Society of Composers, Authors and Publishers' records show that Jamie Starr and Prince are the owners of Tionna Music. Their records also show that "Jamie Starr was elected to membership under the name Prince Rogers Nelson." In the past Jamie Starr has been credited with writing music for Vanity, The Time, Apollonia 6, and all but one song on Sheila E's hit record. It is assumed that (The Artist Formerly Known as) Prince used an alias so as not to steal the thunder of the artists he helped.

45. What novel was the band name "Heaven 17" taken from?

A.) The novel that inspired the name "Heaven 17" was *A Clockwork Orange.* In the book Alex asks a record store clerk, "Do you have Johnny Zhivago? The Heaven 17?" Heaven 17 was formed when an early version of Human League broke up, leaving Martyn Ware and Ian Craig Marsh without a band. They recruited former photographer-turned-singer Glenn Gregory and released their first single in 1981. "(We Don't Need This) Fascist Groove Thing" criticized Britain's racism, and was judged too inflammatory to be played on the radio in the United Kingdom. Instead, the song took off in the nightclubs, and news of Heaven 17 spread by word of mouth. While they never cracked the Top 40 in North America, they racked up several hits in their native Britain ("Temptation" and "We Live So Well"). Marsh and Ware also run the British Electric Foundation (BEF), which has produced singles for Tina Turner, Gary Glitter, and Sandie Shaw.

46. Where did the name "Human League" originate?

A.) Human League was originally called "The Future," but they made a name change after playing the **Star Force video game**. The Human League was one of the opposing forces in the game. The League were pioneers in the field of electro-pop under the guidance of Phillip Oakey, Ian Marsh, and Martyn Ware. The latter two left the band in 1980 to form the influential British Electric Foundation, which produced records for Heaven 17 and others.

47. What movie did rockabilly revivalists The Stray Cats pinch their name from?

A.) The Stray Cats borrowed their name from the name of the band in the **David Essex film Stardust.** The rockabilly trio from Long Island had considerable success with their debut album, which spawned the Top 10 hit "Stray Cat Strut" (#3 1/08/83 *Billboard*).

48. Who won the 1984 *Playboy* Boy George look-alike contest?

A.) Comedian **John Candy** won *Playboy*'s 1984 Boy George look-alike contest.

49. How much did Steve Wozniak, organizer of the US Festival, offer The Eagles to play a reunion concert in 1983?

A.) US Festival organizer Steve Wozniak offered The Eagles **$2.1 million** (including video rights) to perform at the US Festival in 1983. The Eagles flatly refused. This beats the three-thousand-dollar offer that Lorne Michaels made to The Beatles to reform on "Saturday Night Live" in 1976. ("You can divide it up any way you want," said Michaels.

Big Bang! Baby

"If you want to give Ringo less, it's up to you.")

50. What set rock band Stryper apart from most heavy metal bands?

A.) Unlike most heavy metal bands, Stryper **sang for God.** In their live shows singer Michael Sweet, his brother drummer Robert, guitarist Oz Fox, and bassist Tim Gaines used to throw Bibles into the audience, just as some bands throw guitar picks and drumsticks at their fans. The Orange County, California, natives say their name is an acronym for Salvation Through Redemption, Yielding Peace, Encouragement, and Righteousness. Stryper broke into the Top 30 once, with "Honestly" (#23 12/26/87 *Billboard*).

51. Who was the best man at Ron Wood's wedding to Jo Howard in January 1985?

A.) **Keith Richards and Charlie Watts** co-best-manned Ron Wood's wedding to Jo Howard. Mick Jagger was on vacation in Mustique and did not attend the wedding at the five-hundred-year-old St. Mary's Church in Denham, England.

52. What did Police drummer Stewart Copeland's father do for a living?

A.) Police drummer Stewart Copeland's father **worked for the CIA.** Miles Copeland II has written two books outlining his experiences, *The Games of Nations* and *The Real Spy World*.

53. What book was Mark Chapman reading on December 8, 1980?

A.) The day Mark Chapman assassinated John Lennon he was seen waiting for John and Yoko, passing the time by reading *Catcher in the Rye* by J.D. Salinger. Also recovered from the site of the shooting was Chapman's autographed copy of the *Double Fantasy* album.

54. In 1983 John Green released a book called *Dakota Days*, billed as

"The true story of John Lennon's final years." What function did Green perform in the Lennon/Ono household that made him privy to Lennon's deepest thoughts?

A.) John Green was **Lennon's tarot card reader**. His book *Dakota Days* details John and Yoko's life between 1975 and 1980, and makes several outrageous claims. Green takes it upon himself to detail the sexual relationship of the couple, spending many pages describing John's terrible temper. As an example of John's temper, he claims that Lennon, in a fit of anger, kicked Sean when he was a baby. Yoko vehemently denied the accuracy of this book.

55. Where was Prince's film *Purple Rain* shot?

A.) Prince filmed his wildly successful film debut, *Purple Rain*, in his hometown of **Minneapolis.** It was shot in seven weeks, starting November 1, 1983, for the relatively small budget of $7 million. It went on to gross $100 million at the box office, making it one of the most successful rock films of all time. Prince plays The Kid, the musician son of an abusive family who vents his frustrations in his music. Ex-Mod Squad star Clarence Williams III takes a turn as Prince's father, while singer Apollonia essays the role of The Kid's abused girlfriend. The soundtrack from *Purple Rain* was Prince's most successful record to date, spawning five Top 30 singles: "When Doves Cry" (#1 6/09/84 *Billboard*), "Let's Go Crazy" (#1 8/11/84 *Billboard*), "Purple Rain" (#2 10/06/84 *Billboard*), "I Would Die for U" (#8 12/22/84 *Billboard*), and "Take Me With U" (#25 3/02/85 *Billboard*).

56. Which David Bowie film marked Marlene Dietrich's first film appearance in seventeen years?

A.) Marlene Dietrich returned to the screen after a seventeen-year absence in the 1979 film ***Just a Gigolo,*** opposite David Bowie. Bowie describes the David Hemmings-directed film as, "my 32 Elvis movies rolled into one."

57. Who animated the 1980 Pink Floyd film *The Wall*?

A.) The animation sequences in Pink Floyd's *The Wall* were visualized by **Gerald Scarfe.** As an artist, Scarfe's connection with rock and roll goes back many years. In 1967 he designed papier-mâché Beatle statues for the cover of *Time*, and later married Paul McCartney's ex-girlfriend Jane Asher.

58. Who played the alienated Pink in Pink Floyd's *The Wall*?

A.) The lead role of Pink in Pink Floyd's *The Wall* was played by two actors. **Bob (Boomtown Rats) Geldof** played the older Pink, while **Kevin McKeon** played him in the film's flashbacks. Bob Geldof claims to get embarrassed when he sees himself in a video or on the screen, so he refused to see the final product until it opened at the Cannes Film Festival. He forced himself to sit in the theatre, watching *The Wall*, and ultimately he had to concede that he enjoyed it, although he said, "it's extremely weird to see yourself the size of a building."

59. What was the first video that Bruce Springsteen consented to appear in?

A.) Bruce Springsteen's first video appearance was in the Brian DePalma-directed **"Dancing in the Dark."** Jeff Stein, who put together the "You Might Think" video for The Cars, was originally slated to direct, but at the last minute Bruce opted for a more conventional approach, an in-concert clip, to be filmed in St. Paul, Minnesota, during his summer tour in 1984. The release of this video boosted the single to the number 2 position, where it sat for four weeks. Previous to the "Dancing in the Dark" video, Bruce had only released one other clip: a video for "Atlantic City" from the *Nebraska* album was released; Bruce, however, is not seen on screen.

60. Which duo created the Duran Duran "Girls on Film" video, Herbie Hancock's "Rockit," and The Police's "Every Breath You Take,"

"Wrapped Around Your Finger," and "Synchronicity II"?

A.) The creative team behind these videos was **Kevin Godley and Lol Creme**. In the late sixties and seventies they were members of 10CC, releasing such hits as "The Things We Do for Love" (#5 1/29/77 *Billboard*) and "I'm Not in Love" (#2 6/14/75 *Billboard*). They left the band in the latter half of the seventies to pursue solo careers and work in film and video.

61 . Which Eurythmics video, featuring a cow, did Dave Stewart describe as a "three-minute surrealist film"?

A.) Guitarist and songwriter Dave Stewart described The Eurythmics' **"Sweet Dreams (are Made of This)"** (#1 6/18/83 *Billboard*) video as a "three-minute surrealist film." The clip features a cow wandering in and out of a corporate boardroom. This was the first outing for The Eurythmics (Stewart and Annie Lennox had released several unsuccessful albums under the name The Tourists), and was a surprise hit. The album was recorded on a home eight-track tape machine for about seven hundred dollars, with Dave Stewart as a first-time engineer and producer. He claims to have had no idea what he was doing, although he has said, "I knew if I pushed this and that, it would sound like this."

62. Who directed "Hello Again" for The Cars?

A.) The "Hello Again" video for The Cars was directed by pop artist and professional celebrity **Andy Warhol.** Warhol became a media personality, and grandfather of the pop art explosion with works such as the Campbell Soup Can print, the famous Velvet Underground *Banana* album cover, and several cult films, including *Chelsea Girls* starring Edie Sedgwick.

63. How much did the "Jump" video cost Van Halen to produce?

Big Bang! Baby

A.) The video for "Jump" (#1 1/21/84 *Billboard*) was filmed with a hand-held 16mm camera. It was directed by the band and supposedly cost a paltry **six hundred dollars** to make. The song was culled from the *1984* album, which was David Lee Roth's last outing with the band. He left to pursue a solo career, which has been up and (mostly) down since 1985.

64. What movie soundtrack video features a scene with Bill Murray breakdancing?

A.) Bill Murray is seen trying to breakdance in the video for Ray Parker Jr.'s **"Ghostbusters"** (#1 6/30/84 *Billboard*). Ray Parker Jr. started his musical career as a session guitar player for the likes of Marvin Gaye and Stevie Wonder. In the late seventies and early eighties he scored several hits as the lead singer of Raydio before embarking on his solo career.

65. Who played the uptight father in Twisted Sister's "We're Not Gonna Take It" video?

A.) The uptight (and abused) father in Twisted Sister's "We're Not Gonna Take It" (#21 8/18/84 *Billboard*) was played by **Mark Metcalf,** better known as Douglas C. Neidermeyer in *National Lampoon's Animal House.*

66. On August 1, 1981, what was the first video to be shown on MTV?

A.) The first video to be shown on MTV was **The Buggles' clip "Video Killed the Radio Star"** (#40 12/15/79 *Billboard*). Since first broadcasting on August 1, 1981, MTV has revolutionised the way people buy music, and the way artists market their music. Initially MTV only had 2,500,000 subscribers. In the next six years that number would grow to 35,800,000 households. As MTV entered the nineties the number continued to grow, its popularity bolstered by programming like "Unplugged" and "Remote Control."

214

67. Cyndi Lauper was not pleased with the twenty extras hired for the "She Bop" video shoot. What did she do about it?

A.) Cyndi Lauper **personally tinted the hair and redid the make-up** of twenty extras for the shooting of her "She Bop" (#3 7/28/84 *Billboard*) video.

68. Who played Michael Jackson's girlfriend in the video "Thriller"?

A.) Michael Jackson's "Thriller" (#4 2/11/84 *Billboard*) girlfriend was played by **Ola Ray.** Ms. Ray once posed nude in *Playboy*, and had bit parts in *10 to Midnight*, *48 Hours*, and *Night Shift* before being discovered by the gloved one. Jackson, a Jehovah's Witness, came under fire from his church over the "Thriller" video. The church elders were concerned that Michael, by making a video featuring zombies and other creatures of the night, was endorsing the occult. They threatened to ostracize him. To placate the church, Jackson initially wanted to destroy all the copies of the video, a move that would have cost millions of dollars in capital and lost income. He finally settled for a disclaimer at the beginning of the song: "Due to my strong personal convictions, I wish to stress that this film in no way endorses a belief in the occult."

69. Carl Simon's hit single "Anticipation" was used as a jingle for what household product?

A.) Carl Simon's "Anticipation" (#13 1/01/72 *Billboard*) was used as a jingle for **Heinz ketchup**. Since the beginning of rock and roll many artists have lent their personalities and music to television and radio advertising. In 1965 The Supremes could be heard singing Coca-Cola jingles on the radio, and later they did television spots for Arrid Extra Dry. Many rock stars got in on the endorsing action in the eighties after Michael Jackson was paid five million dollars for two Pepsi ads. Other Pepsi ads featured Lionel Richie, Glenn Frey, Tina Turner, David Bowie, and Madonna.

Big Bang! Baby

70. In 1984 Michael Jackson had an accident while filming a Pepsi commercial at the Shrine Auditorium in Los Angeles. What happened?

A.) During the filming of a Pepsi commercial at the Shrine Auditorium in 1984 **a spark from a stage explosion ignited Michael Jackson's hair.** His security chief Miko Brando (Marlon Brando's son) was the first to rush onstage and smother the flames. Jackson was treated for second- and third-degree burns at the emergency room of Cedars-Sinai Medical Center. Later he was transferred to Brotman Memorial Hospital in Culver City for overnight care. The burn was the size of a walnut, and Jackson recovered completely.

71. Name the first song that Spinal Tap's Nigel Tufnel and David St. Hubbins wrote together.

A.) The first song that Spinal Tap's Nigel Tufnel and David St. Hubbins wrote together was **"All the Way Home."** The song appears on the fictitious band's 1992 album *Break Like the Wind*.

72. What was the only Gary Numan song to break into *Billboard*'s Top 10 chart?

A.) Gary Numan's soulless, robotic-sounding **"Cars"** peaked at number 9 on the *Billboard* charts on June 7, 1980. Numan retired from the music business in 1981, just a year after his biggest success, although several live albums, re-issues, and a smattering of new material have been released since then. "I've got a very big fear of being a has-been," Numan told *Trouser Press*'s Jim Green. "I'm getting out of it before I get too involved to get out of it. I have to face not being famous anymore."

73. What was Rocky Burnette's one contribution to the *Billboard* Top 10?

A.) Rocky Burnette placed one song in the *Billboard* Top 10. **"Tired of Toein' the Line"** reached number 8 in July 1980. Burnette comes from a musical family. His nephew Billy Burnette has played with Fleetwood Mac, and as members of Memphis's Rock and Roll Trio, his father and uncle, Johnny and Dorsey Burnette, were pioneers in the world of rockabilly. When Rocky was a child, Eddie Cochran, Gene Vincent, and Elvis were frequent visitors to his house, so a career in music almost seemed a given. "Tired of Toein' the Line" was actually the b-side of the single. The a-side was a tune called "Clowns From Outer Space." Not surprisingly, "Clowns" didn't do very well. Radio programmers liked the flipside better, and with their support Burnette scored his one and only hit.

74. What was Roger Daltrey's only solo Top 20 hit?

A.) Roger Daltrey has had a long and distinguished career as the lead singer of The Who. While his solo albums have sold well, he was only able to place one single in the *Billboard* Top 20. **"Without Your Love"** went to number 20 in November 1980.

75. Who scored a number 5 hit with an English-language remake of Falco's "Der Kommissar"?

A.) The East London and Essex quartet **After the Fire** took an English-language version of the German hit "Der Kommissar" to the number 5 position on the *Billboard* charts in 1983. After the Fire (or ATF for short) released three well-received albums in England before their record company decided to take the best cuts from those records and release one compilation disc in North America. That album yielded two hits, "Der Kommissar" and "Dancing in the Shadows," (number 85, *Billboard* 1983), before the band broke up. Falco's original version of "Der Kommissar" made it to the number 10 spot on *Billboard*'s dance/disco chart in 1983.

76. Which fictitious band's output includes *Intravenous De Milo, The Sun Never Sweats, Brain Hammer,* and *Shark Sandwich*?

A.) The fictitious heavy metal band **Spinal Tap** mentions several of their previous albums in their movie *This is Spinal Tap*, including *Intravenous De Milo, The Sun Never Sweats, Brain Hammer*, and *Shark Sandwich*. The Rob Reiner-directed fake rockumentary documents the English heavy metal band Spinal Tap's ill-fated American Tour. The band suffers through many indignities on the road, including a customs agent finding a cucumber stuffed down bassist Derek (Harry Shearer) Small's tight trousers. *This is Spinal Tap* was released in 1984 to lukewarm response, but has become a cult classic.

77. Who sang with Peter Gabriel on 1986's "Don't Give Up"?

A.) Peter Gabriel and **Kate Bush** dueted on "Don't Give Up," from Gabriel's mega-hit *So*. Gabriel wrote the song after studying a photograph from the American Depression called *This Proud Land*, and relating it to his home country. "Don't Give Up" is his response to the rampant unemployment in Britain. He has said that the song is on the edge of being a cliché, but it was Bush's heartfelt vocal that saved the song, "the way she sang it came across as real."

78. Which science fiction television program inspired a number 1 UK hit for The Firm in June 1987?

A.) The Firm scored a number 1 hit in the UK with "Star Trekkin'" in June 1987. A parody of The Firm's hit, the B-Boys' "Star Wrekkin'," flopped later that same summer. **"Star Trek"** has inspired many songwriters, notably keyboardist George Duke, whose 1976 album *Solo* includes "Spock Gets Funky" and "Vulcan Mind Probe," and T'Pau, who took their unusual name from a Vulcan stateswoman. As well, the psychedelic band Spirit used the sampled voices of Kirk, Spock, and McCoy on their 1977 album *Future Games*.

79. Who did Brian Johnson replace in AC/DC?

A.) AC/DC recruited Brian Johnson to replace gravel-voiced singer **Bon Scott** in AC/DC in 1980. Scott, who had choked to death on his vomit after a bout with the bottle, had been with the band since the mid-seventies, lending vocals to explosive singles like "Dirty Deeds Done Dirt Cheap" and "Big Balls." Brian Johnson was best known for his work with the British heavy metal outfit Geordie. He debuted with AC/DC on the *Back in Black* album, which broke the band into the mainstream, selling over twelve million copies.

80. Who is Stuart Leslie Goddard better known as?

A.) Stuart Leslie Goddard is better known as **Adam Ant.** He formed Adam and the Ants after the break-up of his first band, Bazooka Joe and the B-Sides. In 1979 the original Ants were lured away by pop music Svengali Malcolm McLaren to form Bow Wow Wow with singer Anabel Lwin. The second band of Ants was led by guitarist Marco Pirroni, who with Adam Ant co-wrote all of The Ants' chart toppers. In the United States the band is best known for their 1982 Top 20 single "Goody Two Shoes" (#12 12/11/82 *Billboard*), although they had a string of Top 5 hits in the United Kingdom ("Stand and Deliver," "Prince Charming," "Dog Eat Dog," "Antmusic," and "Kings of the Wild Frontier").

81. Who teamed with rap band Run-D.M.C. for a cover of "Walk This Way" in 1986?

A.) **Aerosmith** and Run-D.M.C. shared label credits on 1986's remake of "Walk This Way." The old Aerosmith chestnut was the first mainstream single to mix rap and rock, a combination that propelled the record into the Top 10.

82. Which progressive rock veterans joined forces to form Asia?

A.) Asia was a progressive rock supergroup formed by drummer **Carl Palmer** (ex-Emerson, Lake and Palmer), guitarist **Steve Howe** (ex-Yes), keyboardist **Geoff Downes** (ex-Buggles and Yes), and bassist and vocalist

John Wetton (ex-Roxy Music and Uriah Heep). Their 1982 eponymous debut album topped the US album charts for over two months, and spawned two Top 20 singles, "Heat of the Moment" (#4 5/01/82 *Billboard*) and "Only Time Will Tell" (#17 8/14/82 *Billboard*).

83. Which Italian-American film star did Bananarama musically pay tribute to in 1984?

A.) Bananarama (Sarah Dallin, Keren Woodward and Siobhan Fahey) paid tribute to their favourite American movie star in 1984's **"Robert DeNiro**'s Waiting." The song only managed number 95 on the *Billboard* charts, but broke into the Top 3 in Britain. Their biggest success came in 1986 with their remake of the Shocking Blue hit "Venus," which topped the charts in the US, a feat they would not repeat. Siobhan Fahey left the band following her marriage to Eurythmic Dave Stewart, and formed Shakespeare's Sister. Woodward and Dallin continued on, adding Jacqui O'Sullivan to the line-up. One album later, 1991's *Pop Life*, O'Sullivan left the band, leaving Woodward and Dallin to forge on as a duo, releasing two albums, 1992's *Please Yourself* and 1995's *Ultra Violet*.

84. Which Bangles' hit appeared on the soundtrack for the film *Less Than Zero*?

A.) The Bangles' remake of Simon and Garfunkel's **"A Hazy Shade of Winter"** appeared on the 1987 soundtrack for the film *Less Than Zero*. The Bangles pushed the song to number 3, beating Simon and Garfunkel's original 1966 chart placing by ten points (#13 11/19/66 *Billboard*).

85. What is Patricia Andrzejewski better known as?

A.) Patricia Andrzejewski is known to the public as **Pat Benatar**. A trained opera singer, Benatar was working as a singing waitress and entering talent shows when she was discovered by rock impresario Rick Newman. He guided her towards the hard rock sound that boosted her up the charts in the early to mid-eighties. In 1985 after a string of hits ("Hit Me With Your Best Shot," "Love is a Battlefield," and "We Belong") and hundreds of live shows, she took some time off to start a family with husband (and band leader) Neil Geraldo.

86. Name the two singers, other than Ozzy Osbourne, who have provided lead vocals for Black Sabbath.

A.) Ozzy Osbourne left Black Sabbath in 1979 citing artistic differences. In 1980 he was replaced by American heavy metal singer **Ronnie James Dio**, who guided the band through three big-selling albums, *Heaven and Hell*, *Mob Rules*, and *Live Evil*. In 1983 **Ian Gillan** took over vocal chores from Dio for one album, *Born Again*. The band called it a day in early 1984, although the original line-up (including Osbourne) reunited for the Live Aid concert in 1985.

87. Whose filmography includes roles in *Union City* (1979), *Roadie* (1980), *Videodrome* (1982), and *Hairspray* (1988)?

A.) **Debbie Harry** of Blondie fame has tried her hand at acting in *Union City* (1979), *Roadie* (1980), *Videodrome* (1982), and *Hairspray* (1988). Aside from acting for the large screen, Debbie provided the theme for Richard Gere's 1980 feature *American Gigolo*. The song "Call Me" was co-written with techno-wizard Giorgio Moroder, and hit number 1 on both sides of the Atlantic.

88. Who was the first artist to simultaneously appear on the *Billboard* charts with a solo single, a duet, and as a member of a trio?

A.) In 1985 **Kim Carnes** was the first artist to appear on the charts with a solo single ("Invitation to Dance"), a duet ("Make No Mistake, He's Mine," with Barbra Streisand), and as a member of a trio (the Top 20 hit "What About Me," with Kenny Rogers and James Ingram). Her breakthrough hit was 1981's "Bette Davis Eyes" (#1 4/11/81 *Billboard*), which stayed at number 1 for nine weeks.

Big Bang! Baby

89. What does Ozzy Osbourne have tattooed on his left hand?

A.) Ozzy Osbourne has **O-Z-Z-Y** tattooed on his left hand — one letter per finger. Osbourne made the headlines in 1981 when he bit the head off a live dove during a meeting with record company executives. He made more headlines later that year when a fan threw a bat onstage during a live show. Thinking it was a stuffed bat he tried to bite the head off. It was a real bat, who bit Ozzy first, forcing him to undergo a painful series of anti-rabies shots.

90. Who was Bruce Springsteen's first wife?

A.) Bruce Springsteen's first wife was **Julianne Phillips.** They were married on May 15, 1985, after having met backstage at one of his concerts just six months before. They were divorced three years later, and Springsteen subsequently married his backup singer Patti Scialfa.

91. Who were Bruce Springsteen's best men at his wedding to Julianne Phillips?

A.) Bruce Springsteen had three best men at his 1985 wedding to Julianne Phillips. Standing up for Bruce were his manager and producer, **Jon Landau,** sax player **Clarence "Big Man, Master of the Universe, Emperor of Everything" Clemons,** and long-time friend and ex-E Street Band guitar player **Miami Steve Van Zandt.**

92. What was the name of Jerry Hall's tell-all book released in 1985?

A.) Mick Jagger's companion Jerry Hall released ***Jerry Hall's Tall Tales*** (written with Christopher Hemphill) in 1985. The book includes warts-and-all stories of her romances with Bryan Ferry and Mick Jagger, as well as anecdotes about Grace Jones and her years as a high-fashion model.

93. What is the name of Grace Jones's character in the 1985 James Bond film *A View to a Kill?*

222

A.) In the 1985 James Bond film *A View to a Kill,* Grace Jones plays a character called **May Day.** The film had another musical connection with Duran Duran scoring a number 1 hit with the title song.

94. Who sang a duet with Annie Lennox on "Sisters are Doin' It for Themselves," taken from the 1985 Eurythmic album *Be Yourself Tonight?*

A.) **Aretha Franklin** teamed up with Annie Lennox on "Sisters are Doin' It for Themselves" on the 1985 Eurythmic release *Be Yourself Tonight.* Several stars make cameo appearances on this album: Stevie Wonder performs a harmonica solo on "There Must be an Angel (Playing With My Heart)," while Elvis Costello lends his vocals to another cut.

95. Which Police video shows Sting wandering through a maze of church candles in slow motion?

A.) In the Police video **"Wrapped Around Your Finger"** Sting is seen wandering through a maze of church candles in slow motion. The clip was produced by Godley and Creme, who shot at sixty frames per second, which is double the normal, so that when played back the video would be in slow motion. To synchronize Sting's mouth to the soundtrack they had to teach him to sing at double speed during the taping of the video, so his lips would be moving in time with the music in the final edit.

96. Which Eurythmics video features cameos by Bananarama, pop singer/transvestite Marilyn, and celebrity look-alikes for Debbie Harry, Liz Taylor, and Sophia Loren?

A.) The Eurythmics video for **"Who's That Girl"** (#21 5/19/84 *Billboard*) features cameos by Bananarama, pop singer/transvestite Marilyn, and celebrity look-alikes for Debbie Harry, Liz Taylor, and Sophia Loren.

223

Big Bang! Baby

97. Where did Nick Lowe get the title for his 1989 "Best of" disc, *Basher*?

A.) Nick Lowe's **father,** who was a pilot in the RAF, nicknamed his son "Basher," which is Battle of Britain pilots' slang. In 1989 Nick Lowe titled his "Best of" collection *Basher* in tribute to his father.

98. Why did Sir Dennis Eton-Hogg sue Spinal Tap?

A.) Sir Dennis Eton-Hogg was the head of Spinal Tap's former record company, Polymer. He sued the band over the **"lack of talent"** clause in their contract. At press time the band and Hogg were still in litigation.

99. Which popular heavy metal band originally recorded under the name The Southern Death Cult?

A.) **The Cult** reached the English charts in 1983 with a collection of radio, stage, and studio sessions released under the name *The Southern Death Cult*. It wasn't until guitarist Billy Duffy and drummer Ray Mondo joined singer Ian Ashbury in 1984 that they became The Cult. As The Cult they enjoyed four years of chart success, placing "She Sells Sanctuary," "Rain," and "Love Removal Machine" in the upper echelons of the Top 10 on both sides of the Atlantic.

100. Which punk band did Captain Sensible play bass for?

A.) Captain Sensible was the bass player for **The Damned.** The Damned set a number of firsts in punk rock. They were the first punk band to release a single (followed by an album), perform on television, and tour the United States. Captain Sensible left the band in 1982 after the success of his solo single "Happy Talk" (#1 1982 *New Musical Express*).

101. Which funk/rock singer occasionally uses the pseudonym

"Incredible" E.G. O'Reilly?

A.) Funk/rock singer **Terence Trent D'Arby** released a single in 1989 under the name "Incredible" E.G. O'Reilly. At age 18 D'Arby (born in New York, 1962) joined the army, and was stationed in Elvis Presley's old regiment in Germany. After his release from duty he relocated to London, where he signed a record deal with CBS. After great success in the UK, he managed to top the American charts in 1988 with "Wishing Well" (#1 2/27/88 *Billboard*) and "Sign Your Name" (#4 6/18/88 *Billboard*), both culled from his debut, *The Hardline According to Terence Trent D'Arby.*

102. What band was Vince Clarke in before forming Yazoo in 1981?

A.) Before forming Yazoo, Vince Clarke played synthesizer in **Depeche Mode**. Clarke was the main songwriter on the band's first album release *Speak and Spell*, and author of their first two Top 20 singles, "New Life," and "Just Can't Get Enough." Clarke left Depeche Mode (he was replaced by Alan Wilder) and teamed up with Alison Moyet to form Yazoo in 1981. (For legal reasons the band was known as "Yaz" in North America.)

103. Which popular "New Romantic" band spawned the part-time groups The Power Station and Arcadia?

A.) Members from **Duran Duran** splintered off to form The Power Station and Arcadia. In 1985 Duran guitarist and bassist Andy and John Taylor joined with singer Robert Palmer to make The Power Station, who hit the Top 10 with their remake of T Rex's "Get It On" (#9 6/22/85 *Billboard*). Arcadia (Simon LeBon, Nick Rhodes, and Roger Taylor) came together later that same year, released one album, and cracked the Top 10 with "Election Day" (#6 11/02/85 *Billboard*), which featured narration by Grace Jones.

104. Which 1988 Steve Earle single featured The Pogues?

Big Bang! Baby

A.) The Pogues played backup to country-rocker Steve Earle on **"Johnny Come Lately"** from the 1988 album *Copperhead Road*. This unlikely collaboration came about after an all-night drinking session that ended up in Livingstone Studios in London, England. The single failed to make an impression on the charts.

105. Who starred in Rob Zombie's favourite movie, *White Zombie*?

A.) *White Zombie* is an obscure 1932 **Bela Lugosi** film. In the movie a young couple gets married on a Haitian plantation run by the conniving Monsieur Beaumont. Beaumont turns to Lugosi's character, Legendre, to turn the young woman into a zombie, so that he may control her mind and, more importantly, her body. Film historians call this one "Lugosi's forgotten masterpiece." Rob Zombie (real name: Robert Cummings) borrowed the name in 1985 when he teamed up with bassist Sean Yseult to form a band (White Zombie) that would combine their affections for hardcore punk, trashy art, gory theatre, and B-movies.

106. Who was the first singer to place singles in the *Billboard* Top 10 black music, disco, pop, MOR, and country charts?

A.) The first singer to place singles in the *Billboard* Top 10 black music, disco, pop, MOR, and country charts was **Sheena Easton.** Singles from the country-flavoured Kenny Rogers duet "We've Got Tonight" (#6 1/29/83 *Billboard*) to her raunchy take on Prince's "Sugar Walls" (#9 1/19/85 *Billboard*) have garnered her airplay on many radio formats. In 1992 she took on the lead female role in a Broadway production of *Man of LaMancha* opposite Raul Julia.

107. Which Frederick Pohl novel inspired the band name "Icicle Works"?

A.) Icicle Works was formed in Liverpool, England in the early eighties by Ian McNabb (vocals/guitar), Chris Layhe (bass), and drummer Chris Sharrock. They took their name from a futuristic Frederick Pohl detective novel titled **The Day the Icicle Works Closed Down**. "We

226

chose the name because it was imaginative," McNabb told *Rolling Stone* in 1984. Icicle Works had one US hit, "Whisper to a Scream (Birds Fly)," which barely breached the Top 40, hitting number 37 in 1984.

108. Who were the only American-based artists to appear on the Band Aid charity single "Do They Know It's Christmas"?

A.) The only American-based artists to appear on the 1984 Band Aid charity single "Do They Know It's Christmas?" were **Kool and the Gang**. Other artists involved in the recording of the song included members of Culture Club, Bananarama, Duran Duran, U2, and solo stars Phil Collins, Sting, George Michael, and Paul Young. Bob Geldof spearheaded a campaign to raise money to aid the citizens of Ethiopia after seeing horrific pictures of that country's famine on television. Geldof oversaw every aspect of the record's manufacture, production, and distribution, ensuring that famine relief received over 96 pence of the £1.35 retail price.

109. What inspired the band name "My Bloody Valentine"?

A.) Singer/guitarist Kevin Shields, drummer Colm O'Ciosoig, vocalist Dave Conway, and keyboardist Tina formed My Bloody Valentine in 1984, naming themselves after **a 1981 low-budget Canadian horror film**. Starring Paul Kelman and Lori Hallier, *My Bloody Valentine* is the grim story of a masked man who kills people with an axe on the eve of the annual Valentine's Day dance.

110. What was the inspiration for the band name "Marillion"?

A.) The Aylesbury, England, progressive rock band Marillion was originally called Silmarillion after **the J.R.R. Tolkien novel**.

111. What was the inspiration for the band name "The Mekons"?

A.) Formed in Leeds, England, in the late seventies, The Mekons took their name from **a 1950s British comic strip called *Dan***

227

Dare. A Mekon was a tyrannical alien that terrorized Earth.

112. What movie was the inspiration for the band name "Ministry"?

A.) Chicago-based Al Jourgensen originally called his band **Ministry of Fear** after **a 1944 Ray Milland film**. Jourgensen came across the offbeat spy melodrama late one night while channel surfing on television. He had been searching for a band name and liked the sound of the film's title. Later he changed the name to Ministry of Truth, then Ministry of Canned Peaches, and then, finally to Ministry.

113. What inspired the band name "The Thompson Twins"?

A.) Fronted by the trio of Tom Bailey (vocals/synthesizer), Alannah Currie (xylophone/percussion), and Joe Leeway conga/synthesizer), The Thompson Twins were actually a seven-piece band. They took their name from a pair of hapless detectives from **Herge's *Tin Tin* comic books**. They scored their biggest North American hit in 1984 with "Hold Me Now" (number 3).

114. What song inspired the band name "Wet Wet Wet"?

A.) Scottish pop band Wet Wet Wet took their name **from a line in the Scritti Politti song "Getting Having and Holding."** Their 1987 debut album, *Popped In Souled Out* (produced in Memphis by veteran soul-producer Willie Mitchell) climbed to number 2 on the UK albums charts. The band was sued by British music legend Van Morrison that same year for the use of his song lyrics in their song "Sweet Little Mystery." The case was settled out of court, and the song reached the British Top 10.

115. What is the longest word ever used in a hit song?

A.) According to British journalists John Tobler and Alan Jones the longest word ever used in a hit song is **Taumatawhaka**

tangihangako ayayauotama teaturipuk akapikimau ngahoronuky pokaiwhenua kitanatahymat akooatan anookawami chitoura — that's 116 letters. Translated into English the unwieldy word means, "A hill whereupon was played a flute of Tamatea, circumnavigator, of lands for his lady love." The Maori word appeared in the British hit "The Lone Ranger" by Quantum Leap. When asked why he included the word in a song about the Lone Ranger, Quantum Leap leader Rupert Hines said, "There were two reasons for using that word. First, we didn't have anything at the start to grab the listener's attention. And then I came across the word, apparently the longest in the world, and decided that, as nobody knows where the Lone Ranger is supposed to come from, we could put forward the theory that it was there."

116. How did the members of The Gap Band come up with their name?

A.) Soul trio The Gap Band created their name as **an acronym for the streets in their neighbourhood** in Tulsa, Oklahoma: **G**reenwood, **A**rcher, and **P**ine. Three brothers, Charles, Ronnie, and Robert Wilson, formed the group in the early seventies, following in the footsteps of their musical cousin Bootsy Collins of Funkadelic. In 1982 they placed two songs in the *Billboard* Top 40: "Early in the Morning" (number 24) and "You Dropped a Bomb on Me" (number 31), although they had better luck on the R&B charts, placing several singles in the Top 10. After the band's dissolution, Charles Wilson played with the Eurythmics.

117. What inspired the band name "Cinderella"?

A.) Cinderella members Tom Kiefer and Eric B. borrowed their heavy metal band's moniker from **a soft-core porn movie** of the same name. The Pennsylvania-based group placed five songs in the *Billboard* Top 40, including "Nobody's Fool" (number 13, 1987) and "Don't Know What You've Got (Till It's Gone)" (number 12, 1988).

118. What well-known British record chain inspired the band name "Bow Wow Wow"?

A.) The members of Bow Wow Wow came together in 1980 at the behest of ex-Sex Pistols manager Malcolm McLaren. He paired Adam Ant's original backup band with singer Annabella Lwin, a fourteen-year-old he had discovered at his local dry cleaner. When they signed to EMI, McLaren came up with the name "Bow Wow Wow" in tribute to Nipper the Dog, the mascot of **HMV Ltd**, a record chain owned by EMI. The band scored two UK Top 10 hits with "Go Wild in the Country" and "I Want Candy" before disbanding in 1983. In the last days of the band a second singer named Lieutenant Lush was introduced to add some zip to the concept. Lush never recorded with Bow Wow Wow, but subsequently did find stardom with Culture Club under the name Boy George.

119. Where did the band name "Love and Rockets" come from?

A.) The band name "Love and Rockets" was borrowed from **the underground comic book** series of the same name. The comics are written and produced by Los Angelenos brothers Gilbert and Jaime Hernandez. Love and Rockets was formed from the ashes of Bauhaus, best known for gloom and doom Goth tunes like the eight-minute epic "Bela Lugosi's Dead." Bauhaus fractured in 1983, with members Daniel Ash (guitar), David J (bass), and Kevin Haskins (drums) leaving to form Tones on Tail, while singer Peter Murphy coupled with Japan's Mick Karn to form Dali's Car. A proposed 1985 Bauhaus reunion was scuttled when singer Murphy backed out at the last minute. The other three decided to continue without Murphy, and formed Love and Rockets. Their sound was a danceable take on the Bauhaus sound, and yielded the hits "Ball of Confusion" and "So Alive."

120. Who are the subjects of the Bruce Springsteen song "Nebraska"?

A.) Bruce Springsteen followed up the enormous success of *The River* with 1982's *Nebraska*. In contrast to the full-frontal musical assault of *The River*, *Nebraska* is forged in a bleak, acoustic style that profiles those left behind by the American dream. The title track is an account of

230

Charles Starkweather and Caril Fugate, the Lincoln, Nebraska, couple who went on a killing spree in 1958.

121. Who produced the original recording of Joan Jett's "I Love Rock and Roll"?

A.) Joan Jett originally recorded "I Love Rock and Roll" in 1978 with producers **Steve Jones and Paul Cook**, ex-Sex Pistols. Their version of the song was only released in Holland as a b-side of "You Don't Own Me," a re-working of the old Leslie Gore hit. While working with producers Ritchie Cordell and Kenny Laguna, Jett recorded a slicker version of the tune in 1981. At first radio stations wanted nothing to do with the tune, but through relentless touring and promotion, Jett created a demand for the song. By early 1982 radio stations were flooded with calls requesting "I Love Rock and Roll," and in March the tune began a reign at number 1 on the *Billboard* charts that lasted seven weeks. Even though she has played the song hundreds of times, Jett never tires of it. "We played a show for the Olympic athletes," she says. "An athlete from Sudan saw me, he was walking down the street in the Olympic Village, and he yelled 'I love rock and roll.' I don't even think he spoke English. The feeling that gave me, it's hard to explain to people."

122. What book inspired the band name "Level 42"?

A.) The Manchester, England-born founders of the band Level 42 took their name from the Douglas Adams novel ***The Hitchhiker's Guide to the Galaxy***. In the book Adams answers the question "What is the meaning of life?" with the flippant answer "42." Level 42 (and the incredible bass-slapping/thumb technique of Mark King) were popular in the UK but their pop/jazz/soul fusion only yielded one Top 10 hit in North America, 1986's "Something About You" (number 7).

123. Who collaborated with Olivia Newton-John on the title track of 1980's *Xanadu*?

A.) Olivia Newton-John and **The Electric Light Orchestra** teamed up for "Xanadu" (#8 8/30/80 *Billboard*), the title track to Newton-John's failed 1980 musical. The movie failed to stir much interest with movie fans, but the soundtrack did well, providing three Top 20 hits for Olivia (one solo, one with ELO, and a duet with Cliff Richard).

124. From which movie did R.E.M. borrow the title for *Life's Rich Pageant?*

A.) When looking for a title for their 1986 release R.E.M. were inspired by the line, "It's all part of life's rich pageant," from the Peter Sellers movie *A Shot in the Dark*. *Life's Rich Pageant*, produced by John Cougar Mellencamp and Don Gehman, became R.E.M.'s first gold record, and produced the single "Fall on Me."

125. Which mid-eighties band did actress Terri Nunn sing with?

A.) Actress Terri Nunn vocalized with **Berlin,** and scored a Top 30 hit in 1984 with "No More Words" (#23 4/07/84 *Billboard*). As an actress Nunn appeared in the disco movie *Thank God It's Friday*, and was nominated for an Emmy for her work on the series "Lou Grant."

126. Who topped the US charts in 1983 with "Come On Eileen"?

A.) The Celtic-influenced "Come On Eileen" (#1 2/26/83 *Billboard*) was a number 1 hit for **Dexy's Midnight Runners.** The band grew out of Kevin (a.k.a. Carlo Rowland) Rowland's late-seventies punk band The Killjoys, who released a single in 1978 called "Johnny Won't Get to Heaven" before changing their musical direction. Dexy's Midnight Runners borrowed their name from a type of speed very popular in their home town of Birmingham.

127. What was the first Queen album to use synthesizers?

A.) The first Queen album to feature synthesizers was 1980's *The Game.* Up until that time their unique operatic sound had been accomplished by studio trickery with man-made sounds. The album *The Game* and its lead-off single, "Play the Game," were the first US chart entries to feature synthesizers.

128. Which Queen video features the members of the band dressed as women?

A.) The video for **"I Want to Break Free"** shows the members of Queen dressed as women. Brian May wears a pink satin slip, with his hair in curlers; John Deacon is a society matron with a fox stole; Roger Taylor is a school girl, with long blonde hair in pigtails; and Freddie Mercury is the moustachioed, leather-skirted dominatrix. The video was shot in support of *The Works*, Queen's 1984 album release.

129. What team was Paula Abdul a cheerleader for?

A.) Paula Abdul started cheerleading for the **Los Angeles Lakers** when she was 17. She began choreographing the cheerleaders shortly afterward. In interviews Abdul takes credit for having changed the style of professional cheerleading. She banished pom poms, and broke new ground by leading her squad into "serious dancing." Her sports choreography was noticed by several record industry insiders, and led to work with The Jacksons and Janet Jackson.

130. Which dance music star had featured acting roles in the sitcoms "Good Times" and "Diff'rent Strokes," and the musical-drama series "Fame"?

A.) **Janet Jackson's** résumé includes featured roles in the sitcoms "Good Times" and "Diff'rent Strokes." It was her work on the series "Fame" that led to the recording of her first album and launched her singing career. She issued two unsuccessful albums before teaming with producers Jam and Lewis, who are responsible for her platinum-selling dance records *Control* and *Rhythm Nation 1814*.

131. Which R&B group's sole attempt at disco was 1980s "Exodisco"?

Big Bang! Baby

A.) **Huey Lewis and the News** took a stab at disco with 1980's "Exodisco." The song fared poorly on the charts, so the band abandoned disco, and turned back to their R&B roots. In 1982 they hit the charts with their second album, *Picture This*. A string of hits followed ("Heart and Soul," "I Want a New Drug," "The Heart of Rock and Roll," and "If This is It"), and they sold over seven million albums. Huey Lewis (real name: Hugh Cregg) made his motion picture debut in *Back to the Future*, for which he also sang the theme song ("The Power of Love") in 1985.

132. Who organized the Artists United Against Apartheid single "Sun City"?

A.) The Artists United Against Apartheid was organized by Bruce Springsteen's ex-guitar player **Little Steven Van Zandt.** Little Steven wrote the protest song "Sun City" (#38 12/07/85 *Billboard*), and arranged for forty-nine artists to lend their vocal and musical accompaniment. The song rails against the practice of apartheid and musicians who play in South Africa's Sun City. All proceeds of this Top 40 song went to aid political prisoners in South Africa.

133. What was the name of Madonna's first movie?

A.) Madonna's first movie was 1981's soft core *A Certain Sacrifice.* In the summer of 1979 Madonna answered an ad seeking "a dark, fiery young woman, dominant, with lots of energy, who can dance and is willing to work for no pay." The ad was placed by director Stephen Lewicki, who was casting the low-budget ($20,000) feature. After sifting through the hundreds of responses to his ad, Lewicki cast Madonna in the lead role of Bruna. In the film Bruna is brutally raped, and with the help of three "sex slaves," she hunts down the rapist, kills him, and performs a sacrificial ceremony with his body. *A Certain Sacrifice* was released in theatres in 1981, and resurfaced on video once Madonna became a superstar.

134. Which future superstar played drums in The Breakfast Club in 1979–80?

A.) **Madonna** played drums with The Breakfast Club in 1970–80. The name of the band was inspired by the early morning breakfasts the band would share after their all-night rehearsals. When singer Angie Smit tired of playing in New York's sleaziest bars and quit the band, Madonna moved from behind the drum kit to centre stage. She left The Breakfast Club after eight months, and formed her own band, known variously as The Millionaires, Modern Dance, and Emanon (read it backwards), before settling on Emmy (one of Madonna's nicknames). Emmy dissolved in 1981 when Madonna decided to become a solo act.

135. Which Irish band graced the cover of *Time* in April 1987?

A.) **U2** were on the cover of *Time* in April 1987. The band was riding high with the success of *The Joshua Tree*, and had just topped the US charts for the first time with "With or Without You." U2 was only the third rock and roll band to adorn *Time*'s coveted cover — The Beatles and The Who preceded them.

136. What is Paul Hewson better known as?

A.) Paul Hewson is better known as **Bono**, the lead singer of U2. The nickname dates back to the late seventies, when he and a group of his friends passed a hearing-aid store called Bonovox on O'Connell Street (opposite the Gresham Hotel) in Dublin. Roughly translated the name means "good voice," so his friends dubbed him Bono Vox, which he felt sounded more like a rock star than Paul Hewson.

137. What is the origin of U2's name?

A.) The name U2 was thought up by **graphic designer Steve Averill.** The band had been called The Hype, but were looking for a new moniker. Averill suggested U2, the name of an American spy plane,

biBang! Baby

a submarine, and a line of Eveready batteries. The band liked the sound of the name, and its pun — "You Too." For a time they used both names, playing one night as The Hype and the next as U2. They officially switched to U2 in 1979.

138. What garden did Yoko Ono dedicate on October 9, 1985?

A.) "This garden, it's a living memorial," said Yoko Ono at the October 9, 1985, dedication ceremonies of **Strawberry Fields** in New York City's Central Park. John Lennon would have been 45 on that day. Yoko's donation of one million dollars helped to revitalize a two-and-a-half-acre part of Central Park, and turn it into Strawberry Fields, an "international garden of peace" in John Lennon's name. The name was taken from the Salvation Army Children's Home in Liverpool, England, that inspired the famous Beatles song. Central Park's Strawberry Fields has been planted with trees, plants, shrubs, and 25,000 strawberry bushes, donated by over one hundred different countries. A plaque reads "Strawberry Fields Forever" — "Imagine All the People Living in Peace," while the word "Imagine" is set into a mosaic pattern on the ground.

Set into a path near Central Park's entrance at 72nd Street in New York, the "Imagine" flat stone monument is the centrepiece of the John Lennon memorial Strawberry Fields.

Photo by Richard Crouse

139. Who was Cyndi Lauper's backup band on her platinum selling debut *She's So Unusual*?

A.) Cyndi Lauper's backup band on her platinum-selling debut *She's So Unusual* was **The Hooters.** After working with Lauper, and writing the hit "Time After Time" (#1 4/21/84 *Billboard*), the Philadelphia-based band was being touted as the next big thing. They proved the rock critics wrong with the release of their debut album. 1985's

Nervous Night failed to live up to expectations, and their first single "All You Zombies," lacked the charm and exuberance of their work with Lauper. "Zombies" barely snuck into the Top 60. They justified their potentially offensive name by claiming that it was the nickname of their keyboard-harmonica.

140. What 1984 song saw a collaboration between Michael Jackson and Mick Jagger?

A.) Michael Jackson and Mick Jagger collaborated on the 1984 single **"State of Shock"** (#3 6/30/84 *Billboard*). The song was taken from The Jacksons' album *Victory*, which was the first time Michael had recorded with his brothers in four years. The Jagger/Jackson collaboration was roundly bludgeoned by the rock press, but the public bought it, propelling "State of Shock" to *Billboard*'s Top 5. Years later Michael expressed his dislike of Jagger. He told friends that Jagger can't sing, and that he almost ruined "State of Shock."

141. Which weight-loss/aerobics guru tried to add "singing sensation" to his résumé with the release of "This Time" in 1982?

A.) Infotainment host and weight-loss/aerobics guru **Richard Simmons** tried to add "singing sensation" to his résumé in 1982 with the release of "This Time," his first single on Elektra Records. The heavily synthesized record was designed to make you feel good about yourself and get up and exercise. Richard sings, "No one means more than you this time," and "Don't you know for *every* change there might be pain inside you?" The song, taken from the album *Reach*, failed to make the charts, and Richard gave up his singing aspirations.

142. Who teamed up in 1986 to release *Phantom, Rocker, and Slick*?

A.) After their defection from The Stray Cats in 1985, **Jim Phantom** and **Lee Rocker** teamed with ex-David Bowie session player **Earl Slick** to form an eighties "supergroup" called Phantom, Rocker, and Slick.

Big Bang! Baby

They released an eponymous album in 1986 to a critical lambasting, and public indifference. After their second album flopped, Phantom, Rocker, and Slick called it quits. The rhythm section returned to their rockabilly roots and reunited with Stray Cat Brian Seitzer. Earl Slick went on to forge a successful career as a session guitar player.

143. Which former Pink Floyd member released a concept album featuring the twin brothers Benny and Billy?

A.) Ex-Pink Floyd bassist **Roger Waters'** 1987 *Radio K.A.O.S.* told the story of Benny, a coal miner with a ham radio, and his twin brother Billy. As the preposterous story unfolds, the inventor of the atomic bomb expresses guilt, Benny moves to America and meets a Los Angeles disc jockey, and Billy saves the world. The disc reached number 50 on the album charts, but did not excite the singles market at all.

144. Who released *Alive, She Cried* in 1983?

A.) *Alive, She Cried* is a live album pieced together from sound checks, and assorted **Doors** gigs from 1968 to 1970. *The Rolling Stone Album Guide* only awarded *Alive She Cried* two stars, placing it in the "fair to poor" category.

145. Who was the lead singer for the hard rock band Blackjack?

A.) The former Michael Bolotin — now called **Michael Bolton** — was the spandex-clad, lion-maned singer of the hard rock outfit Blackjack. Bolton's recording career began at age 15, when his high school band The Nomads was signed to Epic Records. Two unsuccessful singles later they were cut loose, and Michael set out on his own. His solo career fizzled, so he bought some tight pants, permed his hair, and formed Blackjack. Their one and only release stiffed in 1983, leaving Michael free to explore other career options. He made his first big splash as a songwriter. In the mid-eighties everyone from Barbra Streisand to KISS and from Kenny Rogers to Cher covered his songs. In 1987 he stepped back into the spotlight, with a little less hair, and an easy listening approach. "That's What Love is All About" (#19 11/07/87 *Billboard*) was his first Top 20 hit, and paved the way for his brand of overwrought middle-of-the-road tunes.

146. What is the Kalamazoo, Michigan, Burger King's rock and roll claim to fame?

A.) The Burger King in Kalamazoo, Michigan, will go down in rock and roll history books as one of the most famous places **frequented by Elvis Presley** — after his death in 1977. A recent study reported that 7 percent of all Americans think that Elvis is still alive. Given that statistic it is not unusual that he has allegedly been spotted several times: once at Graceland (on the second floor); at a gas station near Nashville; while allegedly working behind the fast food booth at the Air Force Museum in Dayton, Ohio; and on author Gail Brewer-Giorgio's answering machine. The Kalamazoo incident, however, really captured the public's attention. A Michigan housewife claims she spotted him at the drive-through window of the Burger King driving a red Ferrari. Given Elvis's predilection for junk food, many of the Presley faithful felt this sighting might be authentic.

147. Which aptly named rap trio boasted a combined weight of over 750 pounds?

A.) Darren "The Human Beat-Box" Robinson, Mark "Prince Markie Dee" Morales, and Damon "Kool Rock-ski" Wimbley — better known as the **Fat Boys** — boasted a combined weight of over 750 pounds. They are best known for their takes on nostalgic rock songs. In 1987 they scored a Top 20 hit with a rap remake of "Wipeout" (#12 8/08/87 *Billboard*), followed by a rap/dance mix of "The Twist" (#16 7/09/88 *Billboard*), which featured "stupid def vocals" by Chubby Checker. As comedic actors they starred in the 1987 film *Disorderlies*.

148. Who scored a Top 10 hit in 1988 with a rock and roll remake of the Loggins and Messina hit "Your Mama Don't Dance"?

Big Bang! Baby

A.) The Harrisburg, Pennsylvania, rock quartet **Poison** scored a Top 10 hit with their remake of Loggins and Messina's hit "Your Mama Don't Dance" (#10 3/04/89 *Billboard*). The original version of the song broke into the Top 5, finally resting at number 4 in 1972. Poison — Bret Michaels (vocals), CC DeVille (guitar), Rikki Rockett (drums), and Bobby Dall (bass) — went on to break into the Top 5 with "Unskinny Bop" (#3 7/14/90 *Billboard*) and "Something to Believe In" (#4 10/20/90 *Billboard*).

149. Which Canadian group had a number 1 hit with "When I'm With You" in 1988, a full five years after they had broken up?

A.) In one of the more bizarre stories to grace the Top 40, Canadian group **Sheriff** had a number 1 hit with "When I'm With You" (#1 12/17/88 *Billboard*), a full five years after they had disbanded. An American radio station stumbled across the obscure Sheriff album and began to play the song, which became a favourite with listeners. The song's reputation soon spread across the country, and it moved up the charts, despite the fact that the band was no longer together. Sheriff broke up in 1983 with band members Wolf Hassell and Arnold Lanni leaving to form Frozen Ghost, while singer Freddy Curci and Steve DeMarchi put together Alias. Sheriff did not reform after the phenomenal success of "When I'm With You," although they did produce a video to promote the song.

150. Which two artists scored number 1 hit singles with remakes of Tommy James and the Shondells tunes in 1987?

A.) **Billy Idol** (real name: William Broad) and teeny-bopper chanteuse **Tiffany** both scored number 1 hits with remakes of Tommy James and the Shondells songs in 1987. Idol's live take on "Mony Mony" (#1 9/26/87 *Billboard*) entered the charts the same week as Tiffany's version of "I Think We're Alone Now" (#1 9/26/87 *Billboard*). "Mony Mony" remains Billy Idol's only number 1 hit, although he reached number 2 with "Cradle of Love" (#2 6/02/90 *Billboard*) from the soundtrack of the

Andrew Dice Clay film *The Adventures of Ford Fairlane*.

151. Which year's Grammy presentations were dubbed "the Michael Jackson show" by several media watchers?

A.) The Grammy Awards for **1983** (broadcast on February 28, 1984) were dubbed "the Michael Jackson show" after he swept the awards, and added eight awards to his collection (Album of the Year, Record of the Year, Best Male Pop Vocal Performance, Best Male Rock Vocal Performance, Best New Rhythm and Blues Song, Best Male R&B Vocal Performance, Producer of the Year, non-classical (with Quincy Jones), and Best Recording for Children for *E.T.: The Extra-Terrestrial*). He broke a record for most Grammys won in one year formerly held by Roger Miller, who took home six statues in 1965 for "King of the Road." Other big winners that year included Sting, who won the New Song of the Year award for "Every Breath You Take" (#1 6/04/83 *Billboard*), and Culture Club, who were given the nod as Best New Artist.

152. Who were the only Grammy winners to be stripped of their award?

A.) The only Grammy winners ever asked to return their award were **Milli Vanilli** (the name means "positive energy" in Turkish), after it came to light that they had not actually sung on their record. Session singers Johnny Davis, Brad Howell, and Charles Shaw actually supplied the vocals for the dreadlocked duo. They were given the nod as Best New Artist in 1989, despite being voted Worst New Artist in the *Rolling Stone* Critics' Picks Poll. When the fraud was uncovered the press were quick to poke fun at the disgraced singers — *The New York Post* ran the frontpage headline "Milli Vanilli, Phoney Baloney!" Rock critics revelled in the news, as many had reported a rumour that Rob Pilatus and Fabrice Morvan had very little to do with the making of the Milli Vanilli album. Newspapers were delighted to reprint earlier statements by Pilatus like, "Musically we are more talented than Bob Dylan," and "I'm the new Elvis" in stories that exposed their true talents. Arista Records settled a class-action suit out of court, giving former Milli Vanilli fans coupons that could be redeemed for

241

more authentic Arista releases.

153. Which Mötley Crüe album carried a sleeve warning against drunk driving?

A.) Mötley Crüe's 1985 album **Theatre of Pain** included a sleeve warning against drunk driving after singer Vince Neil (real name: Vincent Wharton) was involved in an alcohol-related auto fatality. He was brought up on charges, given twenty days in jail and a large fine, and was commanded to perform two hundred days of community service, performing lectures at schools on the dangers of drugs and alcohol. *Theatre of Pain* produced the Top 20 hit, "Smokin' in the Boys Room" (#16 8/03/85 *Billboard*), a remake of the Brownsville Station tune.

154. Which member of Mötley Crüe did bass player Matthew Tripp claim to have impersonated for two years while the real member recuperated from a serious car accident?

A.) Not since the days of the "Paul is Dead" rumour has a story like this surfaced in rock and roll. Matthew Tripp claims that he stepped in and assumed the role of **Nikki Sixx** onstage and in the studio for two years while Sixx recuperated from a serious car accident. In 1988 he sued the band to gain what he considered to be his rightful share of songwriting royalties. The case is still pending.

155. Who produced Liza Minnelli's 1989 album *Results*?

A.) Neil Tennant and Chris Lowe, better known as the **Pet Shop Boys,** produced Liza Minnelli's 1989 album *Results*, which earned three stars from *Rolling Stone*. The album features orchestration by frequent David Lynch collaborator Angelo Badalamenti, and techno-dance versions of Stephen Sondheim's "Losing My Mind" and Tanita Tikaram's "Twist in My Sobriety." The Pet Shop-penned "Losing My Mind" went Top 10 in Britain.

156. Who scored a number 1 hit with a reggae-styled version of the Neil Diamond song "Red Red Wine"?

A.) The Birmingham, UK, multi-racial reggae group **UB40** scored a number 1 hit with Neil Diamond's "Red Red Wine" in 1988. The 1988 release was a re-issue of an earlier single, which only reached number 34 during its original run in 1984. While the band has consistently released fine records of original material, they have found the most chart success with remakes of popular songs from the sixties. They broke into the Top 30 in 1985 with a cover of the Sonny and Cher chestnut "I Got You Babe" (#28 9/07/85 *Billboard*), with The Pretenders' Chrissie Hynde assisting on vocals. 1990 saw them hit the Top 10 with a reggae-styled "The Way You Do the Things You Do" (#6 10/27/90 *Billboard*). Later that same year they teamed with Robert Palmer for a revival of Bob Dylan's "I'll Be Your Baby Tonight," which cracked the UK Top 20. Their original tunes tend to examine the state of the world and voice their strong political opinions.

157. Which real-life brothers played the vicious Kray siblings in the 1988 film *The Krays*?

A.) **Ex-Spandau Ballet brothers Gary (guitar) and Martin (bass) Kemp** were cast as the Kray brothers — the vicious East End gangsters who ruled London's underground in the 1960s. The portrayal of the brothers spanned the Krays' entire lives, from young up-and-coming killers to the old imprisoned men. *The Krays* was released in 1988 to favourable reviews and box office success on both sides of the Atlantic, and the Kemp brothers garnered good notices for their work.

158. Who is the only artist to ever win Grammys in the four top categories — Album of the Year, Record of the Year, Song of the Year (songwriter's award), and Best New Artist — in the same year?

243

A.) The only artist to ever sweep the Grammys' four top categories — Album of the Year, Record of the Year, Song of the Year (songwriter's award), and Best New Artist — in the same year was **Christopher Cross** in 1980. Paul Simon and Carole King both came close, but failed to pick up the Grammy for Best New Artist. Cross's eponymous debut album produced three Top 20 hits, "Ride Like the Wind" (#2 3/01/80 *Billboard*), "Sailing" (#1 7/05/80 *Billboard*), and "Never Be the Same" (#15 10/25/80 *Billboard*), and sold three million copies. The following year he would lose in the Grammy race, but pick up an Oscar for "Arthur's Theme (Best That You Can Do)" (#1 8/29/81 *Billboard*), the title track of the Dudley Moore film *Arthur*. His last chart entry was 1983's "Think of Laura" (#9 12/24/83 *Billboard*), which gained popularity from the day-time soap opera "General Hospital." The Texas native has since parted ways with Warner Brothers, and produces his records independently.

159. Who was awarded a rhodium-plated disc from *The Guinness Book of World Records* in 1980 for being history's all time best-selling songwriter and recording artist?

A.) **Paul McCartney** was honoured by *The Guinness Book of World Records* in 1980 with a rhodium-plated disc as history's all time best-selling songwriter and recording artist. Rhodium is a precious metal, similar to platinum.

160. Who was the subject of a *Rolling Stone* cover featuring the headline "He's hot, he's sexy and he's dead"?

A.) **Jim Morrison** appeared on a 1981 *Rolling Stone* cover with the headline, "He's hot, he sexy and he's dead." The pouting cover photograph was taken in New York City by *16 Magazine* editorial guru Gloria Stavers in 1968. The story inside focused on the renaissance of Morrison's popularity, ten years after his death. *Rolling Stone* editors call this their most famous, "or notorious," cover line ever.

161. Who was commissioned by dance legend Twyla Tharp to write the score for her hour-long ballet *The Catherine Wheel?*

A.) Dance legend Twyla Tharp commissioned Talking Heads leader **David Byrne** to score her 1981 ballet *The Catherine Wheel*. She had previously used the music of Chuck Berry, The Beach Boys, Bruce Springsteen, and Supertramp in her work, but had never before hired someone from the rock world to write music for her company. The show ran for a month at the Broadhurst Theatre on Broadway before embarking on a North American and European tour. A filmed version of the show appeared on PBS in March of 1983.

Jim Morrison's final resting place at Le Père Lachaise Cemetery, Paris, France. Morrison was interred here after dying of a heart attack following years of drug abuse. Also buried here are Chopin, Moliere, Colette, Marcel Proust, Sarah Bernhardt, Edith Piaf, and Oscar Wilde.

Photo by Anne Yurek

162. Which band recruited Norman Cook (a.k.a. Fatboy Slim) to play bass?

A.) Norman Cook became the bass player for the Hull, England-based group **The Housemartins** in 1985. He performed on all their biggest hits, including "Caravan of Love" and "Happy Hour," before leaving the band, citing a dissatisfaction with the musical direction the group was taking. Since leaving The Housemartins, Cook has formed Beats International (who scored a UK number 1 with "Dub be Good to Me"), and Freakpower, whose song "Turn On Turn In Cop Out" was used as the soundtrack for a major advertising campaign from Levi-Strauss. Next came Pizzaman, and again one of their songs ("Happiness") was used in an advertising campaign, this time for Del Monte. In 1996 Cook

245

adopted the alter-ego of Fatboy Slim, and has released a string of catchy singles, including "The Rockafeller Skank" and "Praise You."

DO YOU REMEMBER?
The 1990s

1. Who said, "I just had a psychedelic experience" after seeing her father perform "Purple Haze" at the 7th Annual Rock and Roll Hall of Fame induction ceremonies in January 1992?

A.) **Roseanne Cash** described watching her father, Johnny Cash, jam "Purple Haze" (with the likes of Keith Richards and Jimmy Page) at the 7th Annual Rock and Roll Hall of Fame induction ceremonies as "a psychedelic experience." The senior Cash was inducted into the Hall of Fame with other music greats like The Yardbirds, Bill Graham, and Doc Pomus.

2. What inspired the title of The Sugarcubes' 1992 release *Stick Around for Joy*?

A.) The Sugarcubes borrowed the title for their 1992 release *Stick Around for Joy* from a **slogan on a Japanese soda pop machine**. This album marked the band's first recording foray outside their native Iceland. Most of the album was laid down at Bearsville Studios near Woodstock, New York.

3. Who shared this secret with concert audiences in 1992: "I am a ... L... L... Lawrence Welk fan."

A.) **k.d. Lang** told audiences in 1992 that she was "a ... L... L... Lawrence Welk fan." Since publicly coming out of the closet, Lang

Big Bang! Baby

has been outspoken on l... l... lesbian issues, most notably in the gay magazine *The Advocate*. Her live show features a set piece with a bubble machine and a chandelier, in tribute to Lawrence Welk.

4. What are Dawn, Terry, Cindy, and Maxine better known as?

A.) Dawn Robinson, Terry Ellis, Cindy Herron, and Maxine Jones are better known as **En Vogue.** A group of singers from the San Francisco area, they were brought together by producers Denzil Foster and Thomas McElroy. En Vogue hit the number 2 spot on the *Billboard* charts in 1990 with "Hold On" (#2 5/12/90 *Billboard*) from their debut album. *People* called En Vogue "The Supremes of MTV" in their Best of Song column in 1992.

5. Which singer made his motion picture debut in Robert Altman's *The Player*?

A.) Country-swing singer **Lyle Lovett** made his motion picture debut in Robert Altman's 1992 film *The Player*. The movie is a satirical look at modern-day Hollywood, with a star studded cast that includes Tim Robbins, Susan Sarandon, Bruce Willis, Whoopi Goldberg, and cameos by some of Hollywood's biggest names. In late 1992 the New York Film Critics Circle named *The Player* as best picture of the year, with Altman picking up Best Director credits.

6. Who posed on the cover of *Rolling Stone* wearing a t-shirt that read "Corporate Magazines Still Suck"?

A.) **Kurt Cobain** of Nirvana posed on the cover of *Rolling Stone* in 1992 wearing a t-shirt that said "Corporate Magazines Still Suck." Cobain was stung by some fans' assertion that by posing on the cover of *Rolling Stone*, he had "sold out."

7. Who sang a duet of "Bohemian Rhapsody" at April 1992's AIDS benefit and tribute to Freddy Mercury?

248

A.) The unlikely duo of **Elton John and Axl Rose** performed "Bohemian Rhapsody" at April 1992's AIDS benefit and tribute to Freddy Mercury. The singers were chosen because Elton John and Mercury were friends, and Axl Rose has said that Queen's music was a big influence on him. Elton teamed with Guns n' Roses later the same year for a live performance of "November Rain." The four-hour benefit concert was beamed out live to an audience of millions, and included stirring versions of Queen's songs by some of today's leading performers. Highlights included George Michael's stirring version of "Somebody to Love," and the Annie Lennox/David Bowie duet on "Under Pressure."

8. Who encouraged you to *Check Your Head* in 1992?

A.) **The Beastie Boys** encouraged the public to *Check Your Head* in 1992. After hitting the top of the charts with their *Licensed to Ill* debut album, the Beasties fell into a commercial slump. Their second release, *Paul's Boutique,* was critically revered, but failed to make any impact with buyers. King Ad-Rock (real name: Adam Horovitz, the son of playwright Israel Horovitz) took a brief vacation from the band to star in 1988's *Lost Angels.* Back in the studio, the band took a different approach on *Check Your Head*, mixing pre-recorded samples and live instrumentation into their song arrangements.

9. What forced Elton John to hop offstage during a 1993 concert in Melbourne, Australia?

A.) A **plague of grasshoppers** invaded a 1993 Elton John concert in Melbourne, Australia, and forced him to prematurely end the show. Newspaper reports said John played for two hours while the insects landed in his hair, clothes, and mouth. He finally stopped the show when the infestation made the stage too dangerous to perform on. The city of Melbourne was invaded by thousands of grasshoppers that flew in from the dry grasslands to the north and northwest of the city. The concert's promoter, Patti Mostyn, expressed surprise that Elton stayed onstage for as long as he did.

Big Bang! Baby

10. Who did Paula Abdul marry in April 1992?

A.) Paula Abdul and **Emilio Estevez** tied the knot in April 1992. Before becoming a recording star Abdul made a name for herself as a choreographer. She won the 1986 MTV Choreographer of the Year Award for her work on Janet Jackson's "Nasty" video. Videos by Duran Duran, ZZ Top, Luther Vandross, and The Jacksons as well as Oliver Stone's *The Doors* all bear the Abdul brand. Her debut album *Forever Your Girl* (1988) broke records when it stayed in the US Top 10 longer than any other artist's debut.

11. Who replaced guitarist Steve Clark in Def Leppard in 1992?

A.) Late Def Leppard guitarist Steve Clark, who died in January 1991 of alcohol-related causes, was replaced by **Vivian Campbell.** No stranger to heavy metal, Viv has played with Dio and Whitesnake. He debuted with Def Leppard at the Freddy Mercury Tribute at Wembley Stadium in April 1992. Clark's death marked the second time tragedy had struck the band: Drummer Rick Allen lost an arm in a car accident on New Year's Eve in 1984. He now plays a specially designed drum kit that allows him to keep time with his feet, and has remained a fully active member of the band.

12. Who released "Peace in LA" as a reaction to the Los Angeles riots in May 1992?

A.) Los Angeles resident **Tom Petty** released "Peace in LA" just two days after the violence began. "There was nothing I could do," he says, "but I didn't want to just sit and watch TV." He donated all the proceeds from the song to the efforts to rebuild the riot-torn areas of Los Angeles.

13. What popular television show featured Bruce Springsteen's first ever TV guest shot?

A.) Bruce Springsteen made his first live television appearance on **"Saturday Night Live"** in May 1992. He debuted his new band, and played three songs from his *Lucky Town* and *Human Touch* albums. "Saturday Night Live" has a tradition of presenting great musical acts, ranging from The Grateful Dead to Ornette Coleman to Stevie Ray Vaughan. The musical guests on "SNL"'s first show in 1975 were Billy Preston and Janis Ian, followed by a Simon and Garfunkel reunion on the second show. Producer Lorne Michaels says that he has only two criteria in selecting the musical acts for the show: they have to sound great and have a large dose of energy in the music.

14. Who did David Bowie marry in April 1992?

A.) David Bowie and supermodel **Iman** were wed twice during 1992. In April they tied the knot in a civil ceremony in Switzerland, then redid their vows in front of friends and family in a Florence church in June. Two versions of the song Bowie composed for the church ceremony, "The Wedding Song," appear on his 1993 release *Black Tie White Noise*. The album opens with an instrumental take on the song and closes with a vocal version, with Bowie crooning about being good, "just like a good boy should." Both had been married before. Iman brought a daughter, Zulekha (age 14), into the marriage, while Bowie has a son Joe (christened Zowie), who was 21.

15. Who caused a stir in 1992 with the song "Cop Killer"?

A.) Rapper **Ice-T** and his speed metal band Body Count grabbed headlines in 1992 with the release of "Cop Killer." Police groups everywhere objected to the theme of the song, in which a psychopath wants revenge on a bad cop. The controversy grew after the L.A. riots, with members of congress, Oliver North, Dan Quayle, and George Bush condemning the tune. Ice-T voluntarily withdrew the song after threats of violence were made against several Warner Brothers executives.

Bang! Baby

16. Who did Edie Brickell marry in June 1992?

A.) Singer Edie Brickell tied the knot with pop legend **Paul Simon** in June 1992. Brickell is best known for the 1989 hit "What I Am" (#7 1/14/89 *Billboard*) with the Dallas-based band New Bohemians. Her father is a pro bowler and is much respected on the bowling circuit. Simon has had several high-profile romances. While in university he briefly dated singer/songwriter Carole Klein, who changed her name and found fame as Carole King. Simon's two-year marriage to actress Carrie Fisher ended in divorce in 1985.

17. Which Elvis Presley image appeared on a US stamp — the heavy Vegas Elvis, or the young rocking singer?

A.) The US Postal Service kicked off its fourteen-part Legends of American Music with a stamp commemorating **the young Elvis** in January 1993. The stamp became one of the biggest-selling stamps in American history, but it was not the first stamp to honour Elvis. New Guinea was the first country to immortalize Presley on a stamp, closely followed by the Republic of Central Africa and Germany. At the time of their issue collectors paid between four dollars and twenty-five dollars for first-day covers of these stamps.

18. Who organized England's first ever National Music Day in July 1992?

A.) **Mick Jagger** organized England's first-ever National Music Day with the assistance of Charlie Watts and Ron Wood. The National Music Day sponsored concerts, parades, and street performances from one end of the country to the other.

19. What was the name of Madonna's steamy big-screen murder mystery, co-starring Willem Dafoe?

A.) The MGM release ***Body of Evidence*** was Madonna's erotic big-screen murder mystery. Madonna plays Rebecca Carlson, who is

252

accused of killing an older, wealthy man with sex. Carlson then seduces, and has an affair with, her lawyer, played by Willem Dafoe. Dafoe's defence rests on the premise that, "it's not a crime to be a great lay." Madonna's best line? "Have you ever seen animals make love, Frank? It's intense." The media focused on the nudity and sex, rather than Madonna's acting ability.

20. Which popular vocal group is comprised of the children of John and Michelle Phillips and Brian Wilson?

A.) **Wilson Phillips** is a group of second-generation music stars. Chynna Phillips is the daughter of a Mama and a Papa — Michelle and John Phillips — while Wendy and Carnie Wilson are the offspring of Beach Boy Brian Wilson. Their 1990 eponymous debut topped the charts, spawning three number 1 singles — "Hold On" (#1 4/07/90 *Billboard*) "Release Me" (#1 7/21/90 *Billboard*), and "You're in Love" (#1 2/23/91 *Billboard*).

21. What is the name of Kurt Cobain and Courtney Love's child?

A.) Kurt Cobain and Courtney Love had a daughter, **Frances Bean Cobain**, who was almost nine pounds at birth. In an interview with *Spin* Love claimed that Frances looked like Yoda. Love, who fronted a band called Hole, came under fire in the September 1992 issue of *Vanity Fare*, where it was suggested that she used heroin while she was pregnant. Both she and her husband, Nirvana's late leader Kurt Cobain, vehemently denied this accusation, with Love saying that she is more disciplined and responsible than the *Vanity Fare* article portrayed her. "I'm not insane," she said.

22. Who are The Rock Bottom Remainders?

A.) The Rock Bottom Remainders are a cover band made up of some of today's best-selling authors. **Stephen King, Matt Groening, Dave Barry, and Amy Tan** perform rock classics like "Louie Louie" and

"Teen Angel." In 1992 they released a video, with the proceeds going to charity. Remainder's merchandise includes t-shirts that read "This band plays music as well as Metallica writes novels."

23. Which alternative band broke into the Top 10 in 1992 with the release of *BloodSugarSexMagik*?

A.) **The Red Hot Chili Peppers** enjoyed their biggest hit to date with 1992's *BloodSugarSexMagik*. The album produced the Top 10 hit "Under the Bridge," and saw them headlining the mega-popular Lollapalooza Tour. The album, a red-hot fusion of funk, speed thrash, rap, and risqué lyrics, was recorded in a haunted house in the Chili Peppers' native Hollywood Hills.

24. Who was Temple of the Dog dedicated to?

A.) The Seattle "supergroup" Temple of the Dog, and their eponymous one-off album, were dedicated to the memory of **Andrew Wood**, the late singer for Mother Love Bone. Wood had been a seminal figure in the Seattle "grunge" scene, but died before attaining the success of some of his friends, notably Nirvana, Pearl Jam, and Soundgarden. In tribute various members of these bands — Soundgarden singer Chris Cornell and drummer Matt Cameron, with Mother Love Bone (later of Pearl Jam) guitarist Stone Gossard and bassist Jeff Ament — recorded *Temple of the Dog*. The CD stiffed upon initial release in 1990, but was quickly reissued in 1992 after the Seattle craze started. Heavy rotation of the "Hunger Strike" video on MTV helped push this album up the charts.

25. Who played Citizen Dick, Matt Dillon's backup group in the film *Singles*?

A.) Matt Dillon's backup group in the movie *Singles* was played by **Pearl Jam.** The film, which is set in Seattle, was shot half a year before Pearl Jam's debut album *Ten* was released. Luckily for the filmmakers, the movie opened just as Pearl Jam was working their way up to the number 2 spot on the charts.

26. Which alternative band released *Psalm 69: The Way to Succeed and the Way to Suck Eggs* in 1992?

A.) *Psalm 69: The Way to Succeed and the Way to Suck Eggs* was the brainchild of Al Jourgensen and **Ministry.** Ministry first came to prominence in the early eighties with the techno-pop stylings of "(Everyday is) Halloween," "Revenge," and "I Wanted to Tell Her." Their sound grew much more aggressive over the years, incorporating speed metal in their industrial music. *Spin* critic Mark Blackwell describes the *Psalm 69* album as sometimes sounding "like a war."

27. Which 1992 movie saw Whitney Houston's acting debut?

A.) Whitney Houston made her acting debut in 1992's ***The Bodyguard,*** opposite Kevin Costner. In the film she plays a singer/actress who is on the bad end of death threats from a deranged fan. Costner is hired to protect her, but they fall in love, which complicates their relationship. The movie earned lukewarm reviews, although it did spawn a successful soundtrack album. Whitney's take on "I Will Always Love You" shot up the charts, hitting number 1 the week the film opened. Neither Costner or Houston were the first choices for their roles. In fact they weren't the second or third choice either. The script was written in the early seventies as a vehicle for Ryan O'Neal and Diana Ross. In the next twenty years many others considered the story — Chaka Khan and Sylvester Stallone, and Debbie Gibson and Dolph Lundgren to name a few.

28. What is the name of Neil Young's sequel to 1972's *Harvest*?

A.) In 1992 Neil Young released ***Harvest Moon,*** the continuation of 1972's *Harvest.* For the recording of *Harvest Moon,* Young gathered all the original players from the *Harvest* sessions. To closely recapture the *Harvest* sound, he insisted that they play the original instruments from those 1972 sessions. Famous friends who reappear on the 1992 album include James Taylor, Linda Ronstadt, and Nicolette Larson.

29. Where did the name for R.E.M.'s 1992 album *Automatic for the People* come from?

A.) R.E.M. named their 1992 release *Automatic for the People* in tribute to their favourite **soul food restaurant** in their home town of Athens, Georgia. At Weaver D's Delicious Fine Foods every customer's whim is met with the reply, "Automatic!" Owner Dexter "Automatic!" Weaver is capitalizing on his new-found fame by selling Weaver D t-shirts and licence plates. For ordering information, write Weaver D's, 1016 Broad Street, Athens, GA 30601.

30. Which seventies rock legend arranged the strings on R.E.M.'s *Automatic for the People*?

A.) The lush string arrangements for R.E.M.'s *Automatic for the People* were done by Led Zeppelin's **John Paul Jones**. Before joining Led Zeppelin John Paul Jones (real name: John Baldwin) was a well-known session player and arranger, having worked on records by Lulu, Donovan, and Dusty Springfield.

31. What mishap almost cost Metallica a lead singer in 1992?

A.) Metallica lead singer and rhythm guitarist James Hetfield was almost killed during a show at Montreal's Olympic Stadium on August 8, 1992, when **he stepped into a special effects flame pod**, inflicting deep second- and third-degree burns on his arms. Luckily his large, double-necked guitar deflected the flames away from his body, but his eyebrows and hair were singed by the blast. A riot ensued later the same night when the show's headliners, Guns n' Roses, cut their show short, citing Axl Rose's voice problems.

32. Which Madonna album was advertised as "Aural Sex"?

A.) Madonna's ***Erotica*** album was advertised as "Aural Sex," in an effort to tie in with her controversial art book *Sex.* The basic tracks for the album were recorded on an eight-track tape deck, to which Madonna would add her vocals. Finishing touches were then added at Soundworks Studio in Manhattan. *Erotica* was kept out of the number 1 spot by Garth Brooks' *The Chase.*

33. Which faded rap star appears with Madonna in her book *Sex*?

A.) Madonna and **Vanilla Ice** posed for several provocative photos for Madonna's 1992 book *Sex*. Madonna said she wanted Vanilla Ice for the "kitsch value." Other models included socialites Daniel de la Falaise and Titiana Von Furstenburg; supermodels Naomi Campbell and Isabella Rossellini; and Julie Tolentino, owner of Manhattan's lesbian Clit Club. The Mylar-encased (to discourage browsing in the store) book sold over 500,000 copies in the first week of its release.

34. Who was *Amused to Death* in 1992?

A.) Pink Floyd founding member **Roger Waters** released *Amused to Death* in September 1992. It was his third solo album since splitting from Pink Floyd in 1983. Waters says that most of the songs developed from watching television and "checking out what's been going on for the last few years." Side musicians on *Amused to Death* include Jeff Beck, Don Henley, Andy Fairweather-Low, Rita Coolidge, and P.P. Arnold.

35. What do the bands Morbid Angel, Carcass, and Deicide all have in common?

A.) The bands Morbid Angel, Carcass, and Deicide are all practitioners of **"death metal."** *Pulse Magazine* calls death metal "the last train out in heavy metal violence." It is characterised by extremely fast

257

guitars, and graphic, gruesome lyrics. Morbid Angel's David Vincent says that there is a lot going on musically in death metal, "like Black Sabbath on a couple of pots of coffee."

36. Who is the boss at More Protein Records?

A.) **George O'Dowd,** better known as Boy George, is the founder of the More Protein label, a subsidiary of Virgin Records. 1992's *Closet Classics, Volume 1* compilation of the label's artists includes classically trained Swiss singer Eve Gallagher, and white female rapper MC Kinky. Protein artists E-Zee Possee had a minor hit with "Love on Love" in 1991. "I wanted to prove to myself, not necessarily others," said George, "that I could do something substantial and classy."

37. Which rock superstar was featured in his own comic from DC Comics in 1992?

A.) **Prince** became part of DC Comics' superhero stable, alongside Superman and The Flash, in 1992 when *Prince: Alter Ego* was released. Splashy cover art was provided by Brian Bolland, known in comic book circles for his work on *Batman: The Killing Joke.* The stories combine events from Prince's life, intertwined with visual representations of his songs. The comic books appeared under DC's Piranha Music label.

38. Who was 3rd Bass ridiculing with their song "Pop Goes the Weasel" in 1992?

A.) Rap band 3rd Bass was poking fun at white rapper **Vanilla Ice** in their 1992 song "Pop Goes the Weasel." MC Serch, head mouthpiece for 3rd Bass, said that Vanilla Ice is the Pat Boone of rap, and hired punk singer Henry Rollins to portray Ice in the video for the song. On their previous album, *The Cactus Album,* they went after MC Hammer, questioning his street credibility. Shortly after the release of "Pop Goes the Weasel" MC Serch left 3rd Bass, releasing a solo album called *Return of the Product.* On his first solo outing he continued to harangue rapper Hammer, rapping, "He'd be my bitch if me and him were in the slammer."

39. Which 1992 movie starred Mick Jagger, Emilio Estevez, and Anthony Hopkins?

A.) Mick Jagger, Emilio Estevez, and Anthony Hopkins all shared top billing in 1992's *Freejack*, a film based on the novel *Immortality* by Robert Sheckley. Jagger plays a twenty-first century bounty hunter who is out to get Emilio Estevez. Supporting actors include Rene Russo, Anthony Hopkins, Jagger's then-wife Jerry Hall, and ex-New York Dolls singer David Johansen.

40. Who are the members of Little Village?

A.) Little Village is a supergroup with drummer **Jim Keltner**, bassist **Nick Lowe,** guitarist and vocalist **John Hiatt,** and slide guitar genius **Ry Cooder**. Their eponymous debut album in 1992 contains a clue to the origins of their name: the song "Don't Bug Me When I'm Working" contains a snippet of a conversation between Leonard Chess and blues great Sonny Boy Williamson. They are arguing over the title of a song. Fed up, Williamson says, "A little village, motherfucker! You name it what you want. You name it your mammy if you want to."

41. How did Michael Jackson offend the people of Abidjan, Ivory Coast, during his visit to Africa in 1992?

A.) Michael Jackson offended the citizens of Abidjan, Ivory Coast, by **holding his nose** while boarding a plane at the airport. The African media jumped all over this insult. *Ivoir'soir*, a large African newspaper, wrote, "The American sacred beast took it upon himself to remind us we are underdeveloped, impure. Our air is polluted, infested with germs. And it's not this mutant genius, this voluntary mutant, this re-created being, bleached, neither white nor black, neither man nor woman, so delicate, so frail, who will inhale it." In response a report from the

259

Jackson camp said that the nose-touching was simply a "nervous twitch."

42. What band did ex-Eurythmic Dave Stewart form after his 1991 split with Annie Lennox?

A.) After Dave Stewart and Annie Lennox decided to dissolve the Eurythmics in 1991, Stewart went on to form **The Spiritual Cowboys.** The eponymous debut from the band was slickly produced, but failed to enjoy any chart action. Many critics likened it to mid-eighties Bowie, with a dash of folk-rock Dylan thrown in. The Spiritual Cowboys were comprised of session players, with only one well-known name in the band — ex-Pretender Martin Chambers on drums.

43. Who has *The Guinness Book of World Records*' title as World's Fastest Rapper?

A.) *The Guinness Book of World Records* handed the title of World's Fastest Rapper to **JC-001** (real name: Jonathan Chandra Pandy). His record-breaking rap included 530 words per minute, 611 syllables per minute, and 10.3 syllables per second. The British rapper was discovered by ex-Eurythmics guitarist Dave Stewart and immediately signed to Stewart's Anxious Records. His debut album, *Blah, Blah,* was produced by funkmeister George Clinton. JC-001 wants to be taken seriously as an artist. In response to those who think of him as a novelty act, he points out that he has more lyrics in one verse of his songs than Lou Reed does on an entire album.

44. Who formed The Ju-Ju Hounds after splitting from Guns n' Roses?

A.) Guitarist **Izzy Stradlin** debuted with the Ju-Ju Hounds after splitting from Guns n' Roses in 1991. Stradlin (real name: Jeffrey Isbell) was one of Guns n' Roses' main songwriters, contributing "Patience," "Pretty Tied Up," and "Right Next Door to Hell" to the G n' R songbook. The Ju-Ju's eponymous debut album features guest spots from Ron Wood, Ian McLagan, and reggae singer Mickey Dread.

45. Who released "Don Henley Must Die" in 1990?

A.) **Mojo Nixon** released the single "Don Henley Must Die" as a follow up to his other "hits" "Debbie Gibson is Pregnant With My Two-Headed Love Child," "Elvis is Everywhere," and "(619) 239-KING." In August 1992 Henley joined Mojo onstage to sing "Don Henley Must Die," a less-than-flattering tribute to the ex-Eagle. After the show Mojo said that Don must "have balls the size of church bells."

46. Which Olympic team used Grateful Dead-designed shirts as their uniform in the 1992 Olympics?

A.) The **Lithuanian basketball team** entered the 1992 Summer Olympics wearing Grateful Dead tie-dyed t-shirts. The shirts were a big hit, and went on sale for forty-three dollars, eventually selling more than eighty thousand. If you are a Dead fan, but too conservative to wear a tie-dyed shirt, don't despair: a Jerry Garcia-designed necktie might be just the thing for you. Bloomingdales (and other fine stores) sold over ten-million-dollars worth of Mr. Garcia's ties in 1992. Even Al Gore, the Vice President of the United States, has been seen wearing a J. Garcia.

47. How did Sinead O'Connor outrage television viewers on October 3, 1992?

A.) Sinead O'Connor upset many viewers of television's "Saturday Night Live" when she **tore up a photograph of the Pope** during her guest spot on the popular comedy show. During her a cappella version of Bob Marley's "War" she destroyed the photograph, while chanting, "You've got to know who the real enemy is. Fight the real enemy." While the show's producers claimed that they were not aware that she was going to deface the photo, other celebrities were quick to comment. Madonna said, "I think there is a better way to present her ideas than ripping up an image that means a lot to other people."

48. Whose trademark is "Is it live, or is it Vig"?

Big Bang! Baby

A.) "Is it live, or is it Vig?" is the trademark of record producer **Butch Vig.** Vig was thrust into prominence after his work with the Seattle grunge band Nirvana. After sales of the Vig-produced Nirvana disc *Nevermind* hit the mega-million stage, his live-off-the-floor sound made him and his Smart Studios (in Madison, Wisconsin) much sought after. His work with Smashing Pumpkins and the Young Fresh Fellows won him the CMJ New Music Producer of the Year Award in 1991.

49. What did Peter Gabriel describe as "the worst job I ever had"?

A.) Peter Gabriel described the **filming of his "Digging in the Dirt" video** as "the worst job I ever had." Gabriel had to lie perfectly still for four hours, with a wasp taped to his face, while snails crawled over his forehead and eyes. The resulting video features a time-lapsed clip of the bug "choreography" and was banned by many television stations: TV programmers deemed the promo too disturbing.

50. Who is the boss at Maverick Records?

A.) **Madonna** is the boss at Maverick Records. She was given the go ahead to set up the label as part of her multi-million dollar deal with Time-Warner, signed in 1992. At press time Maverick had signed several artists. The first band to ink a deal with Madonna was a black rap group called Proper Grounds. They are described as a mix between Public Enemy and Led Zeppelin. Singer Michelle, described as a female Prince, was Madonna's second signing. Maverick's biggest-selling artist is Canadian-born Alanis Morissette.

51. Whose music does cover-band Bjorn Again pay tribute to?

A.) Bjorn Again pays tribute to **ABBA,** the Swedish chart-monsters of the 1970s. Bjorn Again (who hail from Australia) gained great exposure at England's Reading Festival, where they played in support of The Beastie Boys and grunge rockers Nirvana. Their namesake, Bjorn Ulvaeus, is flattered by the impersonation, although he thinks they could use more work on their phoney Swedish accents. He says it is a bit disconcerting that they sound like "the Swedish chef from The Muppets."

52. Which British dance band released a tribute to ABBA in 1992?

A.) *Abba-esque*, an EP with four ABBA techno-soul covers ("Lay All Your Love on Me," "S.O.S.," "Take a Chance on Me," and "Voulez Vous") was released by British dance band **Erasure** in 1992. Main Erasure members Andy Bell and Vince Clarke admit to being long-time ABBA fans, with Bell adding that the Top 40 hasn't been the same since "ABBA's demise." Vince Clarke made his name as a member of Depeche Mode and Yazoo (known as "Yaz" in North America) before teaming with Andy Bell to form Erasure and score hits like "Chains of Love" (#12 9/10/88 *Billboard*) and "A Little Respect" (#14 1/21/89 *Billboard*).

53. What drummer is known as The Stenographer of Soul?

A.) Session drummer **Jim Keltner** is known as The Stenographer of Soul due to his proficiency at programming electronic drums. Keltner is one of rock's most in-demand drummers, having played with the likes of Bob Dylan, Bonnie Raitt, The Travelling Wilburys, Little Village, and Elvis Costello.

54. Who were the Hindu Love Gods?

A.) The Hindu Love Gods were a side project for R.E.M. members **Peter Buck, Michael Mills, and Bill Berry** with eccentric singer/songwriter **Warren Zevon**. An album of blues standards and cover tunes by the Hindu Love Gods was hastily recorded in 1987, during the sessions for Zevon's *Sentimental Hygiene*. The eponymous CD was not issued until 1990. Bill Berry says the album was recorded as a lark, and says that it took as long to record as "it takes to listen to it."

55. Who is Saul Hudson better known as?

A.) Saul Hudson is better known as **Slash** from Guns n' Roses. The guitarist, who has a reputation as a hard drinking, three-pack-a-day smoking wildman, married supermodel Renee Suran in October 1992. His publicist Bryn Bridenthal describes Slash as a "guitar-playing animal," but also as "a romantic" who is "goo goo eyed in love" with his wife.

56. Which Fox TV show used the R.E.M. song "Stand" as its theme?

A.) The R.E.M. song "Stand" (#6 2/25/89 *Billboard*) was used as the theme for the Fox TV show **"Get a Life"** starring Chris Elliot. The band approved of the use of the song. Peter Buck said R.E.M. would not have been agreeable if it was a violent police show, but **"Get a Life"** is "kind of innocuous and okay for kids to watch."

57. Who guests with R.E.M. in the video for "Shiny Happy People"?

A.) **Kate Pierson** of the B-52s guest stars with R.E.M. in their video for "Shiny Happy People." The colourful backdrop that frames the video's action was painted by Ms. April Chapman's 5th grade class at Oglethorpe Avenue Elementary School in Athens, Georgia.

58. Which member of R.E.M. guest stars in the B-52s video for "Deadbeat Club"?

A.) **Michael Stipe** of R.E.M. makes a guest appearance in the 1990 B-52s video "Deadbeat Club" (#30 5/19/90 *Billboard*). B-52s chanteuse Kate Pierson had worked with R.E.M. on their *Out of Time* album, and appeared in the video for "Shiny Happy People," so as part of their work exchange, Stipe returned the favour.

59. Who made a cameo appearance as Percy Shelley in Roger Corman's 1991 movie *Frankenstein Unbound*?

A.) **Michael Hutchence** of INXS played Percy Shelley in Roger Corman's 1991 movie *Frankenstein Unbound*. Michael Stipe of

R.E.M. was also considered for the role, but Hutchence, having starred in the low-budget cult movie *Dogs in Space* in 1987, already had feature film experience and won the role.

60. Who played Jim Morrison in Oliver Stone's 1991 bio-pic *The Doors*?

A.) **Val Kilmer** played Jim Morrison in Oliver Stone's 1991 bio-pic *The Doors*. The other Doors were played by Kyle (Ray Manzarek) MacLachlan, Kevin (John Densmore) Dillon, and Frank (Robbie Krieger) Whaley. Kilmer won kudos for his portrayal of Morrison, with *Q Magazine* saying, "he does an utterly believable impression of the self destructive Lizard King." Meg Ryan co-starred as Morrison's love interest Pamela Courson.

61. Who shared lead vocals with Bart Simpson on "School Day" from *The Simpsons Sing the Blues*?

A.) **David Johansen** (a.k.a. Buster Poindexter) shared lead vocals with Bart Simpson on "School Day." Other guests on *The Simpsons Sing the Blues* include Joe Walsh (guitar: "School Day," "Moanin' Lisa Blues"), B.B. King (guitar: "Born Under a Bad Sign"), DJ Jazzy Jeff (drum programming, keyboards, and scratches: "Deep, Deep Trouble"), Dr. John (piano: "I Love to See You Smile"), and Tom Scott (tenor sax: "Springfield Soul Stew"). Michael Jackson was set to sing a rap duet with Bart, but backed out at the last moment.

62. Who are Jeffrey Townes and William Smith more commonly known as?

A.) Jeffrey Townes and William Smith are more commonly known as **DJ Jazzy Jeff and the Fresh Prince.** The Philadelphia rap duo found chart action with pop-influenced rap tunes like "Parents Just Don't Understand" (#12 6/18/88 *Billboard*) and "A Nightmare on My Street" (#15 8/20/88 *Billboard*). Their 1991 hit "Summertime" (#4 6/29/91 *Billboard*) sampled the Kool and the Gang hit "Summer Madness," and stayed on the charts for thirteen weeks. Will Smith is a double threat — music star and actor. After a successful run on the NBC sitcom "The Fresh Prince of Bel-Air" (a fish-out-of-water story, similar to "The Beverly Hillbillies," with a rap soundtrack), he expanded to the big screen, starring in a string of big-budget films, including *Independence Day* and *Wild Wild West.*

63. Who is Kier Kirby?

A.) Kier Kirby is better known as **Miss Lady Kier,** the feminine member of Deee-Lite. The band is based in New York, but the members are multi-national in origin. Miss Lady Kier hails from Youngstown, Ohio, while Super DJ Dmitry was born in Kiev, Soviet Union, and Jungle DJ Towa Towa is from Tokyo, Japan. The group borrowed their name from the Cole Porter song "It's De-lovely." Their sole entry in the Top 5, "Groove is in the Heart" (#4 10/20/90 *Billboard*), features backup vocals by funkmeister Bootsy Collins and A Tribe Called Quest's rapper Q-Tip.

64. In "L.L. Cool J" what do the initials stand for?

A.) L.L. Cool J, or **Ladies Love Cool James**, is the stage name of Queens, New York rapper, James Smith. He revolutionized rap in 1987 with the release of "I Need Love" (#14 8/15/87 *Billboard*), the first rap ballad. L.L. Cool J broke further ground at the 1991 MTV Video Awards when he led a live band, rather than the usual turntable set-up favoured by most rappers. His biggest commercial success was 1991's "Around the Way Girl" (#9 1/05/91 *Billboard*), which had a fifteen-week run on the charts. As an actor L.L. Cool J can be seen in supporting roles in 1985's *Krush Groove*, the 1991 Christmas release *Toys* with Robin Williams, and 1999's *Deep Blue Sea* and *Any Given Sunday.*

65. Who attended the Academy Awards ceremony with Madonna in 1991?

A. Michael Jackson and Madonna attended the Academy Awards ceremony together in 1991. After the show they reportedly stripped to their birthday suits and gave one another the once over. When asked to elaborate on the nature of their relationship Madonna said that they get together and compare bank accounts.

66. Which rap superstar played a cop in 1991's *New Jack City*?

A. Rapper **Ice-T** starred opposite Judd Nelson in 1991's *New Jack City*. Ice-T received good reviews for his portrayal of an undercover cop who attempts to topple an enormous drug empire. Ice-T is one of the main exponents of "gansta-rap," a tough street-level brand of music, characterised by boasting and violent imagery. It is ironic that Ice-T made his film debut playing a police officer, when, in 1992 his thrash-metal song "Cop Killer" raised the ire of everyone from local police organizations to George Bush.

67. Who released the first live rap album?

A. The first live rap album was released by **Vanilla Ice** in 1991. The album, *Extremely Live,* was the Miami Lakes native's second release, and featured live versions of tunes from his first album, and four new studio tracks, including a rap version of "Satisfaction." *Extremely Live* stiffed, selling only a fraction of what its predecessor sold.

68. What was Madonna's *Truth or Dare* called in the UK?

A. Madonna's all access behind-the-scenes concert movie *Truth or Dare* was retitled ***In Bed With Madonna*** for release in the United Kingdom. The Alek Keshishian film is an intimate look at Madonna's 1990 *Blond Ambition Tour*, and features cameo appearances by Warren

A backstage pass for Madonna's 1990 Blond Ambition world tour.

WORLD TOUR
90
MADONNA
BLOND
AMBITION

267

Beatty, Kevin Costner, and an Evian bottle.

69. What was the name of Paul McCartney's classical music debut?

A.) In 1991 Paul McCartney debuted his fully orchestrated, autobiographical, eight-movement **Liverpool Oratorio.** The ninety-seven minute work, co-written with American-born composer Carl Davis, met with mixed reviews from the British press. McCartney responded to critics who suggested that he stick to pop music: "I don't see any fences between pop and classical music. To me, writing any kind of music gives me a kick." He admits that he can't read or write music, and notes that composing classical music has been a welcome challenge. "The *Liverpool Oratorio* evolved from my normal music and stretched it a bit." In 1997 McCartney released a second classical outing, *Standing Stone*, a seventy-five-minute composition featuring an orchestra and chorus. *The Los Angeles Times* gave it a mixed review, at once calling the piece "painfully hokey," and able to "stop a listener short with its sheer musicality." *Standing Stone* topped the classical music charts in 1997 (selling 2,800 copies in the first week) making it his first number 1 album in a decade.

70. Whose 1967 hit "At the Zoo" was released as a children's book in 1991?

A.) **Simon and Garfunkel** had a hit with "At the Zoo" (#16 4/01/67 *Billboard*) in 1967. Twenty-four years later Paul Simon (with illustrator Valerie Michaut) released a children's picture book based on the fanciful song. The song translated easily, except for the line "The zoo keeper is very fond of Rum." You can't mention alcohol in a kids' book, so Rum became Rum the Beaver, and is seen snuggling with the zoo keeper.

71. According to *Forbes,* who raked in $115 million dollars in 1990/91?

A.) **New Kids on the Block** topped the *Forbes* list, which reveals who the highest paid people in the country are. The magazine

268

reported that Joe McIntyre, Donnie Wahlberg, Danny Wood, and Jordan and Jon Knight raked in $115 in 1990/91. The second and third place honours were taken by Bill Cosby and Oprah Winfrey.

72. Who was the first rap star to have his own Saturday morning cartoon show?

A.) Rapper **Hammer** (real name: Stanley Kirk Burrell) joined the ranks of The Jackson 5 and The Partridge Family with the debut of his Saturday morning cartoon show, *Hammerman,* in 1991. As a child, Burrell was nicknamed Hammer because of his strong resemblance to "Hammerin'" Hank Aaron. He was known as MC Hammer in the late eighties, but dropped the "MC" in 1991 for the release of *Too Legit to Quit.*

73. Which Michael Jackson video featured cameos from Bart Simpson and Macaulay Culkin?

A.) Both Macaulay Culkin and Bart Simpson were featured in Michael Jackson's ***"Black or White"*** video. The long form video is eleven minutes long, and was the lead single off Jackson's first release for Sony Records, *Dangerous.*

74. Who is the lead singer for Mr. Bungle?

A.) Faith No More crooner **Mike Patton** fronts the art/thrash band Mr. Bungle. Using the alias Vlad Drac he helps the band create their unique industrial/reggae/punk/circus fusion music. Their eponymous 1991 debut album was produced by avant-garde musician John Zorn.

75. Which soul singer appeared on "The Oprah Winfrey Show" in August 1990 celebrating the loss of 122 pounds?

A.) **Luther Vandross** has battled a weight problem all his life. After enduring a six-month liquid-only diet in 1990, his waist size shrank

Big Bang! Baby

from 54" to 34" and he dropped 122 pounds. In August 1990 he told Oprah Winfrey that it was a difficult process, but worth it, now that his weight was down "hopefully for the last time."

76. Who was Lucky Wilbury?

A.) Lucky Wilbury was **Bob Dylan**'s pseudonym on the first Traveling Wilburys album. The other Wilburys were Roy Orbison (Lefty Wilbury), Tom Petty (Charlie T. Jr.), Jeff Lynne (Otis Wilbury), and George Harrison (Nelson Wilbury). As Wilbury legend has it, they were all half-brothers — sired by Charles Truscott Wilbury — who travelled the world in search of musical inspiration. On their second album, *Vol. Three,* they adopted new pseudonyms — Spike Wilbury (Harrison), Muddy Wilbury (Petty), Clayton Wilbury (Lynne), and Boo Wilbury (Dylan).

77. Which symphony orchestra sued Michael Jackson in 1992?

A.) **The Cleveland Orchestra** sued Michael Jackson (and won) to receive credit and royalties from a sixty-seven-second snippet of their performance of Beethoven's Symphony No. 9 used on Jackson's *Dangerous* album. The sample of their work is heard at the beginning of "Will You Be There." The lawsuit named Michael Jackson and his company, MJJ Productions, Epic Records, and Epic's parent company, Sony Music Entertainment.

78. Which rapper co-starred with Robin Williams in 1992's *Toys?*

A.) **L.L. Cool J** plays a special-forces son of an evil military uncle who battles Robin Williams for control of a toy factory in 1992's *Toys.* This was not L.L. Cool J's (real name: James Smith) motion picture debut. For example, he had a cameo appearance opposite Michael J. Fox in *The Hard Way*, which he says was easy: "All I had to do was crack a joke, and sit behind a desk." His role in *Toys* was much more complex, "I had to think and believe," he says, "I almost had to hypnotize myself."

270

79. Which folk/rock singer allegedly gave actress Daryl Hannah a black eye and broke her finger in 1992?

A.) Long-time beau **Jackson Browne** allegedly gave Daryl Hannah a black eye and broke her finger in September 1992 when she tried to end their relationship. She found comfort in the arms of John F. Kennedy Jr., while Browne's friends came to his defence, publicly touting his non-violent nature and his easy-going manner.

80. Who was Italian model Carla Bruni referring to when she announced in 1992: "He's a fossil. His wife can keep him"?

A.) Italian model Carla Bruni was trying to squelch rumours of an affair between her and **Mick Jagger** in 1992 when she announced, "He's a fossil. His wife can keep him." In July of that year wife Jerry Hall left Jagger, claiming he had run off with Bruni shortly after Hall had given birth to their daughter Georgia May. The couple reunited later in the year. Jagger made light of his marital woes when as a presenter at an awards ceremony he thanked Woody Allen and Mia Farrow for publicizing their marital troubles and "making rock and roll marriages look normal."

81. Who said in 1992: "You know, Bush is always comparing me to Elvis in sort of unflattering ways. I don't think Bush would have liked Elvis very much, and that's just another thing wrong with him"?

A.) The public first became aware of **Bill Clinton**'s admiration for Elvis Presley when he appeared on Charlie Rose's talk show and sang a verse of "Don't Be Cruel" early in the 1992 presidential race. In one of the greatest public relations manoeuvres of his campaign Clinton then donned a saxophone and played "Heartbreak Hotel" for a June episode of "The Arsenio Hall Show." George Bush frequently took jabs at Bill Clinton's well-known love of Elvis Presley. In August 1992 Bush commented on Clinton's policy switches, "First one side, then the other. He's been spotted in more places than Elvis Presley." Bush used the E.P. analogy once again in October when he announced, "I finally figured out why he compares himself to Elvis. The minute he has to take a stand on something, he starts wiggling." Clinton countered Bush's statements by saying, "You know, Bush is always comparing me to Elvis in sort of unflattering ways. I don't think Bush would have liked Elvis very much, and that's just another thing wrong with him."

82. What was the most popular souvenir on U2's 1992 *Achtung Baby* Tour?

A.) The most popular souvenir on U2's 1992 *Achtung Baby* Tour was the ***Achtung Baby* condom,** which outsold all other merchandise, including tour programs and t-shirts.

83. Who is older: Mick Jagger or the President of the United States, Bill Clinton?

A.) **Mick Jagger** is older than Bill Clinton. In fact, if Clinton went to a party with Brian Wilson, George Clinton, Eric Clapton, Jerry Garcia, and James Brown, they could all call him junior.

84. Which former child star unveiled a line of perfumes for the Christmas market in 1992?

A.) **Michael Jackson** unveiled both the Legend de Michael Jackson cologne for men, and Mystique de Michael Jackson perfume for women in late 1992. The bottles featured a holographic image of the gloved one. The cosmetics were dubbed "Attic Stuffers" by *Entertainment Weekly*, with one reviewer suggesting that the people who bought this stuff wouldn't actually use it, but buy it for its kitsch value.

85. In the film *Spice World* what is written on the Spice Bus's licence plate?

A.) In *Spice World* the band drives around in a bus with the vanity plate **5GIRLS**. The 1997 film follows The Spice Girls and their fictional entourage as they film a documentary on "the real Spice Girls." Cameo appearances in the film include Roger Moore and Elvis Costello.

86. Who offended the residents of Evansville, Indiana, by calling their town "boring" and comparing it to Prague?

A.) **Madonna** filmed part of the 1992 movie *A League of Their Own* in Evansville, Indiana. Accompanied by her entourage, she spent almost three months in this small town. During her stay she gave an interview to *TV Guide*. She said that the town was "boring," comparing it to Prague, Czechoslovakia, and complained that she couldn't even get MTV at her rented house because there was no cable. The townspeople struck back at her by arranging a "Madonna Get a Life" rally, which was televised by news stations all over the country.

87. Who did dancers Oliver Crimes, Kevin Seta, and Gabriel Trooping sue in 1991?

A.) In 1991 dancers Oliver Crimes, Kevin Seta, and Gabriel Trooping sued **Madonna**, Boy Toy Inc., and *Truth or Dare*'s distributor Miramax Films. The three were dancers on the 1990 *Blond Ambition* Tour, and were included in the documentary *Truth or Dare*. The suit charges Madonna with "invasion of privacy, fraud, and deceit, intentional misrepresentation, suppression of fact, and intentional infliction of emotional distress." The dancers claim that they weren't told the film was going to be released commercially, and they felt they were not adequately compensated for their work. The outcome of the case is still pending.

88. What play marked Madonna's Broadway debut?

A.) In 1988 Madonna made her debut on Broadway in David Mamet's *Speed-the-Plow* at New York's Royal Theatre. She played the office temp opposite two Hollywood vultures, played by Joe Mantegna and Ron Silver. The critics were not kind, with *CAS*'s Dennis Cunningham reporting, "She moves ... as if she were operated by remote control." Clive

273

Barnes of the *New York Post* suggested that while she has some charm, she is not ready to "light the lamps on Broadway."

89. Who appeared to knock himself out at the 1992 MTV MusicVideo Awards?

A.) Nirvana bassist **Krist Novoselic** appeared to knock himself unconscious at the 1992 MTV Music Video Awards. One highlight of the awards show was Nirvana playing their song "Lithium." After the song was over, Nirvana proceeded to smash their instruments. Novoselic threw his bass straight up in the air, only to have it come straight back down and conk him on the head. He fell to the stage and lay there while his bandmates continued to trash their instruments. There were no further reports on the head-banger's condition.

90. Which white rapper caused a sensation with his ads for Calvin Klein underwear in 1992?

A.) Almost every magazine on earth featured the **Marky Mark** ad for Calvin Klein underwear in 1992. The ads showed a shirtless Marky, whose denims had slipped down to reveal his black Calvin skivvies. One magazine reported that stolen poster-sized copies of the ad (meant for bus stops) were selling for between seventy-five and one hundred dollars on the black market in Los Angeles. His sensational success with the Calvin Klein ads prompted *Cosmopolitan* to label him "the king of the undie world."

91. How did David Bowie select the songs for his 1990 greatest hits tour?

A.) David Bowie selected the songs for his 1990 greatest hits tour by setting up a 1-800 number and **allowing fans to phone in and vote** for the songs they would most like to hear. The "Dial A Dave Fave" line results were then tabulated, and formed the basis of his live show. Bowie announced that this would be the last time that fans would have a chance to hear these songs done live. "I'm not retiring," he said, "but I'm afraid it will probably be the last time I play those songs."

92. What charity did the proceeds from the *Red, Hot and Blue* compilation albums benefit?

A.) All proceeds from the release of the *Red, Hot and Blue* albums and accompanying video benefited various **AIDS charities.** The first benefit album featured modern interpretations of Cole Porter songs. Artists who donated their talents include Annie Lennox ("Ev'ry Time We Say Goodbye"), The Pogues and Kristy McColl ("Miss Otis Regrets"), Fine Young Cannibals ("Love for Sale"), Neneh Cherry ("I've Got You Under My Skin"), the Neville Brothers ("In the Still of the Night"), and David Byrne ("Don't Fence Me In"). Videos for the project were directed by Derek Jarman and Jim Jarmusch, among others.

93. Why is Billy Idol seen using a cane in his 1990 video "L.A. Woman"?

A.) Billy Idol is seen using a cane in the 1990 video "L.A. Woman" because of injuries sustained in a **motorcycle accident** in February 1990. His Harley-Davidson collided with a truck in Hollywood. Idol was taken to the Cedars-Sinai Medical Center where he underwent a seven-hour surgery to correct a fractured leg and arm. During his post-surgery therapy Idol experienced some pain, and was forced to walk with a cane. Ironically, Idol was in Hollywood working on his *Charmed Life* album.

94. Which socially aware singer refused to appear on an episode of "Saturday Night Live" featuring shock comedian Andrew Dice Clay?

A.) In May of 1990 **Sinead O'Connor** was booked as the musical guest on an episode of "Saturday Night Live" that was to be hosted by shock comedian Andrew Dice Clay. O'Connor refused to appear on the show, and released a statement that said, "I feel it shows disrespect — it would be nonsensical to expect a woman to perform songs about women's experiences after a monologue by Clay." O'Connor's decision confounded

275

BigBang! Baby

"SNL" producer Lorne Michaels, who said, "We weren't asking her to embrace Andrew Dice Clay. We were asking her to sing two songs."

95. Which of The Spice Girls has a gold tooth?

A.) **Sporty Spice** (her birth certificate reads Melanie Jayne Chisholm) is the only Spice Girl with a gold tooth. Look for it on the upper left, second incisor.

96. Which heavy metal band was implicated in a double suicide in 1990?

A.) In August 1990 heavy metallers **Judas Priest** faced charges in a Reno, Nevada, court that alleged subliminal messages on their 1978 *Stained Glass* album encouraged two teenagers to kill themselves in 1985. Relatives asserted that the two boys were Judas Priest fans, and were driven to suicide by the lyrics of two songs, "Beyond the Realms of Death" and "Heroes End." An "expert" testified for the prosecution that the songs contained backwards Satanic messages. He claimed that the words "Do it, do it" (just one of several "Satanic" messages he uncovered) encouraged the boys to form a suicide pact. The band denied any wrongdoing, and told *The New Musical Express*, "There has not been one subliminal message or devil worshipping suggestion on any Judas Priest record ever. They may wear studs and leather onstage but that's just an image, it's just entertainment." In September 1990 Judas Priest was cleared of all charges.

97. Whose ass did Frank Sinatra want to kick in September 1990?

A.) Frank Sinatra offered to "kick **Sinead O'Connor's** ass" in September 1990 after she refused to allow the US national anthem to be played before her concert at the Garden Arts Center in New Jersey. Sinead found herself in the centre of another controversy over this one. Several of her shows were picketed, and some radio stations asked their listeners to smash her records, while others actually smashed her records

276

on the air. Rapper Hammer jumped on the bandwagon and publicly offered to pay her plane fare back to Ireland. To try and ease tensions Sinead released a statement that explained that she meant no disrespect to Americans, but she never allows national anthems to be played before her concerts in any country, "not even my own."

98. Which Grateful Dead icon has a brand of ice cream named after him?

A.) In 1990 Ben and Jerry's (Vermont's Finest All Natural Ice Cream) unveiled the Cherry Garcia flavour in honour of Grateful Dead icon **Jerry Garcia**. Ben and Jerry pay tribute to their heroes by turning them into "living flavours." They are very careful who they choose to immortalize in ice cream. At press time only one other sixties figure had been so honoured — Woodstock MC Wavy Gravy. The Wavy Gravy flavour is a caramel-brazil nut ice cream, with caramel fudge, chocolate chunks, and Rainforest tidbits. Company chairperson Ben Cohen said they chose Wavy Gravy because "he symbolizes taking sixties values, peace and love, and turning them into action in the nineties." The Wavy Gravy flavour is sold in the world's first tie-dyed ice cream containers.

99. What number appears in several scenes of The Spice Girls' movie *Spice World*?

A.) Careful viewing of The Spice Girls' 1997 cinematic debut will reveal the repeated use of **the number 19**. The Spice Bus is number 19, their flight to Milan is number SG 1919, and the return flight to London is number 1819. The repetition of the number was a tribute to the band's handlers, a company known as Management 19.

100. How many times do The Spice Girls sing the word "wanna" in their 1997 hit single "Wannabe"?

A.) The Spice Girls sing the word "wanna" **twenty-eight times** during their number 1 single "Wannabe." For the record, they also use the word "really" twenty-six times. "Wannabe" established The Spice

Big Bang! Baby

Girls as international superstars, hitting the top spot on the charts in both Europe and North America. Written by The Spice Girls, with producers Richard Stannard and Matt Rowe, "Wannabe" started off as a lark in the studio. "You know when you're in a gang and you're having a laugh and you make up silly words?" says Mel C. on the genesis of the tune. "Well we were having a giggle and we made up this silly word, zigazig-ha. And we were in the studio and it all came together in this song. It only took about thirty minutes to write and we demoed it up fast. As soon as we recorded it, we knew we wanted it to be our debut single."

101. Which Grammy-winning composer/producer accidentally struck, and almost killed, singer Ben Vereen on Malibu's Pacific Coast Highway in 1992?

A.) In June 1992 **David Foster** was driving home from a session (he was working on Michael Bolton's album *Timeless (The Classics)*) on an unlighted stretch of Malibu's Pacific Coast Highway when he struck, and almost killed, singer Ben Vereen. He tried to avoid hitting the singer by slamming on his brakes, but to no avail. Vereen was tossed forty feet by the impact, then rolled another fifty feet before coming to rest in the road. Foster called for help on his cellular phone, before he realized the man he had struck was Ben Vereen, an old friend and collaborator. Vereen was rushed to hospital, and was in surgery for five hours. Two more operations were required to correct a fractured femur in his left leg and an infection in his abdomen. Vereen recovered completely from the accident.

102. What 1992 television show gave us the chart-topper "How Do You Talk to an Angel"?

A.) Fox TV's **"The Heights"** — a mix of *The Buddy Holly Story* and "Beverly Hills 90210" — gave us the 1992 chart-topper "How Do You Talk to an Angel." The show is based on the trials and tribulations of a struggling rock band. Real-life actor/musician James Walters sang the MOR ballad, although he has said he would be happier playing the blues. The soundtrack album *The Heights* features a Walters-penned blues song called "So Hot," dedicated to his then-fiancée Drew Barrymore.

103. Which singing superstar wrote in 1992, "I wouldn't want a penis"?

A.) In one of the tamer sections of her randy coffee-table book *Sex*, **Madonna** wrote, "I wouldn't want a penis. It would be like a third leg. It would seem like a contraption that would get in the way." *Sex* is a collection of photos based on Madonna's sexual fantasies. Appearing with Madonna are a collection of male strippers, faded rap stars (Vanilla Ice), socialites, and supermodels. An *Entertainment Weekly* survey reports that there are eighty-four nipple shots, nine men in dog collars, six things that look like they could hurt, and zero photos of Isabella Rossellini that Lancome could use.

104. Will cows give more milk if they listen to Guns n' Roses or Garth Brooks?

A.) Fifteen-year-old Bethany Lynn Welch ascertained that cows will give more milk listening to country singing star **Garth Brooks** than heavy metallers Guns n' Roses. She conducted her experiment for her high school science class in Ashland, Ohio.

105. Which two cool rappers appear in the 1992 Walter Hill flick *Trespass*?

A.) Rappers **Ice-T** and **Ice Cube** appear in the 1992 Walter Hill action flick *Trespass*. The movie centres around two firemen who find an envelope containing newspaper clippings about a fifty-year-old church robbery, and a map to the stolen loot. Their search for the booty leads them to an abandoned warehouse, and an encounter with some drug dealers. The balance of the movie is a showdown between the good guys and the bad guys. The movie opened to respectable reviews, with most critics praising the rappers' acting style. *Trespass* was originally called *Looters*, and was scheduled for release during the L.A. riots of May 1992. To avoid any connection with the riots the film's producers

BiGBang! BabY

changed the name and bumped up the release date.

106. Who was booed off the stage at the 1992 Bob Dylan Tribute Concert at Madison Square Garden?

A.) Rock chanteuse/trouble-maker **Sinead O'Connor** was booed off the stage at the 1992 Bob Dylan Tribute Concert, which came only two weeks after she tore up a picture of the Pope on "Saturday Night Live." The incident made headlines, overshadowing the rest of the concert, a who's who of rock and roll — everyone from George Harrison to John Mellencamp to the O'Jays and back to Lou Reed appeared in this four-hour tribute to one of rock's great poets. Sinead publicly chastised Bob Dylan for not defending her at the concert. She felt that Dylan, who became a folk hero for his protest songs, should have been more vocal in his support. In *Time* she rhetorically asked, "Why doesn't he take his responsibility?" and felt that Dylan should have talked directly to the audience, rather than trying to comfort her backstage. Sinead has been no stranger to controversy during her career, and from the sounds of the *Time* interview she has no plans to tone down her outrageous public persona. O'Connor was quoted as saying that people are asleep and need a shock to make them "stand up and listen."

107. Who was the first act in UK chart history to have their first four singles go to number 1?

A.) **The Spice Girls** were the first act in UK chart history to have their first four singles go to number 1. Their history-making run at the charts started with their debut single "Wannabe," and continued with their next three releases, "Say You'll Be There," "2 Become 1," and "Who Do You Think You Are" b/w "Mama." In early 1997, just as the fourth record was entering the number 1 slot in the UK, "Wannabe" hit the pinnacle on the *Billboard* charts, knocking Toni Braxton's "Un-Break My Heart" out of the top spot after an eleven-week run.

108. Which alternative bass player helped designer Christian Francis Roth

280

put together a line of "grunge" clothes in 1992?

A.) Sonic Youth's bassist **Kim Gordon** acted as editor for Christian Francis Roth's 1992 "grunge" collection. Grunge is a fashion style that originated in the Seattle, Washington, area. Young people in Seattle dressed in layers of clothing — t-shirts covered by flannel shirts and tights (or long johns) worn under shorts. For the originators of grunge it wasn't a fashion statement, but a necessary way of life. The flannel shirts were warm, and available for next to nothing at local thrift stores and K-Marts. The tights-under-shorts look was originally adopted by cyclists who found jeans too restricting, but needed something on their legs to protect them from the damp Seattle air. The whole effect is much like these people got dressed in the dark — the clothes don't match in the traditional way. Flannel is mixed with polka-dot t-shirts and multi-coloured striped shorts, or whatever was available at the thrift store for very little money. With the success of grunge bands like Nirvana and Pearl Jam, it was just a matter of time before their manner of dress became a trend. Among the high fashion designers taking the plunge into grunge were Marc Jacobs, who created sheer silk plaid "flannel" blouses and Martin Margiela and Rei Kawakubo, who left their clothes unfinished, or designed them to be worn inside out. It goes without saying that the originators of the trend — mostly musicians from Seattle — found it a bit strange that their thrift store garb had gone high fashion. "It's a bunch of fashion people jumping on a bandwagon," said Pearl Jam bassist Jeff Ament.

109. Whose photo did Madonna tear into pieces (a la Sinead) after her performance on "Saturday Night Live" in early 1993?

A.) Madonna had just finished singing "Bad Girl" (from her *Erotica* album) for her January 1993 performance on "Saturday Night Live," when she imitated Sinead O'Connor and tore up a picture of **Joey Buttafuoco.** He was the alleged lover of Amy Fisher — a Long Island teenager who was convicted of shooting Buttafuoco's wife, and who became the subject of three (and counting) television movies. Months earlier Sinead had created a storm by defacing a picture of the Pope and

BiBang! Baby

exhorting "Fight the real enemy" on the same television program.

110. Which animal rights activist once said that McDonald's should be bombed because "animals die for Big Macs"?

A.) **Chrissie Hynde** of The Pretenders is the militant vegetarian and animal rights activist who once said that McDonald's should be bombed because "animals die for Big Macs." In late 1992 Hynde made her first visit to a McDonald's in over twenty years when a McD's in Amsterdam began offering all-vegetable hamburgers. "I like it," she said, "but it could use some more soy." Hynde was one of twenty animal rights activists invited to sample McDonald's attempt at vegetarian cuisine. The new "Groenteburger" (veggie burger) was a pattie made of mashed potatoes, carrots, peas, and onions topped with pickles, chives, and cottage cheese on a sesame-seed bun. This was the second time McDonald's had offered vegetarian fare. In the early sixties they presented the Hula Burger, a pineapple ring on a bun, smothered in melted cheese. The Hula Burger proved too loopy for Middle America, and was discontinued after a short test run.

111. Which of Michael Jackson's sisters headlined the show at Paris's legendary cabaret The Moulin Rouge?

A.) The scandal-seeking sister **La Toya** Jackson headlined the show at Paris's legendary cabaret The Moulin Rouge. She was hired to boost the revenues of the once-glamorous club, and while she apparently put on an entertaining show, audiences were not that interested in seeing Michael Jackson's sister. She left The Moulin Rouge after just five months of her one-year contract.

112. Who did Elizabeth Taylor call "the least weird man I have ever known"?

A.) Elizabeth Taylor called **Michael Jackson** "the least weird man I have ever known" during an interview with Oprah Winfrey as part of "Michael Jackson talks to Oprah Winfrey." This TV special was

282

broadcast live to over 36 million people in February 1993 from Neverland, Jackson's $22-million estate near Santa Barbara, California. Jackson wanted to use the interview as a forum to clear the air, and to dispel many of the rumours that had been printed in tabloid newspapers all over the world. During the interview Jackson discussed his plastic surgery, saying that you could count his operations "on two fingers"; he went on to say that plastic surgery is very common in Hollywood. He revealed that as a child he was beaten by his father Joseph, which confirmed the allegation made by his sister La Toya in her 1992 tell-all book (which Jackson claims not to have read). In reference to his love life, Jackson said that he has been in love twice, once with Brooke Shields, and once with someone he refused to name. He stated that he wanted to propose marriage to Elizabeth Taylor, but never did. At this point Liz, who was watching the interview off-camera jumped in to reassure the viewers that she had never proposed to him either. The most startling revelation in the ninety-minute interview had to do with Jackson's skin colour. Oprah asked Michael if he was bleaching his skin. He admitted that his skin is turning lighter, but denied that it was the result of a chemical treatment. "I have a skin disorder which destroys the pigmentation of my skin," he explained, adding that it was a problem he could not control. He uses a heavy coat of make-up to even out the blotchy hue of his complexion. At the time of its airing "Michael Jackson Talks to Oprah Winfrey" was the fourth highest rated television broadcast of all time (excluding Super Bowls), falling just behind "M*A*S*H"'s final episode, "Dallas"'s *Who Shot J.R.?*, and the television movie *The Day After*.

113. Which controversial rapper commented on the Los Angeles riots by saying, "If black people kill black people every day, why not have a week and kill white people?"

A.) Controversial rapper **Sister Souljah** (real name: Lisa Williamson) raised the ire of President Clinton and many media watchers when she commented (in reference to the L.A. riots), "If black people kill black people every day, why not have a week and kill white people?" She later

283

clarified the remark by adding that she was referring to a hypothetical gang member who had become desensitised about killing. During his presidential campaign Clinton zeroed in on this remark, comparing Sister Souljah to Ku Klux Klan leader David Duke, and saying that her remarks were "filled with hatred." Their ongoing debate during the campaign filled hundreds of column inches in newspapers all over North America. Sister Souljah is much in demand on the lecture circuit, where she speaks about African history (she graduated with honours from Rutgers University), and what she perceives to be the racist policies of the government. She began her rap career as a guest vocalist on the Public Enemy album *Apocalypse '91*, and has released several solo albums. *360 Degrees of Power* showcased her radical theories, with the song "The Hate That Hate Produced" being her most vitriolic attack on racial politics. Although her records have failed to make an impression in the sales department, she remains one of the most important and outspoken voices in the rap community.

114. Who replaced Jim Morrison in the reformed Doors at the 1993 Rock and Roll Hall of Fame Awards?

A.) Pearl Jam singer **Eddie Vedder** stepped in to replace the late Jim Morrison at The Doors' reunion set at the 1993 Rock and Roll Hall of Fame Awards. Vedder originally turned down the offer to front the reformed band, but changed his mind after listening to a Doors' greatest hits tape during a long car trip. Later he joked that the only other possible replacement for the Lizard King was William Shatner, so he figured he may as well step in. At the awards ceremony the new Doors tore through spirited versions of "Roadhouse Blues," "Break On Through," and "Light My Fire." On behalf of the Morrison family, Jim Morrison's trophy was accepted by his sister, Anne Churning.

115. Which rocker's film résumé includes roles in *Married to the Mob, The Silence of the Lambs, Twin Peaks: Fire Walk With Me,* and *Little Buddha?*

284

A.) Singer/songwriter **Chris Isaak** did cameo roles in *Married to the Mob*, *The Silence of the Lambs*, and *Twin Peaks: Fire Walk With Me*. Bernardo Bertolucci's *Little Buddha* marked Isaak's first lead role. He described the part as "the Fred MacMurray" character, as he plays an architect with a ten-year-old son. His main problem with the role was trying to tone down his rock and roll image. Isaak says they spent a great deal of time washing the brylcream out of his hair, but he thinks he stills looks "a little too rock and roll" in the picture. The filming of the movie took him to Katmandu, Nepal, and Seattle. Isaak is best known for his Top 10 hit "Wicked Game" (#6 1/19/91 *Billboard*) from the David Lynch film *Wild at Heart*.

116. Which sixties legend's offspring fronts The Wallflowers?

A.) **Bob Dylan**'s youngest son Jakob Dylan writes songs and plays rhythm guitar and piano for the L.A. band The Wallflowers. Critics have noted that he didn't inherit the nasal vocal stylings of his dad, but bears a closer resemblance to John Prine. The Wallflowers' eponymous 1992 debut album, with its rootsy feel, has been favourably compared to The Band, with Jakob's songwriting earning high praise. The band began in 1990 as a loose group that would jam every Tuesday night at Canter's Deli in Hollywood. They soon gained a following, and turned Canter's into a hot spot each and every Tuesday. At the time of the release of the debut album Jakob told *The Toronto Star*'s Peter Howell that he hopes one day in the future when someone expresses an interest in listening to some Dylan, the reply will be "Which Dylan?"

117. Which legendary gospel/soul singer appeared on a 1991 episode of "Murphy Brown," and sang a duet with an off-key Candice Bergen?

A.) **Aretha Franklin** appeared on a 1991 episode of the hit sitcom "Murphy Brown," and sang "A Natural Woman (You Make Me Feel Like)" with an off-key Candice Bergen. On a more serious note Aretha recorded several duets in the eighties. In 1985 she guested with Annie Lennox and The Eurythmics for the Top 20 hit "Sisters are Doin' It for

Themselves" (#18 11/02/85 *Billboard*). A duet with George Michael, "I Knew You Were Waiting (For Me)" (#1 3/07/87 *Billboard*), hit the top spot in 1987, two years before she entered the studio with Elton John to record "Through the Storm" (#16 4/29/89 *Billboard*).

118. Who was briefly Axl Rose's famous father-in-law?

A.) Axl Rose married Erin Everly in 1990, making **Don Everly** of The Everly Brothers his famous father-in-law. The Guns n' Roses hit "Sweet Child of Mine" (#1 7/23/88 *Billboard*) was written in tribute to Erin. The marriage only lasted three weeks, so Don and Axl never did find the time to record that long-awaited Guns n' Roses/Everly Brothers collaboration — perhaps a remake of the 1960 Everly hit "So Sad (To Watch Good Love Go Bad)" would have been appropriate. More recently Axl has been keeping company with supermodel Stephanie Seymore.

119. Which Eric Clapton song swept the 1992 Grammys?

A.) **"Tears in Heaven,"** Eric Clapton's touching tribute to his late son, swept the 35th Annual Grammy Awards, winning Record of the Year, Song of the Year, and Best Male Pop Vocal. That same year Clapton also picked up Grammys for Album of the Year (*Unplugged*), Best Rock Vocal (*Unplugged*), and Best Rock Song ("Layla"). "I feel incredibly guilty for winning all these awards," said a humble Clapton, adding that he didn't feel he deserved to win anything for "Tears in Heaven" because "there were better songs. But I thank you." In his final speech of the evening, an emotional Clapton dedicated the awards to his son, who died in 1991.

120. What rumour did Michael Jackson put to rest at the 35th Annual Grammy Awards in 1993?

A.) Michael Jackson was awarded a special Grammy Legend Award at the 35th Annual Grammy Awards. It was presented by his sister Janet, who made a moving speech about her superstar brother. When

286

Jackson took the stage he hugged his sister, and began his acceptance speech with, "I hope this finally puts to rest another rumour that has been in the press for too many years — **me and Janet really are two different people."** Later in the show, host Garry Shandling continued the joke by commenting that he too would like to put an end to the long-time show business rumour that he and Tina Turner were the same person.

121. Which Florida band released a rock opera about the music business titled *Five Steps to Getting Signed*?

A.) *Five Steps to Getting Signed*, a satirical rock opera dissecting the music business, was independently issued by the Florida band **The Goods.** The opera follows a young band's progress from formation to hassles with record companies. A list of the CD's songs tells the whole story: "Managers," "We Need a Demo," "Creating a Buzz," and "Rejection."

122. Who produced The Butthole Surfers' debut album, *Independent Worm Saloon*?

A.) Legendary alternative rock nutbars The Butthole Surfers enlisted the aid of Led Zeppelin's **John Paul Jones** to produce their major label debut, *Independent Worm Saloon*. Before joining Led Zeppelin, Jones did session work for many of Britain's biggest acts. More recently he worked with R.E.M. on their *Automatic for the People* CD. As well as manning the board for the Surfers, he also lent his bass playing to their first-ever acoustic track, "Goofy's Concern." Other cuts on the album include "Dispute About T-Shirt Sales" and "Ballad of a Naked Man."

123. Which late soul singer's daughter released her debut album in 1993, titled *Love for the Future*?

A.) **Nona Gaye, the daughter of the late soul singer Marvin**, made her debut in 1993 with *Love for the Future*. The album featured no less that nine producers, and tunes like "I'm Overjoyed" and "The Things We All Do for Love," which *Spin* described as "sleek, stylish singles."

124. Who agreed to pay The Rolling Stones $45 million for three new albums and the rights for seventeen albums from their back catalogue?

A.) In 1994 The Rolling Stones inked a deal with **Virgin Records** that will pay them $45 million for three new albums and the rights to seventeen albums, dating back to 1971. An *Entertainment Weekly* article analysed the deal, and weighed all the relevant factors: many of the seventeen albums from the back catalogue were duds, and mean little in terms of generating any new sales; they speculate that the Stones are getting too long in the tooth to mount the massive promotional tours of old; Keith Richards and Mick Jagger seem to have made their solo careers a priority; original bassist Bill Wyman just quit the band; and the Stones' last three albums only sold 3.5 million albums — combined. Based on this data the experts at *Entertainment Weekly* believed that Virgin paid too much for the Stones.

125. What is the English translation of the German band name "Einsturzende Neubauten"?

A.) The English translation of the German industrial band name Einsturzende Neubauten is **"collapsing new buildings."** The name represents the band's manifesto to create music from the sounds of destruction.

126. What inspired the band name Everything But the Girl?

A.) The duo of Tracey Thorn and Ben Watt met while studying at Hull University in England. Their unusual name was borrowed from **a furniture store called Everything But the Girl**. The owners of the store boasted "everything but the staff is for sale."

288

127. What inspired Elvis Costello to write and produce the classically influenced *The Juliet Letters*?

A.) Elvis Costello was inspired to write and produce his 1993 release *The Juliet Letters* after reading **the true story of a Veronese professor who answered letters written to Juliet Capulet.** Costello teamed with the Brodsky Quartet and produced a suite for voices and strings. Critical reaction was mixed, but, writing in *Spin*, musicologist and producer Hal Wilner called *The Juliet Letters* "an incredible journey," and "one of Costello's best."

128. Who was the first artist to refuse a Grammy Award?

A.) **Sinead O'Connor** was the first artist ever to refuse a Grammy Award. She won in 1990 for Best Alternative Music Performance for *I Do Not Want What I Haven't Got*. When the nominations were announced she issued a statement declaring that if she won she would not accept the trophy. She told Arsenio Hall that "it represents everything I despise about the record industry." She also said that she felt that the Grammys rewarded commercial success over artistic integrity. After her boycott of the Grammys she also announced that she would, in the future, also skip the MTV Awards and the American Music Awards. The public and media alike were quick to take shots at her, with disc jockey Rick Dees reporting that his station had been inundated with calls from irate listeners, who objected to O'Connor's views.

129. Which white rapper made headlines in 1993 when charges of racism, homophobia, and criminal behaviour were levelled at him by the Committee Against Anti-Asian Violence?

A.) **Marky Mark,** brother of New Kids on the Block singer Donnie Wahlberg, was accused of participating in a racially motivated act of violence against two Vietnamese men. The Committee Against Anti-Asian Violence organized an anti-Mark rally in New York's Times Square after they received information that Marky Mark had assaulted the two

289

Asians in the spring of 1988. Police records say that he beat one with a wooden pole and punched the other in the face. The police report goes on to say that he called them "slant-eyed gooks." In response to the Committee Against Anti-Asian Violence, Marky Mark issued a statement denouncing racially motivated violence, and chalked up the incident as the "act of a foolish kid." He claims he was simply trying to steal a case of beer from one of the men. The courts imposed a two-year suspended sentence in the case, and Marky served forty-five days in jail. Previously, in 1986, Marky also ran afoul of the law after he was allegedly caught throwing rocks and yelling, "Kill the niggers," at a group of black children. While defending himself against the charges from the Committee Against Anti-Asian Voilence, Marky Mark found himself in hot water with the Gay and Lesbian Alliance Against Defamation after an appearance on a British television show. He appeared with reggae singer Shabba Ranks, who advocated violence against gays, saying "if you forfeit the laws of God Almighty, you deserve crucifixion." On the show Marky applauded Ranks' candour, and performed a song with him. Later Marky explained that he wasn't agreeing with Shabba, but "defending his right to say it." To help clear the air, Marky agreed to appear in an anti-bias public service announcement.

130. What is the name of the skin disorder that has made Michael Jackson's skin appear lighter?

A.) Michael Jackson suffers from a non-contagious skin disorder known as **vitiligo,** which destroys the skin's pigment cells. He went public with the news during a live television interview with Oprah Winfrey in February 1993. Winfrey point-blankly asked Jackson if he was bleaching his skin. "I have a skin disorder which destroys the pigmentation of my skin," he replied, without mentioning the name of the disease. He wears a heavy coat of make-up to even out his blotchy complexion. Vitiligo affects both blacks and whites, with almost one in every one hundred people suffering some form of it.

131. Who were the d.j.'s who added a heavy dance beat to Suzanne

Vega's a cappella tune "Tom's Diner," turning it into a huge hit?

A.) Two mysterious Bristol, England, d.j.'s who call themselves **DNA** remixed Suzanne Vega's a cappella tune "Tom's Diner" (#5 11/03/90 *Billboard*), adding a heavy dance beat, and turned it into a huge international hit. The trouble was they hadn't received authorization from A&M to remix the song. However, there is no arguing with success, and when the tune hit the UK Top 3 and the *Billboard* Top 5, A&M quickly legitimised the release.

132. Whose first solo album starts with the line, "Hello, this is the operator with a collect call from the L.A. county jail from Tommy. Will you accept the charges?"

A.) **Ex-Mötley Crüe drummer Tommy Lee**'s 1999 solo debut, *Methods of Mayhem,* begins with an operator patching a collect call through from the L.A. county jail. The line is a reference to the four months Lee spent in lock-up for assaulting his wife, Pamela Anderson Lee. Featuring guests like Snoop Dogg and Kid Rock, the album is Lee's first attempt at solo stardom since leaving Mötley Crüe in April 1999. A raucous collection of heavy metal-rap fusion, *Methods of Mayhem* features Lee's first attempts at rapping, or "delivering lyrics with a rhythmic execution," as he calls it.

133. What is Calvin Broadus's stage name?

A.) Calvin Broadus acquired the name **Snoop Doggy Dogg** because of his resemblance to the Peanuts character Snoopy. His father remembers that Snoop "had a lot of hair on his head as a baby and looked like a little dog." In March 1998 he dropped the "Doggy" from his name, and subsequent album releases have been issued under the simpler Snoop Dogg moniker.

134. Which singer-songwriter never leaves home without a Tupperware container of Homer, Alaska, soil?

BigBang! Baby

A.) **Jewel** Kilcher was raised in Homer, Alaska, with her parents and two brothers in a home situated on an eight-hundred-acre plot of land. With no running water (just an outhouse in the yard) or TV, Jewel kept busy tending horses and working in the family's garden. By age 6 she was performing with her parents as part of their singing-songwriting duo, displaying an unusual talent she picked up from her Swiss-born grandfather — yodeling. Re-locating to San Diego, she performed in coffee-houses, and in 1994 recorded her first album, *Pieces of You*. The album went un-noticed for fourteen months, until Atlantic Records put the full weight of their promotional prowess behind the single "Who Will Save Your Soul" (said to be only the third song she ever wrote). A combination of relentless touring and well-placed television appearances propelled the single to number 11 on the *Billboard* charts. A second single, "You Were Meant for Me," went to number 2 in May of 1997. Two years after its release, *Pieces of You* had gone triple platinum. During this time of intense touring, Jewel got into the habit of always carrying a Tupperware container of Homer, Alaska, soil with her to remind her of her roots.

135. What is the title of Fiona Apple's sophomore album?

A.) Fiona Apple's sophomore album has one of the longest titles in rock and roll history. Here we go: ***When the Pawn Hits the Conflict He Thinks Like a King What He Knows Throws the Blows When He Goes to the Fight and He'll Win the Whole Thing 'Fore He Enters the Ring There's No Body to Batter When Your Mind is Your Might So When You Go Solo, You Hold Your Own Hand and Remember That Depth is the Greatest of Heights and If You Know Where You Stand, Then You Know Where to Land and If You Fall It Won't Matter, Cuz You'll Know That You're Right.*** In case you have lost track, that's ninety words. Apple explains that the title was originally a poem she wrote while on the road promoting her first album. It was written in response to critics who had been harsh in their assessment of her first album. "It's telling me that when everyone's being mean to me, I shouldn't believe it,"

292

she explained. "Do not think that you're wrong because people are saying that you are."

136. What are the three categories of inductees at the Rock and Roll Hall of Fame?

A.) The three categories of inductees at Cleveland's Rock and Roll Hall of Fame are: **Performers, Non-performers, and Early Influences**. Artists become eligible for induction twenty-five years after the release of their first record.

137. Which member of Korn held a part-time job as an autopsy assistant for the Kern County coroner's office?

A.) Korn front man **Jonathan Davis** worked as an autopsy assistant for the Kern County coroner's office (just north of Los Angeles) from his senior year in high school until joining Korn at age 22. He reports it took a little time to warm up to the idea of working with corpses, but later found the work to be "a rush." In an interview with *The New York Times* he said, "There's some kind of power involved when you're cutting up a human body."

138. How did Stone Temple Pilots' Scott Weiland and Robert DeLeo meet?

A.) Scott Weiland and Robert DeLeo first met **at a Black Flag concert** in Long Beach, California, and made the unsettling discovery that they were both dating the same woman. Instead of fighting for the woman's honour, the pair started jamming together — Weiland on guitar and vocals, DeLeo on bass. In time, the two-timing woman moved to Texas, and the guys moved into her apartment, forming a band called Mighty Joe Young. That moniker had to be changed when it was discovered that there was already a blues man who owned the name. Inspired by the S.T.P. Motor Oil logo, they came up with the name Stone Temple Pilots, which they claim has no meaning, hidden or otherwise.

139. Which two Quentin Tarantino movies did The Fun Lovin' Criminals sample on their single "Scooby Snacks"?

A.) The Fun Lovin' Criminals borrowed substantial amounts of dialogue from two Quentin Tarantino movies, **Reservoir Dogs and Pulp Fiction,** for their single "Scooby Snacks." They didn't ask for permission to sample the movies, and after some legal maneouvring Tarantino was awarded a co-writing credit on the song.

140. Whose house appears on the picture sleeve for the Oasis single "Live Forever"?

A.) The members of Oasis paid tribute to one of their musical heroes on the picture sleeve for their single "Live Forever." The house on the sleeve is **John Lennon's** home at 251 Menlove Avenue in Woolton, England. After the death of his mother, Lennon lived in this home with his Aunt Mimi and Uncle George Smith. Julia Lennon was struck and killed by a car driven by an off-duty policeman just down the block from the Menlove house in July 1958.

141. Who was Nirvana's first drummer?

A.) Before settling on Dave Grohl, Nirvana worked with four different drummers. The first, **Aaron Bruckhard**, joined the group in 1987, and was fired later that same year after he was stopped for drunk driving while driving Kurt Cobain's car. Bruckland went on to play drums for a thrash-metal band called Attica, while maintaining a day job laying insulation. Other Nirvana drummers included Dale Crover (1988 and 1990), Dave Foster (1988), and Chad Channing (1988–90).

142. Which band was given veteran reporter Sam Donaldson's stamp of approval to run for president?

A.) **The Smithereens** appeared with Sam Donaldson on "The Tonight Show" in the summer of 1992. During the course of the show, the band and the reporter became unlikely friends. In fact they even posed for a photo together, which eventually became the image on The Smithereens' Christmas card later that year. At the end of the show as Leno said goodnight to the audience, Sam Donaldson turned to the band and commented that since it was an election year he felt that, "you guys should run for president."

143. What did the police find in Kurt Cobain's pockets on his first arrest for vandalism?

A.) Kurt Cobain was arrested several times for vandalism in Aberdeen, Washington, mostly after drunken spray-painting sprees. On his first bust the arresting officer emptied Cobain's pockets, and according to the police report found **one guitar pick, one key, one can of beer, one mood ring, and most unfortunately, one *Millions of Dead Cops* cassette.**

144. Who was the first artist of the 1990s to turn someone else's actual recording into a hit song?

A.) **MC Hammer** appropriated Rick James' "Super Freak," turning it into one of the first mainstream hip-hop singles, "U Can't Touch This." Hammer says he got the inspiration to write the song while walking on an airport runway, humming "Super Freak." The phrase, "You can't touch this," just popped into his head, and he says he created the song there and then. Shortly afterward he sampled the entire song with a new vocal, and scored a Top 10 hit.

145. Who wrote Sinead O'Connor's 1990 number 1 hit single "Nothing Compares 2 U"?

A.) Sinead O'Connor recorded **Prince**'s "Nothing Compares 2 U" on the advice of her manager and close friend Fachtna O'Ceallaigh. Two days before they were scheduled to shoot the video for the song, O'Connor had a rift with O'Ceallaigh that broke up their partnership.

Big Bang! Baby

O'Connor later said that thinking about O'Ceallaigh during the shoot helped her cry on cue for the cameras. "Nothing Compares 2 U" stayed in the number 1 position for four weeks.

146. Who scored a number 1 hit in 1992 with the song "I'm Too Sexy"?

A.) Sussex, England, natives Richard and Fred Fairbrass, better known as **Right Said Fred,** took "I'm Too Sexy" to the top of the *Billboard* charts in 1992. The brothers were managing a gymnasium in London called The Dance Attic during the day, and working on their music at night. The pair came up with "I'm Too Sexy" after hearing a bass tape loop playing over and over on their computer. They made up the nonsense lyrics on the spot, taking their inspiration from the narcissistic attitude they saw everyday at The Dance Attic. To test the song, they used it as a workout tune at their gym. Buoyed by the response they received, the brothers re-mixed "I'm Too Sexy" and pursued a record deal. The song was held out of the number 1 spot in the UK by Bryan Adams' "Everything I Do (I Do For You)," but held the number 1 position in the United States for three weeks.

147. How old were the members of Kris Kross when they recorded their number 1 hit "Jump"?

A.) *Billboard* called them "baby rappers," and while they weren't exactly infants, they weren't far off. Kris Kross's Chris Smith (Mack Daddy) and Chris Kelly (Daddy Mack) were only **twelve and thirteen years old** respectively when they recorded "Jump." The song was written by producer Jermaine Dupri after attending a hip-hop concert. During the show he watched the crowd jump up and down. "Rappers had been doing it and I said we should make a record like this," said Dupri. "I went home and wrote the song in an hour."

148. Who is "Salt" and who is "Pepa"?

A. Salt-n-Pepa are hip-hop pioneers. They were one of the first rap groups to cross over to the pop charts, and one of the few groups of their genre completely comprised of women. They are: **Cheryl "Salt" James and Sandy "Pepa" Denton**. Pamela Greene is their d.j. The rappers met while working at Sears in Brooklyn. One afternoon a co-worker asked them to lend some vocals to a project he was working on. The song was called "The Show Stoppa," and was an answer to Doug E. Fresh and Slick Rick's "The Show." The girls agreed to rap on the song, which was released under the band name "Super Nature." "The Show Stoppa" became a minor hit, reaching number 46 on the R&B charts. The rapping pair decided to pursue a career in music. Taking their name from a line in "The Show Stoppa," Salt-n-Pepa signed a record deal with rap independent Next Plateau. Their debut *Hot, Cool and Vicious* produced three singles that dented the R&B charts, but it wasn't until a San Francisco d.j. remixed "Push It" that the group had a major hit. "Push It" rose to number 9 on the pop charts, and was nominated for a Grammy in 1988. Other hits include "Let's Talk About Sex" (#13 10/12/91 *Billboard*), "Shoop" (# 4 10/23/93 *Billboard*), and "Whatta Man," (#3 1/29/94 *Billboard*).

149. Who was the first rap star to emerge from Seattle?

A. **Anthony Ray, a.k.a. Sir Mix-a-Lot** was the first rap star to emerge from Seattle. In the early eighties he got his nickname while d.j.-ing an inner-city club in Seattle's Central Ghetto district. In tribute to his hometown, Sir Mix-a-Lot executive-produced 1993's *Seattle: The Dark Side* album, a collection of rap and R&B acts from the western city. Sir Mix-a-Lot is best known for his two-million selling, Grammy Award-winning single "Baby Got Back" (#1 5/2/92 *Billboard*), a song that celebrates large-bottomed women.

150. Who is the bass player in the rock band Dogstar?

A. *Matrix* star **Keanu Reeves** plays bass in the rock band Dogstar. The band was formed in 1990 by Reeves and two friends,

Big Bang! Baby

vocalist/guitarist Bret Domrose and drummer Rob Mailhouse. Despite a national tour to support their debut album, 1996's *Our Little Visionary,* the album failed to yield any hit singles.

151. What was the name of NBA superstar Shaquille O'Neal's debut album?

A.) Shaquille O'Neal's solo rap debut was 1993's platinum-selling *Shaq Diesel*. His second record, 1994's *Shaq-Fu Da Return,* was a successful follow-up, spawning the Top 20 single "Biological Don't Matter." In 1996 Shaq established his own label, an off-shoot of Interscope Records called TWIsM (The World Is Mine).

152. Which producer has had the longest chart span of number 1 songs?

Television's favourite cartoon family — The Simpsons.

Photo courtesy of Rhino Records

A.) Among the many credits in his prodigious career, **famed producer Sir George Martin** can claim the longest chart span of number 1 songs by a producer in the history of rock and roll. He first entered the *Billboard* charts in 1964 as the mastermind behind The Beatles' "I Want to Hold Your Hand" (#1 1/25/64 *Billboard*), and last entered the charts with Elton John's "Candle in the Wind 1997" (#1 10/11/97 *Billboard*). The span between the tunes? Thirty-three years, eight months, and two weeks.

153. Who sang the "Plow King Theme" on episode 68 of *The Simpsons*?

A.) Homer Simpson purchases a snowplow and goes into business as Mr. Plow on the November 19, 1992, episode of *The Simpsons.* His drinking buddy Barney gets into the act, starting a rival company, and hires **Linda Ronstadt** to sing the "Plow King Theme" on television commercials. In the jingle Ronstadt sings, "Mr. Plow is a loser and I think he is a boozer."

154. Who is the only Spice Girl with a pierced tongue?

A.) Melanie Janine Brown a.k.a. **Mel B**. a.k.a. Scary Spice is the only Spice Girl with a pierced tongue.

155. Which of The Spice Girls has the most tattoos?

A.) The Spice Girl with the most body art is **Sporty Spice** (real name: Melanie Jayne Chisholm). She has three tattoos: two on her right upper arm — a band and a Chinese symbol meaning Women and Strength — and a large cross on her upper left arm. Other Spice Girls tattoos include Ginger Spice's (real name: Geradine Halliwell) panther tattoo on her lower back and Mel B.'s stomach art.

156. Which Janet Jackson single was her first sole writing credit?

A.) Janet Jackson's "**Black Cat**" marked the first time she was the sole writer on any of her singles. The song was number 1 for one week in October 1990, her fourth record to hit the top of the charts.

157. Which movie soundtrack features the track "Gangsta's Paradise"?

A.) Coolio's (real name: Artis Ivey Jr.) hit single "Gangsta's Paradise" is featured on the soundtrack of the 1995 film ***Dangerous Minds***, starring Michelle Pfeiffer. In the film Pfeiffer plays an ex-marine who becomes a ghetto high school teacher. On the strength of his record "Fantastic Voyage," rapper Coolio was invited to submit a theme song. He wrote "Gangsta's Paradise" in three hours, using the song "Pastime Paradise" from Stevie Wonder's *Songs in the Key of Life* as a melodic starting point. Wonder didn't like the song initially. He was concerned about the vulgarities that Coolio had peppered through the lyrics of the re-vamped tune. Once the lyrics were cleaned up, Wonder gave his permission, and the song was added to the soundtrack of *Dangerous*

Minds. "Gangsta's Paradise" stayed at number 1 on the *Billboard* charts for three weeks in September 1995.

158. How many weeks did Mariah Carey and Boyz II Men spend at number 1 with "One Sweet Day"?

A.) "One Sweet Day," performed by Mariah Carey and Boyz II Men, spent **sixteen weeks** at the number 1 spot of the *Billboard* charts in 1995/96 before being knocked off by Celine Dion's "Because You Loved Me" (#1 03/23/96 *Billboard*). The tune is the longest running number 1, breaking the record previously held by (in a three-way tie) "I Will Always Love You" (#1 11/14/92 *Billboard*) by Whitney Houston, "I'll Make Love to You" (#1 8/13/94 *Billboard*) by Boyz II Men, and "Macarena (Bayside Boys Mix)" by Los Del Rio, all of which held the top spot for fourteen weeks.

159. What does Edie Brickell's father do for a living?

A.) Singer Edie Brickell's father is a **professional bowler** known as "The Fort Worth Southpaw."

160. Who was the late Tupac Shakur's infamous mother?

A.) Late rapper Tupac Shakur was the son of **Afeni Shakur**, known as one of the leaders of the New York City chapter of the Black Panther party.

161. Which dance-pop artist first made her mark as head cheerleader for the NBA Los Angeles Lakers?

A.) **Paula Abdul** first came to the notice of music industry insiders as the head cheerleader for the Los Angeles Lakers. As a result of her carefully choreographed routines on the basketball court, she started fielding calls from the Jackson brothers asking her to choreograph their first video. She later worked on videos by Janet Jackson, Dolly Parton,

Debbie Gibson, Warren Zevon, and ZZ Top, as well as "The Tracy Ullman Show." During the shoot of "Velcro Fly" by ZZ Top she mentioned to Warner Brothers executive Jeff Ayeroff that she would be interested in recording her own album. He subsequently moved to Virgin Records, and immediately signed Abdul to a recording contract. At Virgin she produced many hits, including "Straight Up" (#1 12/24/88 *Billboard*), "Forever Your Girl" (#1 4/01/89 *Billboard*), "Cold Hearted" (#1 7/08/89 *Billboard*), and "Opposites Attract" (#1 1/06/90 *Billboard*).

162. Which member of Bruce Springsteen's E Street Band is a trained gymnast?

A.) E Street guitar player **Nils Lofgren** is a trained gymnast. He can frequently be seen bouncing on a trampoline onstage, and during the *Tunnel of Love* tour taught Bruce Springsteen to tumble. Springsteen then used his new-found skill to start many of the shows on that tour.

163. Why was the cover of U2's *Achtung Baby* banned from some American record stores?

A.) The cover montage of U2's 1991 *Achtung Baby* was deemed objectionable by several store chains in the United States **because of a small photograph of a nude Adam Clayton**. The full frontal shot of the bassist was covered up in the initial printings of the record, and completely removed in later pressings.

164. Who was the spokesman for Black Death vodka?

A.) The makers of Black Death vodka chose **Guns n' Roses guitarist Slash** as their spokesman. The ad campaign, featuring the notoriously hard-living Slash, played up on the idea that alcohol was poison. The ads were too controversial for most outlets, and despite the celebrity endorsement, the vodka never made much of an impact with drinkers.

301

165. Which nineties shock rock star attended the Heritage Christian School in Canton, Ohio?

A.) **Brian Warner (aka Marilyn Manson)** attended Canton, Ohio's Heritage Christian School, entering the curriculum in Grade 6. His former principal, Caroline Cole commented, "I'd like to ask (Marilyn Manson), 'Did I influence you in any way to this lifestyle?' I keep thinking, 'Wow, did I do something I should have done differently?'"

166. Which alternative rock legend signed on to become a scriptwriter for Ted Turner's World Championship Wrestling in 1999?

A.) Former Hüsker Dü front man **Bob Mould** took a job as scriptwriter for Ted Turner's World Championship Wrestling in 1999. According to one report his duties include "spending his days thinking of ever more new and inventive uses for folding chairs, trash cans and peroxide." In the early eighties Hüsker Dü Mould pioneered the fusion of punk, metal, and pop, a style the media soon labeled "alternative rock." He continued to make fine records throughout the eighties and nineties. After Hüsker Dü split, Mould formed Sugar, whose album *Copper Blue* was voted 1992's Album of the Year by *The New Musical Express*.

167. Which rapper successfully sued the makers of St. Ides Malt Liquor?

A.) Although the makers of St. Ides Malt Liquor had used Ice Cube as a celebrity spokesman, another rapper wasn't pleased to be included in their marketing strategy. **Public Enemy's Chuck D** had long been an outspoken opponent of malt liquor sales, both in interviews and song. He sued St. Ides in 1991 when they used his voice in an advertisement without his permission. The case was settled, to Chuck D's benefit, in 1993.

168. Why was Ted Nugent arrested in January 1993?

A.) Guitarist Ted Nugent ran afoul of the Cincinnati police in January 1993 when **he shot flaming arrows into the crowd at a Damn Yankees show**. He was charged with a misdemeanour fire code violation and fined $1,000.

169. Why did the all-vegetarian band Flesh for Lulu choose their unusual name?

A.) The all-vegetarian band Flesh for Lulu chose their strange name **after seeing sixties pop icon Lulu buying a hamburger at the Victoria Station McDonald's restaurant.** Lulu (real name: Marie Lawrie), is best remembered by North Americans for her number 1 single "To Sir With Love" (#1 9/23/67 *Billboard*) from the film of the same name starring Sidney Poitier.

170. Who was bumped from "The Tonight Show" guest roster in March 1993 after protests from gay-rights groups?

A.) Following protests from gay-rights activists, Jamaican dancehall superstar **Shabba Ranks**' appearance on "The Tonight Show" was cancelled in March 1993. The brouhaha started in December 1992 when Ranks told a British television show that he agreed with Buju Banton's controversial song "Boom Bye Bye," which advocated the killing of gay men. "If you forfeit the laws of God Almighty you deserve crucifixion," said Ranks. After a series of cancelled live and television appearances, Ranks had a change of heart. To silence his critics he issued a statement saying that he regretted his inflammatory remarks, and did not approve of "any act against homosexuals."

171. What is the name of the boy pictured on Nirvana's *Nevermind*?

A.) The naked baby floating after a dollar bill on the cover of Nirvana's *Nevermind* album is **Spencer Eldon**. Eldon was four months old at the time of the shoot, earning a paltry $250 model's fee, now safely invested in a bank account. The cover photograph was snapped by Kirk Weddle, a long-time friend of Spencer's parents. In fact, he was such a good friend, he had even taken a mail-order minister's course to legally marry the couple. The famous cover photo was taken at the Pasadena Aquatic Center, with Weddle taking only one roll of film. The winning photo, culled from a series of ten shoots with different babies, was left un-retouched, with the exception of an airbrushed dollar bill dangling from a hook added at Kurt Cobain's request.

172. How many calories will you burn if you sing Whitney Houston's "The Greatest Love of All" thirteen times in a row?

A.) According to Daiichikosho, a karaoke company from Japan, singing Whitney Houston's "The Greatest Love of All" thirteen times in a row will burn off **two hundred calories**. They have designed a system that allows you to count the amount of calories burned while singing. A computer analyses a performer's voice, then tabulates how many calories they expend when the song is over via a printed data report. Songs are rated based on the length of the song, its tempo, and its volume.

173. What was the name of model Naomi Campbell's ill-fated R&B/rock album?

A.) In 1994 model Naomi Campbell released an R&B/rock album titled **Babywoman**. It flopped, reportedly only selling 175 copies in its first two weeks. England's *Daily Mirror* reviewed it, with the sarcastic line, "Don't give up the day job, Naomi."

174. How many children would Michael Jackson like to have?

A.) Michael Jackson told a reporter he would like to sire **ten children**, just like his father. He and ex-wife Debbie Rowe had two kids together, Prince Michael and Paris Katherine, but he wants more. "I thought I was prepared because I read everything about child rearing but it's so much more exciting than I ever imagined. The only regret I have is that I wish I had done it earlier."

175. Which famous play inspired Courtney Love to name her band "Hole"?

A.) Courtney Love chose the band name "Hole" after reading the line, "There's a hole burning deep inside me," in **Euripides' play** *Medea*.

176. Who was awarded more gold and platinum records than anybody else in the twentieth century?

A.) According to the Recording Industry Association of America, **Elvis Presley** was awarded more gold and platinum records than anybody else in the twentieth century. Although he has no diamond awards (signifying sales of more than ten million copies), Elvis sold more than 77 million records, and both *Elvis' Golden Records* and *Elvis' Christmas Album* have been certified six-times platinum.

The last photo of Elvis and The Jordanaires, taken at RCA Studio B in Nashville, Tennessee. Left to right: Neal Matthews, Gordon Stoker, Elvis, Hoyt Hawkins, and Ray Walker.

Photo courtesy of Gordon Stoker

177. According to the Recording Industry Association of America, who was the top female rock artist of the twentieth century?

A.) The Recording Industry Association of America has certified **Madonna** as the top female rock artist of the twentieth century. Other winners include: Garth Brooks as the top country artist; *The Bodyguard* the top soundtrack; Michael Jackson the top R&B artist; Bob Marley's *Legend* the top reggae album; TLC's *CrazySexyCool*

Big Bang! Baby

the top hip-hop album; and Boston's self-titled debut the top debut album.

178. What was the best-selling album of the twentieth century?

A.) **The Eagles' *Their Greatest Hits 1971–1975*** was the best-selling album of the twentieth century according to the Recording Industry Association of America. The album narrowly edged out its competition, Michael Jackson's *Thriller,* by one million units. At the end of the century, *Their Greatest Hits* had been certified twenty-six times platinum.

179. Who was the first musician to be inducted to the Rock and Roll Hall of Fame three times?

A.) On March 6, 2000, **Eric Clapton** became the first musician to be inducted into the Rock and Roll Hall of Fame three times. He was first honoured as a member of The Yardbirds, and again as a member of Cream. His third induction was in tribute to his solo work.

INDEX

BiBang! Baby

Q

R

Big Bang! Baby

ſ

317

www.ingramcontent.com/pod-product-compliance
Lightning Source LLC
Chambersburg PA
CBHW081323090426

42737CB00017B/3012